20th Century Heroes

20th Century Heroes

A compilation of profiles originally published in
THE NEW AMERICAN magazine.

American Opinion Publishing, Inc.

Appleton, Wisconsin

First Printing . . . . October 2000

American Opinion Publishing, Inc.
P.O. Box 8040
Appleton, Wisconsin 54912
(920) 749-3784

Printed in the United States of America
Library of Congress Control Number: 00-135828
ISBN: 0-9645679-1-1

Dedication

This history of "20th Century Heroes" has been made possible by a generous gift from Mrs. A.T. "Betty" Bliss of Scottsdale, Arizona, in memory of her husband, a true American Patriot:

A.T. Bliss.

About This Book

The profiles contained in this volume were originally published in THE NEW AMERICAN magazine as the "20th Century Heroes" series, which appeared in installments from May 24, 1999 to June 5, 2000.* The scope of the series was limited to those heroes who contributed significantly to the cause of liberty.

Our selection was also intended to illustrate that admirable people can be found fighting for freedom in many lands and in many different fields of endeavor. However, the roster presented herein is by no means exhaustive. While the term "hero" is used far too promiscuously in contemporary society, there are many who have earned that title who are not included among the 25 profiled in this book.

For the sake of convenience, we have organized the essays in categories that emphasize a particular aspect of heroism. However, it should be understood that heroism is a compound virtue consisting of many noble traits. Of course, these virtues overlap, and were displayed — to a greater or lesser extent — by all of the worthy figures profiled in these pages.

---

* A few minor revisions have been made, including the use of expanded photo captions in many of the profiles.

Table of Contents

Heroes for All Time

During the 20th century, 25 extraordinary individuals — among many — helped steer the course of history away from the tyranny of the Total State.

by Gary Benoit

On the surface at least, the tragic history of the last century does not appear to offer much hope for the survival of our Christian-style civilization. "What's past is prologue," the Bard observed almost 400 years ago. The 20th-century prologue to the new millennium could be described as the rise of the Total State — the totalitarian "isms"

Lindbergh

Washington

Smoot

(Communism, Nazism, Fascism), under which the ruling elite exercise absolute power without any religious, moral, or legal constraints.

The Total State, and the corrupting influence it has had on those who have administered it, has resulted in what Professor R.J. Rummel calls "a plague of Power." In his 1994 book *Death by Government*, the professor, who has spent many years studying government mass murder, recounts:

In total, during the first eighty-eight years of [the 20th century], almost 170 million men, women, and children have been shot, beaten, tortured, knifed, burned, starved, frozen, crushed, or worked to death; buried alive, drowned, hung, bombed, or killed in any other of the myriad ways governments have in-

flicted death on unarmed, helpless citizens and foreigners. The dead could conceivably be nearly 360 million people. It is as though our species has been devastated by a modern Black Plague. And indeed it has, but a plague of Power, not of germs.

Professor Rummel notes that "the more power a government has, the more it can act arbitrarily according to the whims and desires of the elite, and the more it will make war on others and murder its foreign and domestic subjects."

Although America has not yet experienced the full-fledged, unbridled power of the Total State, our movement in this direction under the false flags of "New Dealism" or "Liberalism" has been unmistakable. Hungarian expatriate Balint Vazsonyi, in his book *America's Thirty Years War* (1998), warns that "all aspects of our lives — and all of our institutions — have been moving in one direction: away from America's founding principles.... And every time we move away from America's founding principles, we move in the direction of the sole realistic alternative" — what we call here the "Total State," what Vazsonyi calls in his book "The Idea."

Vazsonyi notes that "The Idea ... has gone through countless transformations and as many versions" — including Communism and National Socialism (Nazism), both of which he lived under in his native Hungary. "The Idea has been successfully installed in America's schools," he says, "as well as in most of the information and entertainment media.... And, as high school textbooks, college courses, television newscasts, or national newspapers attest, the purpose is the *transformation* of America."

Yet, in spite of the bloodiness and oppressiveness of the last century, history also provides much cause for hope. It shows, for example, that the rise of the Total State is not the product of some uncontrollable wave of the future but of the deliberate actions of evildoers who have conspired to oppress their fellow man and who have waged war against God and His laws. It also shows that free peoples do not want to be enchained, that the oppressed do not love their servitude, and that the enemies of freedom must always operate covertly and under false flags. This is because man is not the malleable creature the coercive utopians claim him to be; he is instead blessed by God with a free will that cannot be broken and an immortal soul that cannot be destroyed. In every age and in every land, regardless of how prevalent amorality or despotism may have been, man has exercised his free will for good as well as for evil.

In their study *The Lessons of History* (1968), Will and Ariel Durant note that history is not merely "a warning reminder of man's follies and crimes," but also "an encouraging remembrance of generative souls … a celestial city, a spacious country of the mind, wherein a thousand saints, statesmen, inventors, scientists, poets, artists, musicians, lovers, and philosophers still live and speak, teach and carve and sing." The 20th century — even though marred with unbridled collectivism and conspiracy — has produced many such "generative souls," including heroic individuals from various walks of life who have bravely challenged the collectivist tide and contributed significantly to the cause of freedom. The fact that a century as morally bankrupt as the 20th has been blessed with the noble actions of many such great men and women is proof positive that hope still "springs eternal" and that others will surely follow in their footsteps — no matter how desperate or despotic the times may become.

Twenty-five of these extraordinary individuals are profiled in this book. (These profiles originally appeared as a series of articles in THE NEW AMERICAN. Other worthy candidates could have been profiled, space permitting.) In one of these profiles — the one honoring World War II freedom fighter Draza Mihailovich — Fr. James Thornton observes: "Without heroes and without heroic sacrifices, there would be no liberty, no law, no order, no justice, no civilization, no great nations or peoples, and no history as we understand that word. Without heroes, such records as might exist among men would be squalid tales of cravenness and brutality." But thanks to heroes, the history of the 20th century is not confined to "squalid tales of cravenness and brutality." Liberty, law, order, justice, civilization, and great nations and peoples still exist, even though all are under attack. Without 20th century heroes, the Total State would have triumphed long ago; because of them we still have the opportunity to save our Christian-style civilization.

Heroes are staunch individualists, willing to go against the popular opinions of the day, willing to take the road "less traveled by," willing to go against the odds, willing to do what is right because it is right and for no other reason. Oftentimes they are mavericks — like Charles Lindbergh, who honored America by his bold flight across the Atlantic.

Heroes "must not only demonstrate

Franco

Pinochet

Mihailovich

Chiang

Newsmakers

tenacity and spirit, but must be prepared to die for their cause," Fr. Thornton points out. So it was with Mihailovich, who fought valiantly to rid his beloved Serbian homeland of both Communist and Nazi invaders, but who was eventually betrayed by the West and executed by the Communists. And so it was with two other heroes featured in this volume: U.S. Army Captain John Birch, who was brutally murdered by our supposed Chinese Communist "allies" just 10 days following the end of World War II; and African leader Moise Tshombe, who died under suspicious circumstances in an Algerian prison.

Other heroes did not actually die at the hands of the enemy but were put through the torments of hell, oftentimes in Communist gulags. Yet they never faltered; they never bent a knee to the Total State; they never lost their abiding faith; they never betrayed their God. The Communists and other practitioners of the Total State could break their bodies, but they could not conquer their souls. So it was with Hungary's Jozsef Cardinal Mindszenty, who proved to his Communist torturers that faith is one weapon tyrants cannot overcome. The cardinal's example was so powerful that he became a living symbol of faith and freedom to his fellow Hungarians.

The heroes profiled herein came from disparate backgrounds, many of them without rank or privilege, confirming that heroic qualities extend outward from the soul and not inward from the environment. Booker T. Washington was born into poverty and slavery in 19th century America, yet became a widely respected leader of Black Americans by the 20th. "When persons ask me in these days how, in the midst of what sometimes seem hopelessly discouraging conditions, I can have such faith in the future of my race in this country, I remind them of the wilderness through which and out of which, a good Providence has already led us," said this emancipator by example. Dan Smoot (still living) pulled himself up by the bootstraps to go from a 14-year-old orphan-hobo to a G-man bat-

MacArthur

Patton

tling internal subversion to an independent broadcaster reaching millions with the freedom philosophy.

"Heroes may ... be reviled for a time, and it may be many years before their motives and the significance of their sacrifices are widely understood," observes Fr. Thornton. Many of the heroes in our series have been reviled — General Franco, Senator Joseph McCarthy, and the still-living General Pinochet to name just a few. But whether or not they one day receive the recognition they deserve depends on what the new generation of heroes does to expose and oppose the opinion cartel's propaganda and to set the record straight.

In Joseph McCarthy's case at least, new evidence released from Soviet archives shows that (surprise!) the Communists had infiltrated the U.S. government just as he had claimed. Yet, in spite of these recent revelations, and in spite of McCarthy's care never to identify anyone as a Communist who was not, the great anti-Communist senator is reviled as much as ever. Why the continuing smear, decades after his death? Part of the answer must be that the subverters of our free institutions fear exposure — and they are hoping against hope that no one

will dare follow in his footsteps.

Of course, none of the heroes honored in this book was perfect; all of them were sinners. Yet, by the grace of God, they were able to perform heroic deeds in spite of man's fallen nature and, in many cases, to rally their countrymen in defense of freedom.

In spite of the obstacles, a number of the 20th century heroes we've profiled have enjoyed amazing success in their war against the collectivist conspiracy. In Chile, General Pinochet stepped in just in time to prevent his

Mindszenty

Heroes are staunch individualists, willing to go against the popular opinions of the day, willing to take the road "less traveled by," willing to go against the odds, willing to do what is right because it is right and for no other reason.

country from becoming a full-fledged Communist dictatorship resulting in the elimination of basic rights and the liquidation of the opposition. His military coup a success, Pinochet then used his powers, not to oppress his fellow Chileans, but to deliver peace, freedom, stability, security, economic growth — and even a proposed Constitution that the Chilean people accepted overwhelmingly. Finally, just as he promised he would do, he voluntarily stepped down, handing the reins of government back to civilian leaders.

Spain's General Franco performed a similar rescue mission, defeating the Communists who were already firmly entrenched in his country. Years later, he refused to enter WWII on the side of the Axis powers and refused to help Hitler seize Gibraltar. That heroic stand, by a weakened nation still recovering from the Spanish Civil War, against a mighty military machine that had already overrun

France, made the difference in keeping the Mediterranean open to the Allies. In neighboring Portugal, Dr. António de Oliveira Salazar reluctantly left his beloved academia to serve his country as Finance Minister and then as Prime Minister, during which time he delivered his homeland from anarchy and totalitarianism and provided 40 years of stability and growth.

Switzerland's General Henri Guisan united and inspired his countrymen to defend their homeland against a planned Nazi invasion. Swiss citizen-soldiers were implored to fight to the death, and to resort to "cold steel" should their ammunition run out. So successful and formidable was Guisan's mobilization — entailing not just an "army" but a whole people — that the Nazis decided the subjugation of Switzerland would be too costly. During WWII, Switzerland became a haven for more than 300,000 refugees, including 25,000 Jews.

The Congo's Moise Tshombe led the Katangan province of that terrorist-ravaged land to independence, order, and

freedom. For a limited time, in this one sector of the dark continent, the flame of liberty burned brightly. It took an invasion of United Nations "peacekeeping" forces to extinguish it.

China's Generalissimo Chiang Kai-shek eventually lost his years-long fight to prevent Mainland China from falling to the Communists. That tragic defeat was the result, not of any lack of resolve on his part, but of betrayal by the West. But Chiang did not allow betrayal to discourage him, and he refused to give up the freedom fight. Reestablishing his government on the island of Formosa (Taiwan), he created a beacon of hope and freedom that shone in stark contrast to the despair and slavery on the mainland.

Chiang's accomplishments appear all the more amazing when the Orient's lack of a centuries-old tradition of freedom and individual worth is taken into consideration. He had his faults to be sure, but he willingly cast aside the "warlord" system he had inherited in order to bring the Western tradition to the Orient. In so doing, he instilled an unyielding love of freedom in the minds and hearts of millions who had not previously experienced it. Another Oriental profiled in our series, South Korea's Syngman Rhee, breathed the fire of freedom into his homeland.

Other great heroes who have successfully fought the totalitarian tide include American Generals Douglas MacArthur and George Patton, two of the greatest military minds this country has ever produced. MacArthur's brilliant Inchon landing resulted in the speedy defeat of the Communist forces in Korea. But U.S. policy makers nullified this victory by placing unprecedented restrictions on MacArthur's forces. Eventually MacArthur was relieved of command and Korea became the first war America did not win.

Taft

McCarthy

Benson

Dies

But upon returning home, the old soldier — whose 52 years of military service epitomized "duty, honor, country" — spoke out. In an address to a Joint Session of Congress he recounted: "Why, my soldiers asked of me, surrender military advantages to an enemy in the field? I could not answer." "War's very object is victory — not prolonged indecision," he stated. "In war, indeed, there can be no substitute for victory."

While General MacArthur was defeating the Japanese forces in the Pacific through a series of flanking maneuvers that kept American casualties to a minimum, General Patton was steamrolling through North Africa, Sicily, and then Europe — also with minimal casualties compared to those he inflicted upon the enemy. But Patton's advance was stopped within 50 miles of Berlin, not by the German Army but by an incredible order to *withdraw* 100 miles westward over captured territory. The Soviets, meanwhile, *advanced* westward, extending Communist tyranny throughout much of Eastern Europe, including East Germany. "[T]he tin-soldier politicians in Washington and Paris … have allowed us to kick hell out of one b****** and at the same time forced us to help establish a second one as evil or more evil than the first," Patton complained in an off-the-record press conference.

But not all U.S. politicians were duplicitous betrayers. The featured American political heroes in this book include, in addition to Senator Joseph McCarthy, Senator Robert Taft, Secretary of Agriculture Ezra Taft Benson, and Congressman Martin Dies. Dies, in fact, as chairman of the House Committee on Un-American Activities, was viciously attacked for his effective exposure of Communist subversion in the 1930s and '40s, just as McCarthy was viciously attacked for his effective exposure of Red subversives during the 1950s.

Other heroes fought for the preservation of our Christian-style civilization without the benefit of public office. Those whose chosen weapon was the pen included free market champion Ludwig von Mises, journalist John T. Flynn, novelist Taylor Caldwell, John Birch Society founder Robert Welch, and Christian apologists G.K. Chesterton and C.S. Lewis. Each of these individuals made a significant contribution to the freedom fight; each confirmed the old adage that the pen is mightier than the sword. But in our view, the greatest of this exemplary group was Robert Welch, not because he was a better writer or had his books more widely distributed, but because he had the vision, determination, and tenacity to found an organization for the preservation of freedom and to lead that concerted effort for the next 25 years.

"[S]imply publishing good books, articles, and pamphlets, and even getting them distributed, is not, by itself, enough to win this battle," Welch once observed. "This literature must be read, it must be put to use, and it must be a part of an overall, concerted plan of action. And this is exactly what The John Birch Society has been doing, and must continue to do in the future."

Caldwell

Robert Welch named his organization after Captain John Birch, having detected in his study of Birch's relatively short life the embodiment of the American ideal — an ideal possessed not only by Birch but by others, in spite of the tragic times in which they lived. As Welch put it in *The Life of John Birch* (1954), "the fact that cultural traditions and ethical forces still at work can produce one such man is clear proof that they are still producing others like him. Of the slowly built hereditary and environmental molds, into which such youth were poured, many have now been smashed altogether, and many more have their sidewalls badly cracked; but many still remain unreached by the stresses of political tyranny and the erosion of moral anarchy around us. The output of these molds can still save our civilization."

Steve Bonta, in his moving essay on the soldier-missionary, reflects:

Chesterton

Flynn

von Mises

Mises Institute

Liberty, law, order, justice, civilization, and great nations and peoples still exist, even though all are under attack. Without 20th century heroes, the Total State would have triumphed long ago; because of them we still have the opportunity to save our Christian-style civilization.

In many respects, John Birch is a far more typical hero than others we have profiled in these pages. Unlike the statesmen, the generals, the scholars, the writers, and others who have left their mark on our tragic century, he led a modest, self-sacrificing existence and died a martyr's death without public acclaim. It never occurred to him to do other than what was right; he was unencumbered by the moral ambiguities associated with power politics. He defined all of his hopes and ambitions in terms of serving his God, his family, and his fellow men.

Bonta continues: "John Birch, in a word, belonged to that most heroic of all classes of human beings — the so-called common men and women who, in order to preserve our civilization, have fought, suffered, and died by the countless millions." A few of these so-called common heroes are known to us; many more are not. Many of these heroes labored for a lifetime for what was right and true — sometimes in simple ways such as by faithfully supporting their family, church, and community; sometimes (when the opportunity arose) in more spectacular ways.

In his best-selling book *Tortured for Christ* (1967), Rev. Richard Wurmbrand informs us of a Romanian pastor whom the Communists "tortured with red-hot iron pokers and with knives. He was beaten very badly. Then starving rats were driven into his cell through a large pipe.

He could not sleep, but had to defend himself all the time. If he rested a moment, the rats would attack him." Rev. Wurmbrand continues:

He was forced to stand for two weeks, day and night. The Communists wished to compel him to betray his brethren [in the underground church], but he resisted steadfastly. In the end, they brought his fourteen-year-old son and began to whip the boy in front of his father, saying that they would continue to beat him until the pastor said what they wished him to say. The poor man was half mad. He bore it as long as he could. When he could not stand it any more, he cried to his son, *"Alexander, I must say what they want! I can't bear your beating any more!"* The son answered, "Father, don't do me the injustice to have a traitor as a parent. Withstand! If they kill me, I will die with the words, 'Jesus and my fatherland.'" The Communists, enraged, fell upon the child and beat him to death, with blood spattered over the walls of the cell. He died praising God.

On the threshold of the new millennium, those who have given up — who claim that it's too late, that the freedom fight has already been lost, that the triumph of the Godless Total State is inevitable — should be told about the selfless sacrifice of this heroic 14-year-old boy. They should be told how, in a Communist torture chamber, without any hope of escape, this brave lad proclaimed his love of God and country. And they should be told of his exact words, words that should apply to any one of us should the occasion arise: "Withstand! If they kill me, I will die with the words, 'Jesus and my fatherland.'"

Birch

Welch

Those who claim that the tide of collectivism cannot be reversed should be reminded of the astonishing accomplishments of the 25 "20th Century Heroes" we've profiled. They should be reminded that America and other lands have not only had many wonderful heroes but have them still. And they should be presented with these poignant words of Edmund Burke: "How often has public calamity been arrested on the very brink of ruin by the seasonable energy of a single man?... One vigorous mind without office, without situation, without public functions of any kind ... I say one such man confiding in the aid of God, and full of just reliance in his own fortitude, vigor, enterprise, and perseverance, would first draw to him some few like himself, and then that multitudes hardly thought to be in existence, would appear and troop about him."

Burke also succinctly stated: "When bad men combine, the good must associate; else they will fall one by one, an unpitied sacrifice in a contemptible struggle." We should draw inspiration from the champions of freedom who have preceded us, become involved ourselves, and trust in God. If enough of us do so, the new century should turn out to be much brighter than the last. ∎

Martial Valor

The 20th century was an age of total warfare, with all of its attendant horrors. But even amid the savagery of war some men have distinguished themselves through acts of nobility, sacrifice, and courage. The lives and careers of Generals Douglas MacArthur and George Patton exemplified patriotism, personal honor, inspired leadership, and battlefield genius.

As the leader of Yugoslavia's "Chetnik" forces, Draza Mihailovich fought to protect his people from both Germany's National Socialists and the Communists; he also participated in the rescue of more than 500 American airmen who were shot down by the Nazis during World War II. After the betrayal of his people into the hands of Tito's Communists, Mihailovich was captured, made the subject of a Communist show trial, executed, and buried in an unmarked grave — a martyr to the cause of freedom.

Following the Hitler-Stalin pact of 1939 and the subsequent Nazi conquests in Europe, only one nation on the continent resisted the totalitarian tide: tiny, landlocked Switzerland. Defying both the Axis — which was drawing up invasion plans — and the defeatism of the Swiss central government, General Henri Guisan, commander-in-chief of Switzerland's militia during World War II, gathered his top officers at Rütli Meadow and ordered them to defend their homeland at any cost — and with their bare hands, if necessary. Rallying his countrymen to the cause of "spiritual national defense," General Guisan preserved Switzerland's independence and neutrality, and spared his nation from the horrors of history's most destructive war.

Duty, Honor, Country

Throughout his illustrious life, General Douglas MacArthur modeled the priorities of a true patriot.

by Robert W. Lee

Many U.S. military leaders have been so fundamentally sound in character and upstanding in their personal lives that they serve as positive role models for adults and youth alike. George Washington, Robert E. Lee, and John J. Pershing come readily to mind. And so does Douglas A. MacArthur, one of the most brilliant military strategists and astute statesmen that our country has produced.

MacArthur was born in Little Rock, Arkansas on January 26, 1880. He was homeschooled during his early years, so was steeped in fascinating stories of military history and patriotism told by his father, Arthur MacArthur, who had enlisted in the Union Army at 17 to fight in the Civil War. The elder MacArthur's experiences during the war, and subsequent Indian fighting in the West, were related to his three sons not to induce a lust for battle, but to instill such character traits as love of country, honor, duty, morality, and fairness. Douglas MacArthur would exemplify those attributes throughout his own adult life. Even in war, MacArthur's credo was not simply that there is no substitute for victory, but that victory should be achieved as quickly and humanely as possible, with as few casualties on all sides as possible. William Manchester, in his less than favorable biography of the general entitled *American Caesar* (1978), notes that in both World War II and Korea, MacArthur's 89 amphibious assaults resulted in the lowest casualties suffered by any of the American field commanders.

Douglas MacArthur graduated from the U.S. Military Academy at the top of his class in 1903, recording the highest marks at West Point in a quarter century. Indeed, by the end of his third year he was named First Captain, West Point's highest military award. He was one of only a handful in the history of the Academy to garner both honors.

His first assignment after graduating was to help map the Philippines. He also served for two

years as an aide to President Theodore Roosevelt, and by the time the U.S. entered World War I had advanced to the rank of colonel. During the war, he became chief of staff of the famous 42nd Division, and later commanded the 84th Infantry Brigade.

Germany's use of poison gas was a serious threat to Allied forces. MacArthur, however, roamed the battlefields without a gas mask as a gesture of defiance to the enemy and to instill courage in his men. Twice during fighting in France he was caught in poison gas attacks, but refused to be hospitalized. To pause for such medical attention would have meant leaving his men, and he firmly believed that an officer's place was with his troops. Even though one of the gassings left him violently ill, he did not allow it to interfere with his duties.

MacArthur was officially lauded for bravery in action (General Pershing described him as "the greatest leader of troops we have") and was promoted to Brigadier General in 1918. The next year he was appointed superintendent of West Point, where he successfully undertook the chore of upgrading the institution's already lofty military and academic standards. He returned to the Philippines in 1922 for three years as commander of the Philippine Division, and in 1930 was named a full general and appointed Army

chief of staff, the youngest in U.S. history.

General MacArthur was by then increasingly concerned about the growing menace of Communism, both at home and abroad. During an address to the graduating class of the University of Pittsburgh in 1932 he warned: "Pacifism and its bedfellow Communism are all about us. In the theaters, newspapers and magazines, pulpits and lecture halls, schools and colleges, it hangs like a mist before the face of America, organizing the forces of unrest and undermining the morals of the working man."

In the summer of that year, the "forces of unrest" were mobilized by the Communist Party in an attempt to provoke a violent confrontation between the Army and some veterans groups that were seeking cash bonuses from Congress. Soldiers under MacArthur's command squelched a Red-instigated riot of 5,000 marchers without fatalities, or serious injuries, or so much as a shot being fired. Some of his left-wing critics still attempt to portray him as the villain in the incident, but one of the Communists who organized the march would later testify that "General MacArthur put down a Moscow-directed revolution without bloodshed, and that's why the Communists hate him."

MacArthur formally retired from the Army in 1937 and spent the next four years as military adviser for the Philippines to help that island nation prepare for a possible Japanese attack. He was recalled to active duty by President Franklin D. Roosevelt in July 1941 to command U.S. forces in the Far East. When the Japanese attacked the Philippines on December 8, 1941, MacArthur's forces were isolated, but fought bravely before being forced to retreat to the Bataan Peninsula due to a lack

"War's very object is victory — not prolonged indecision. In war, indeed, there can be no substitute for victory."
— Douglas MacArthur

of reinforcements and supplies that were instead being sent to Europe to help England and our "ally," Soviet Russia.

MacArthur's forces continued to resist courageously, and it was his defense of Bataan that earned MacArthur a Medal of Honor, our nation's highest military award for bravery. The accompanying citation stated:

For conspicuous leadership in preparing the Philippine Islands to resist conquest, for gallantry and intrepidity above and beyond the call of duty in action against invading Japanese forces, and for the heroic conduct of defensive and offensive operations on the Bataan Peninsula. He mobilized, trained, and led an army which has received world acclaim for its gallant defense against a tremendous superiority of enemy forces in men and arms. His utter disregard of personal danger under heavy fire and aerial bombardment, his calm judgment in each crisis, inspired his troops, galvanized the spirit of resistance of the Filipino people, and confirmed the faith of the American people in their Armed Forces.

In March 1942, President Roosevelt ordered MacArthur to Australia to command Allied forces in the Southwest Pacific. After arriving at his new post, MacArthur lamented leaving his men in the Philippines and made his famous promise, "I shall return."

The return trip began in late 1942 when MacArthur opened a three-year offensive that by early 1944 had freed most of New Guinea, New Britain, the Solomons, and the Admiralty Islands. His promise was fulfilled on October 20, 1944, when he led the invasion of Leyte Island. Within six months, virtually all of the Philippine Islands were free.

At one point during the remaining weeks of the war, MacArthur relates in his 1964 memoirs *Reminiscences*, he "received a shocking order from Washington to release seventy of my transport ships at once. They were to return to San Francisco and be used to carry supplies and munitions to the Soviet forces at Vladivostok." He registered a vigorous protest, since the "abrupt removal of these transports endangered the entire Philippine campaign and threatened the loss of thousands of our men fighting in north Luzon." Washington ignored his pleas, and years later the move would return to haunt MacArthur in Korea. As he revealed in *Reminiscences*, instead of go-

ing to the Soviets, "all of the supplies carried to Vladivostok, by those ships, and hundreds of thousands of other tons, were eventually used in Korea by the Communist governments of North Korea and China against our own forces."

In December 1944, MacArthur became the Army's first five-star general. The following April, he assumed command of all U.S. Army forces in the Pacific. On August 14, 1945, President Truman announced that the Japanese had accepted Allied surrender terms, and named MacArthur supreme commander for the Allied Powers to receive the surrender and to rule post-war Japan. MacArthur accepted the Japanese surrender aboard the battleship *Missouri* on September 2, 1945.

After the war, MacArthur was subjected to intense pressure by some elements of the Washington establishment that

were anxious to humiliate the Japanese and reduce their country to servitude by destroying its industrial potential. MacArthur quickly made it clear, however, that he was not bent on revenge, but rather hoped to return Japan to the community of respectable nations as soon as possible. To accomplish that objective, he concluded that it would be necessary to work through the existing Japanese government, since he was convinced that the Japanese would not take orders from a foreigner for long.

His policy was firm, but fair. He issued orders through the military government to disarm and demobilize Japan's military forces, destroy the power of the war lords, substitute civics for military training in the schools, allow women to vote, give the nation a constitutional government similar to our own, and stymie the influence of Communist agitators who worked from the beginning to undermine

Determined return: MacArthur wades ashore at Leyte Island in the Philippines on October 20, 1944. Two years earlier, following a desperate but ill-fated defense of the Philippines for which he won a Medal of Honor, the General had departed the fortress of Corregidor with the immortal words, "I shall return." Within six months of his landing on Leyte's east coast the entire Philippine Islands were free.

Gen. MacArthur signs acceptance of Japan's surrender, aboard *USS Missouri*, September 2, 1945.

his efforts and further increase animosity between the U.S. and Japan. As a result, the Japanese, who had feared fierce retribution, came to revere MacArthur as a wise and compassionate administrator. His death on April 5, 1964 was mourned by many nations, but none more so than Japan. Former Premier Shigeru Yoshida expressed his country's sentiment when he stated, "I cannot forget the great achievement of the general in rebuilding our nation out of the ashes of defeat." Douglas MacArthur's administration of post-war Japan had demonstrated that he was not merely a great military leader, but a skilled and humane statesman and diplomat as well.

On June 25, 1950, six divisions of Communist North Korean troops invaded South Korea. On July 9th, the 70-year-old "retired" general was once again called to active duty, this time to serve as Supreme Commander for United Nations forces in the Far East.

MacArthur apparently did not realize the ominous significance of this initial step in placing the U.S. military at the behest of the UN, but he would eventually experience personally some of the sinister and essentially treasonous implications of the move.

Initially, MacArthur's greatly outnumbered forces had their backs to the wall to the point that the combined U.S. and South Korean troops faced possible annihilation. But with one of the great military maneuvers of all time — the famous amphibious landing assault at Inchon — MacArthur completely reversed the course of the war.

Inchon, located on Korea's West Coast some 24 miles southwest of Seoul, is the port for the South Korean capital. Troops of the U.S. 10th Corps landed on September 15, 1950. The assault was extraordinary because extreme tides in the area varied by more than 30 feet, which meant that the assault had to be timed literally to the minute to avoid having our

landing craft and other ships trapped on mud flats. Both the Joint Chiefs of Staff and MacArthur's own staff considered the operation too risky (one estimate placed the odds of success at roughly 5,000 to 1), but that only firmed up MacArthur's resolve to proceed, since it convinced him that the enemy would conclude the same, so be caught completely off guard. The landing cut between North Korean troops in the south and Communist forces farther north. With supply lines severed, the Communists were soon routed in the south and North Korean troops were driven out of control in the north. The war appeared to be won. General MacArthur had again displayed extraordinary military competence that had defeated an adversary with a minimal loss of life and limb on both sides.

But then, as one observer subsequently noted, "we snatched defeat from the jaws of victory." On November 26, 1950, four Red Chinese armies stormed across the Yalu River into North Korea. MacArthur had a few weeks earlier ordered the destruction of bridges across the river, but his order had been countermanded by Washington. He was stunned. Writing in *Reminiscences*, he recalled: "I realized for the first time that I had actually been denied the use of my full military power to safeguard the lives of my soldiers and the safety of my army. To me, it clearly foreshadowed a tragic situation in Korea and left me with a sense of inexpressible shock."

MacArthur described how he became "worried by a series of directives from Washington which were greatly decreasing the potential of my air force. First I was forbidden 'hot' pursuit of enemy planes that attacked our own. Manchuria and Siberia were sanctuaries of inviolate protection for all enemy forces and for all enemy purposes, no matter what depredations or assaults might come from there. Then I was denied the right to bomb the hydroelectric plants along the Yalu. The order was broadened to include every plant in North Korea which was capable of furnishing electric power to Manchuria and Siberia. Most incomprehensible of all was the refusal to let me bomb the important supply center at Racin, which was not in Manchuria or Siberia, but many miles from the border, in northeast Korea. Racin was a depot to which the Soviet Union forwarded supplies from Vladivostok for the North Korean Army. I felt that step-by-step my weapons were being taken away from me."

An earlier policy decision by our government helped assure that the Red Chinese would have plenty of manpower available for the invasion. One of the most incredible incidents of the war occurred on June 27, 1950, when President Truman ordered our Seventh Fleet into the Formosa Strait, supposedly to protect Free China (Formosa) from military action by Red China, but in reality to protect the Red Chinese who would soon be attacking our forces in Korea. MacArthur recalled how the decision to move his troops into North Korea following the Inchon landing had confronted him with a

grave problem. "It immediately raised the shadow of Red Chinese intervention," since "the possibility of such an intervention had existed ever since the order from Washington, issued to the Seventh Fleet in June, to neutralize Formosa, which in effect protected the Red China mainland from attack by Chiang Kai-shek's force of half a million men. This released the two great Red Chinese armies assigned to the coastal defense of central China and made them available for transfer elsewhere." Not until February 2, 1953, after irreversible damage had been done, did President Eisenhower announce in his first State of the Union message that he was "issuing instructions that the Seventh Fleet would no longer be employed to shield Communist China" from attack by Chiang Kai-shek's forces because "we certainly have no obligation to protect a nation fighting us in Korea."

It was later learned that the Chinese had been assured in advance that MacArthur's hands would be tied. MacArthur wrote:

That there was some leak in intelligence was evident to everyone. [Brigadier General Walton] Walker continually complained to me that his operations were known to the enemy in advance through sources in Washington.... Information must have been relayed to them, assuring

that the Yalu bridges would continue to enjoy sanctuary and that their bases would be left intact. They knew they could swarm down across the Yalu River without having to worry about bombers hitting their Manchurian supply lines.

He then cited an "official leaflet" published by Red Chinese General Lin Piao, which bluntly acknowledged: "I would never have made the attack and risked my men and military reputation if I had not been assured that Washington would restrain General MacArthur from taking adequate retaliatory measures against my lines of supply and communication."

MacArthur did not disobey orders, but expressed his frustration and displeasure with this no-win, protect-the-enemy policy that he was convinced would prolong the war and cause the deaths of needless thousands of his troops. At the request of House Minority Leader Joseph Martin (R-MA), he catalogued some of his concerns in a private letter to the congressman. Representative Martin, without consulting MacArthur, subsequently made the letter public, which served as an excuse for President Truman to remove MacArthur from his command on April 11, 1951. Six months earlier, during a meeting with the President at Wake Island, Truman had pinned the General's fifth Distinguished Service Medal on his

Corbis

On the Korean front: MacArthur completely reversed the course of the Korean War through his brilliant Inchon landing. But the incredible restrictions placed on MacArthur by Washington, and the removal of MacArthur from command, snatched defeat from the jaws of victory.

shirt, and said that MacArthur had "so inspired his command by his vision, his judgment, his indomitable will, and his unshakable faith, that it has set a shining example of gallantry and tenacity in defense and of audacity in attack matched by but few operations in military history."

The war dragged on for two more years, resulting in stalemate with a truce agreement signed on June 27, 1953. Approximately three-fourths of the U.S. casualties suffered during the war occurred after MacArthur was fired.

With the war over, a parade of embittered generals (including James A. Van Fleet, Mark Clark, and George Stratemeyer) joined MacArthur in testifying before Congress about the incredible restrictions under which they were forced to operate. General Clark, who was UN Commander in Korea when the war ended, had been assigned the task of negotiating with the North Koreans as the war wound down. He signed the armistice agreement for the United States, but would later lament that he had "gained the unenviable distinction of being the first United States Army commander in history to sign an armistice without victory."

MacArthur returned to the United States a hero. He defended his policies in an address before a joint session of Congress, during which he stated: "I know war as few other men now living know it, and nothing to me is more revolting. I have long advocated its complete abolition as its very destructiveness on both friend and foe has rendered it useless as a means of settling international disputes." He insisted, however, that "once war is forced upon us, there is no other alternative than to apply every available means to bring it to a swift end. War's very object is victory — not prolonged indecision. In war, indeed, there can be no substitute for victory." He recalled an old barrack ballad from his West Point days that says, "Old soldiers never die, they just fade away," and concluded with the memorable words: "And like the old soldier of that ballad, I now close my military career and just fade away, an old soldier who tried to do his duty as God gave him the light to see that duty. Good-bye."

MacArthur returned to private life once again. But on May 12, 1962, he returned to West Point, where he was awarded the Sylvanus Thayer Medal, the Academy's highest honor. In his impromptu response to the presentation, known to history as his Farewell Address, he focused on the three beacons which had guided his half-century of military service spanning three wars: "Duty-Honor-Country." He told the cadets, "Those three hallowed words reverently dictate what you ought to be, what you can be, and what you will be.

They are your rallying points; to build courage when courage seems to fail; to regain faith when there seems to be little cause for faith; to create hope when hope becomes forlorn." In closing, he reflected: "The shadows are lengthening for me. The twilight is here. My days of old have vanished tone and tint; they have gone glimmering through the dreams of things that were.... But in the evening of my memory, always I come back to West Point. Always there echoes and re-echoes in my ears — Duty-Honor-Country. Today marks my final roll call with you. But I want you to know that when I cross the river my last conscious thoughts will be of the Corps — and the Corps — and the Corps. I bid you farewell."

General MacArthur "crossed the river" on April 5, 1964. President Herbert Hoover, who also passed away in 1964, accurately assessed his contribution to our country when he stated on one occasion: "There is no way to measure the service General MacArthur has given the American people. He is the greatest general and one of the greatest statesmen of our nation's history. He is the greatest combination of statesman and military leader that America has produced since George Washington.... General MacArthur may say, 'Old soldiers never die, they just fade away.' Physically they will. But the great deeds of men live forever after them." ■

20th CENTURY HEROES

Liberty's Steamroller

A cultured, perceptive man of principle, General George S. Patton fought for freedom as one of America's greatest military geniuses.

by William Norman Grigg

Corbis

O God, thou art my God; early will I seek thee; my soul thirsteth for thee, my flesh longeth for thee in a dry and thirsty land, where no water is; To see thy power and thy glory, so as I have seen thee in the sanctuary....

My soul followeth hard after thee. Thy right hand upholdeth me. But those that seek my soul, to destroy it, shall go into the lower parts of the earth. They shall fall by the sword.... But the king shall rejoice in God; every one that sweareth by him shall glory, but the mouth of them that speak lies shall be stopped.

— From Psalm 63
General Patton's favorite Bible verse

"**P**iety" is not a word commonly associated with the memory of General George S. Patton, also known as "Old Blood and Guts" — a man quite properly regarded as the embodiment of America's martial tradition. The late George C. Scott's Oscar-winning film portrayal of Patton, which was as much caricature as tribute, has immortalized the general as a human juggernaut to whom everything, including worship, was subordinated to an all-consuming passion for war. But as his posthumously published memoir *War As I Knew It* documents, Patton was a cultured and perceptive man of principle for whom war was a means of protecting freedom.

Although his granite-willed determination to destroy the enemy's capacity for warfare is well known, Patton's capacity for melancholy reflection upon war's ugliness is not. Upon arriving in Normandy, Patton noted in his journal that he attended a Field Mass "where all of us were armed. As we knelt in the mud in the slight drizzle, we could distinctly hear the roar of the guns, and the whole sky was filled with airplanes on their missions of destruction ... quite at variance with the teachings of the religion we were practicing."

George Gosselin, a much-decorated veteran of

"I am a strong believer in prayer. There are three ways that men get what they want: by planning, by working, and by praying. Any great military operation takes careful planning.... But between the plan and the operation there is always the unknown.... Some people call that getting the breaks; I call it God."

— *General Patton*

Patton's army, observed that while the general was a "taskmaster" who demanded exemplary order and discipline within the ranks, he was also a man of profound and sincere faith. It should not be forgotten, wrote Gosselin, that "this man, who was so hard on himself and others, was totally soft on God." "I am a strong believer in prayer," declared General Patton on one occasion. "There are three ways that men get what they want: by planning, by working, and by praying. Any great military operation takes careful planning. Then you must have well trained troops to carry it out. But between the plan and the operation there is always the unknown. That unknown spells success or failure. Some people call that getting the breaks; I call it God. God has His part or margin in everything. That's where prayer comes in."

As a believer, Patton's God was Christ, not Mars. As a master strategist given to fits of tactical genius he couldn't explain, Patton understood the need for focused ruthlessness in confronting an insurgent foe; as a Christian, he understood and practiced the virtue of mercy in dealing with a conquered enemy. These complementary aspects of Patton's personality were on display during an interview with the Vicar of Sicily after Patton's forces routed the Italian Army. "I assured him," wrote Patton, "that I was amazed at the stupidity and gallantry of the Italian Army; stupid, because they were fighting for a lost cause, and gallant, because they were Italians." Patton asked the Vicar to call upon the Italians to surrender in order to prevent needless bloodshed. "As a matter of fact," wrote Patton, "I called off the air and naval bombardments we had arranged, because I felt enough people had been killed, and felt that with the drive of the 2nd Armored Division we could take the place without inflicting unproductive losses on the enemy."

On another occasion, Patton referred reproachfully to what he called "the seemingly barbaric bombardment of the centers of cities" during the war, a practice that did not comport with Patton's sense of martial chivalry and the moral principles of just warfare. "Kill all the Germans you can," urged the general during the Third Army's unprecedented drive across Europe, "but do not put them up against a wall and kill them. Do your killing while they are still fighting. After a man has surrendered, he should be treated exactly in accordance with the Rules of Land Warfare, and just as you would hope to be treated if you were foolish enough to surrender. Americans do not kick people in the teeth after they are down."

George Smith Patton was born in California in 1885, and at the age of five he informed his parents of his intention of becoming a "great general." "When he learned to read, the first book he bought was a history of decisive battles," recounted Colonel Robert S. Allen in *Lucky Forward*, his memoir of serving in Patton's Third Army. "In school he was always organizing sham battles. On his honeymoon in France, he took his young bride to historic battlefields and fortresses. Later, when stationed in Hawaii, he and his wife and young children would stage assault landings while on sailing trips. Even when playing his beloved polo, and fox hunting, he played at war." Patton received his Cavalry commission in 1909. After representing the U.S. at the 1912 Olympic Games, Patton took part in General John J. Pershing's punitive raid into Mexico in 1916. Pershing took Patton to France in 1917 as a staff captain, and Patton finished World War I as a commander of a tank brigade.

During a mere 13 months of combat command in World War II — a little more than a month in northern Africa, 38 days in Sicily, 318 days in northwest Europe — Patton gradually showed himself to be America's greatest fighting general. Under his command, the Third Army killed or captured 1.4 million soldiers of the Third Reich, while enduring the lowest casualty rate of any Allied army in the European Theater of Operations (ETO). A strategic assessment of Allied generals compiled by the German *Oberkommando Herres* (high command) described Patton as "the most modern, and the only, master of the offensive" among Allied commanders: "Patton is the most dangerous general on all fronts. The tactics of other generals are known and countermeasures can be effected against them. Patton's tactics are daring and unpredictable. He fights not only the troops opposing him, but the Reich."

This ironic tribute from Patton's enemies is made more ironic still in light of the post-war smear campaign, mounted by Soviet sympathizers in the press and acted upon by a pro-Soviet political establishment, depicting the general as a covert

Know the past: Through diligent study of military history, Patton was able to get inside the head of an enemy, even predicting in 1937 a Japanese sneak attack against Pearl Harbor.

Nazi sympathizer. "It is not an exaggeration to state that Patton fought two wars in the ETO: one against the enemy and one against higher authorities for the opportunity to fight the enemy," notes Colonel Allen. After Germany surrendered on May 7, 1945, Patton realized that our Soviet "allies" — who had begun the war as co-aggressors with National Socialist Germany — were in fact our enemy, and he urged his superiors to evict the Soviets from central and eastern Europe.

In a conversation with then-Undersecretary of War Robert P. Patterson that took place in Austria shortly after the Nazi surrender, Patton complained that the "point system" being used to de-mobilize Third Army troops was destroying the Third Army, and creating a vacuum that the Soviets would exploit. "Mr. Secretary, for God's sake, when you go home, stop this point system; stop breaking up these armies," pleaded the general. "Let's keep our boots polished, bayonets sharpened, and present a picture of force and strength to these people [the Soviets]. This is the only language they understand." Asked by Patterson — who would become Secretary of War a few months later — what he would do, Patton replied: "I would have you tell the [Red Army] where their border is, and give them a limited time to get back across. Warn them that if they fail to do so, we will push them back across it."

Patton knew that the Red Army was weak, under-supplied, and vulnerable, and that if Europe were to be freed from totalitarian despotism, the West would have to act before the Soviets consolidated their position. "Oh George," came the condescending reply from Patterson, "you … have lost sight of the big picture."

That "big picture," as leftist historian Arthur Schlesinger Jr. explained in the July/August 1995 issue of *Foreign Affairs*, "was to commit the United States to postwar international structures before [victory] … could return the nation to its old habits." In order to keep our nation entangled in the growing network of international bodies, a credible foreign menace was needed, and the Soviets were perfectly cast in the part. "It is to Joseph

Rommel (standing, front), like other German generals, knew Patton was the Allies' only "master of the offensive." Heading the 2nd U.S. Corps., Patton proved it, whipping the vaunted Afrika Corps.

Stalin that Americans owe the 40-year suppression of the isolationist impulse," wrote Schlesinger with approval.

Had Patton been permitted to drive the Soviets from Europe, millions of people would have been spared decades of abject oppression, and the criminal elite that continues to dominate most of eastern and central Europe might never have come to power. Patton understood, and warned his superiors, that if the Soviets were allowed to consolidate their grip, "we have failed the liberation of Europe; we have lost the war!" Patton, an honorable and patriotic man, was apparently unable to accept the fact that while he and his soldiers fought to liberate their fellow men from tyranny, those above him in policy-making positions were seeking to control the world, not to emancipate it. Thus Patton was traduced in the servile press as a covert "Nazi sympathizer" and stripped of his command shortly before his fatal automobile accident on December 9, 1945.

Patton "was a man who trained and disciplined his mind and body nearly every day of his life for the role he had always known he was to play," recorded Patton's nephew, Fred Ayer, Jr., in his book *Before the Colors Fade: Portrait of a Soldier*. "[He was] a

man who believed in the aristocracy of achievement and in the sanctity of his country's course. He was conceited, sometimes ruthless, often inconsiderate and outwardly very, very tough. He was often too much the impetuous showman and yet a deep and careful thinker. But he was also magnificently well-read, deeply religious, softhearted, emotional and easily moved to tears."

It is quite likely that Patton possessed the finest military mind our nation ever produced, and that mind was the result of a deep and expansive study of history. "Papa always told me that the thing was to be a good soldier," recalled the general. "Next was to be a good scholar." It was Patton's scholarly exertions that made his soldierly exploits possible. "To be a successful soldier you must know history," Patton advised in *War As I Knew It*. "Read it objectively. Dates and even the minute details of tactics are useless. What you must know is how man reacts. Weapons change, but man who uses them changes not at all.... To win battles you do not beat weapons — you beat the soul of man, of the enemy man." Because he was a diligent student of the past, noted Ayer, Patton "would accurately be able to foretell much of the future."

Not only was Patton an omnivorous

reader, he was blessed with uncanny powers of retention, and could quote extensively from nearly anything he read — the Bible, military history, Shakespeare, even the Koran (which he read as preparation for his arrival in northern Africa). While Patton was stationed in Hawaii as a colonel, he maintained a personal library containing hundreds of books — histories, biographies, memoirs, and political works — nearly all of which had been read and annotated with margin notes.

His preternatural gifts of retention and recall proved indispensable during the Third Army's mad dash across Europe. "He collected maps the way some men do art treasures," recalls Colonel Allen. "He knew the entire road net of France and Germany by memory, and the details of every major battlefield." Before his arrival in Normandy, Patton devoured Douglas Southall Freeman's *The Norman Conquest,* paying particular attention to the roads used by William the Conqueror during his campaigns in Normandy and Brittany almost nine centuries earlier. Using those ancient roads, explained Patton, provided his army with valuable avenues of attack "when the enemy resorts, as he always does, to demolition."

Patton's diligent study of military history could have spared our nation one of its most painful defeats, had Patton's superiors been willing to listen to him. In 1937, during his assignment in Hawaii, then-Colonel Patton composed a detailed report predicting, in unsettling detail, the sneak attack by Japan against Pearl Harbor four years later. Taking note of the fact that Japan's 1904 sneak attack upon Russian forces at Port Arthur began the victorious campaign in that war, Patton warned that "an attack like that is perfectly feasible if we're off guard.... They haven't forgotten how well it worked." Patton's astute assessment, if followed, may have saved countless American lives, but his superiors had a different agenda. "I turned [the report] in to the ranking naval officer of the command and he just put it in his safe," Patton recalled later. "Nobody else had the combination except his own houseboy, [who] was, of course, a good loyal Japanese.

Nobody ever saw the report again — not on our side, anyway."

As this incident illustrates, Patton's devoted study and his intuitive gifts allowed him to get inside the head of an enemy, in this case the Japanese. He proved to be an equally pellucid student of the German military as well. "I have studied the German all my life," reflected Patton in *War As I Knew It*. "I have read the memoirs of his generals and political leaders. I have even read his philosophers and lis-

Badge of courage: Patton believed, "All men are frightened.... The courageous man ... forces himself, in spite of his fears, to carry on."

tened to his music. I have studied in detail the accounts of every damn one of his battles. I know exactly how he will react under any given set of circumstances. He hasn't the slightest idea what I am going to do. Therefore, when the time comes, I'm going to whip the hell out of him."

"Throughout his life, [Patton] completely dominated every unit he commanded," recalled Colonel Allen. "Yet in dominating, he did not domineer. Patton always led men. He did not rule them. This vital distinction explains many things about him. It explains why the troops called him 'Georgie.' Why his men and units were always the most soldierly, the most effi-

cient, the most aggressive, and cockiest. Why he always got so much out of them." "I served with General George S. Patton," proudly recalls military historian Porter B. Williamson in his book *Patton's Principles*. "No man served *under* Gen. Patton; he was always serving *with* us."

Patton's well-publicized contempt for soldiers who professed to suffer from "battle fatigue," or who had dodged combat through self-inflicted wounds, was the obverse of his respect for personal courage. In *War As I Knew It*, the general recalled that whenever he would come across a soldier with self-inflicted wounds, "I would ... say, 'Now, all of you other soldiers listen,' and would use about three lines of choice profanity and state that, by wounding himself, he not only showed he was a coward, but also added to the labor and risk of the brave men who did not use this means of getting out of battle."

While Patton certainly understood the horrors of combat, he also understood that it was useless to "take counsel of one's fears" when there were battles to fight. "I don't admit the existence of battle fatigue, because in war you can't admit the existence of things like that," he explained. "Once you concede its reality, you admit the reality of demoralization. You can't win battles with demoralized troops." Nor did he allow himself ever to display even the slightest hint of fear or doubt in the midst of battle. "Patton was scared, discouraged, and weary on many occasions, as he would frankly admit *afterward*," notes Colonel Allen. "He never claimed to be devoid of fear. It was not unusual for him to return from the lines and relate that he had been frightened."

"If we take the generally accepted definition of bravery as a quality which knows no fear, I have never seen a brave man," reflected Patton. "All men are frightened. The more intelligent they are, the more frightened they are. The courageous man is the man who forces himself, in spite of his fears, to carry on. Discipline, pride, self-respect, self-confidence, and the love of glory are attributes which will make a man courageous even if he is afraid."

Center of Military History

"Talk with the troops," Patton demanded of his officers. "They know more about the war than anybody. Make them tell you all of their gripes."

Among Patton's keys to victory were preparation and discipline. "A pint of sweat saves a gallon of blood," he noted in his memoirs, and he had the advantage of inheriting an exceptionally well trained Third Army from Lt. General Courtney H. Hodges. He also demanded that his army meet the highest and least forgiving standards of discipline and comportment, because it is through discipline that men overcome their fears on the battlefield.

"All human beings have an innate resistance to obedience," wrote Patton. "Discipline removes the resistance and, by constant repetition, makes obedience habitual and subconscious. Where would an undisciplined football team get?... Battle is more exigent than football. No sane man is unafraid in battle, but discipline produces in him a form of vicarious courage which, with his manhood, makes for victory. Self-respect grows directly

from discipline. The Army saying, 'Who ever saw a dirty soldier with a medal?' is largely true."

Patton also displayed "intense loyalty to his men," recalled Colonel Allen, and he gave personal attention to men of outstanding courage. On one occasion he came across a soldier who had been run over by a tank and nearly cut in two. The general personally administered morphine and tended to the injured man as he succumbed to his fatal injuries. According to Patton, nearly 80 percent of an army commander's mission "is to arouse morale in his men." Patton's carefully cultivated image — the spit-shined cavalry boots, ivory-handled revolvers, the bulldog demeanor — was not merely an exercise in vanity, but a reflection of his leadership strategy.

Patton was also "the only army commander in the ETO who was briefed by enlisted men," notes Allen. "He listened

to them as attentively as he did to officers." Patton demanded that the officers "talk with the troops": "They know more about the war than anybody. Make them tell you all of their gripes. Make sure they know we are doing everything we can to help them. The soldiers have to win the war. We cannot do it." Williamson points out that while Patton understood and strictly enforced the discipline of rank, he readily mingled with his men. "He talked with all of the soldiers," writes Williamson. "He touched the soldiers with a handshake or a slap on the back." Although Patton's insistence upon obedience to uniform regulations was legendary, he also respected those soldiers who had dirtied themselves in combat, and no soldier "was so dirty or greasy that Gen. Patton would decline to shake his hand.... If a man deserved a compliment, Gen. Patton would snap to attention and salute the man for his work." Patton was also "the only senior ETO commander who always thanked and commended his troops upon the completion of a campaign, not with a merely perfunctory 'well done' statement, but a heartfelt message that he wrote himself," recalls Colonel Allen.

Williamson testifies that the respect shown by Patton to his troops was heartily reciprocated: "When we were in the dust and dirt of the desert and the salute was not required, I have seen soldiers try to form a straight line and salute Gen. Patton when he would drive past their area." The devotion of Patton's men, summarizes Colonel Allen, was the product of "three deep-seated beliefs: That he was invincible in battle; that he was loyal to his men and always looked out for their interests; that he was as courageous as he demanded others should be."

Following the Allies' disastrous loss to Rommel's German-Italian Panzer army at Tunisia's Kasserine Pass in February 1943, Patton was appointed to replace Lt. General Lloyd Frendenall as head of the 2nd U.S. Corps. Upon taking command of a demoralized force that had suffered great losses in men, matériel, and momentum, Patton —

Patton displayed intense loyalty to his men and he gave personal attention to men of outstanding courage. On one occasion he came across a soldier who had been run over by a tank and nearly cut in two. The general personally administered morphine and tended to the injured man as he succumbed to his fatal injuries.

at the time a two-star general — issued what he described as "a simplified directive of war: Use steamroller strategy; that is, make up your mind on course and direction of action, and stick to it." But he understood that strategic inflexibility depends upon tactical flexibility: "[I]n tactics, do not use steamroller strategy. Attack weakness. Hold them by the nose and kick them in the pants."

Few if any field commanders in history have been as tactically adaptable as Patton, and while he was an assiduous student of both warfare and history, he was quite at a loss to explain his gifts. "Whether these tactical insights of mine are the result of inspiration or insomnia, I have never been able to determine, but nearly every tactical idea I have ever had has come into my head full-born, much after the manner of Minerva from the head of Jupiter," Patton reflected. But his tactical decisions always served his overall strategy, which was rooted in Napoleon's maxim that "the purely defensive is doomed to defeat."

"Wars are not won by defensive tactics," he explained. "Pacifists would do well to study the Siegfried and Maginot Lines, remembering that these defenses were forced; that Troy fell; that the walls of Hadrian succumbed; that the Great Wall of China was futile; and that, by the same token, the mighty seas which are alleged to defend us can also be circumvented by a resolute and ingenious oppo-

nent," admonished the general. "In war, the only sure defense is offense, and the efficiency of offense depends upon the warlike souls of those conducting it."

"General Patton always hated those military and political leaders who delayed, regrouped, consolidated gains, defended land, dug foxholes, or would permit any act which would prolong the war without any thought of the soldiers on both sides that would die from the delay," observed military historian Porter B. Williamson. "It's a waste of fine young men to stay in fixed positions and see who can send over the most shells," ex-

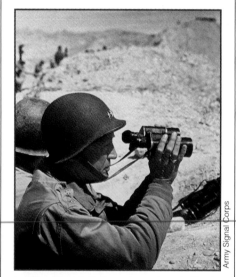

Looking ahead: Patton, shown here in North Africa, recognized not only the nature of the Nazi enemy but of the Soviet "ally." When Germany was defeated, he warned that "the tin-soldier politicians in Washington and Paris ... have allowed us to kick hell out of one b✱✱✱✱✱✱ and at the same time forced us to help establish a second one as evil or more evil than the first." "We're headed down another long road to losing another peace," he predicted.

Army Signal Corps

plained General Patton. "It costs too many men to stay in fixed positions where the enemy can strike. We will keep moving and the enemy will always hit where we have been and not where we are. When the enemy is firing at where we have been, we can tell exactly where they have their firepower. We will move fast and destroy the enemy where he can be easily killed." To his Third Army Pat-

ton attached the nickname "Hell on Wheels" — an apt summary of his strategic vision. Patton's key tactical insight was, "Never let the enemy pick the battle site. We will fight where we want to fight and not where the enemy wants to fight. We will always keep the odds on our side."

During his 13 months in combat in WW II, recalls military historian Colonel Paul D. Hawkins, Patton "never issued a defensive order. His theory — attack, attack, attack, and, when in doubt, attack again — shortened the war by never giving the enemy a chance to organize or reorganize enough to make a concerted attack against him." Although Patton, like most men of accomplishment and ambition, had a flair for self-promotion, he readily acknowledged that his successes were not the product of his unaided genius and the disciplined, capable troops under his command. "God has been very good to us," he acknowledged on the eve of his dramatic relief mission at Bastogne. "We have never retreated; we have suffered no defeats, no famine, no epidemics. This is because a lot of people back home have been praying for us. We have to pray for ourselves, too."

By September 1944, the Patton-commanded Third Army had blitzed across France, crushed German defenses, and was poised to strike at the very heart of the Reich. Within sight of the German border, Patton's drive literally ran out of gas and ammunition. Supreme Allied Commander General Dwight Eisenhower had diverted the crucial supplies from Patton's Army to British Commander Bernard Montgomery, who was staging an airborne invasion of Holland. Montgomery's operation was a debacle that cost the lives of 17,000 British and American soldiers, while Patton, immobilized by the diversion, could only watch in impotent frustration. "It was my opinion that this was the momentous error of the war," Patton wrote in his memoir.

As journalist Jeffrey St. John wrote in an earlier profile of Patton in THE NEW AMERICAN, "Stopping Patton's army from a thrust into Germany prolonged the war and cost greater Allied casualties." Patton, who understood that to make war means to sacrifice the lives of good men, found the needless waste of lives unconscionable. Compounding this outrage, observes St. John, was the fact that Eisenhower's decision "gave the Soviets the necessary time to advance toward Germany from the east and to occupy Eastern Europe. Eisenhower's later decision to allow the Soviets to capture Berlin has been defended on the grounds of saving lives — but he threw away lives earlier by halting Patton in August 1944. Keeping Patton from taking Prague proved equally favorable to the Soviets."

In April 1945, the Third Army had crossed the Rhine, rolled across Germany, and were within 50 miles of Berlin, when Patton's superiors issued a nearly inexplicable order: He was ordered to withdraw 100 miles west, over captured territory. The vacuum was quickly filled by the Red Army, which swarmed over Czechoslovakia and eastern Germany.

"This war stopped right where it started," observed Patton during a closed, off-the-record press conference on May 8, 1945. "Right in the Hun's backyard which is now Hitler's graveyard. But that's not the end of this business by any means. What the tin-soldier politicians in Washington and Paris have managed to do today is another story you'll be writing for a long while.... They have allowed us to kick hell out of one b****** and at the same time forced us to help establish a second one as evil or more evil than the

first. We have won a series of battles, not a war for peace. We're headed down another long road to losing another peace."

Over the next several months, as Patton's understanding of the betrayal grew, he became resolved to speak out publicly. "I will resign when I have finished this job [as military governor of Bavaria], which will be not later than Dec. 26," wrote Patton in an October 1945 diary entry. "I hate to do it, but I have been caged all my life, and whether they appreciate it or not, America needs some honest men who dare say what they think, not what they think people want them to think."

Unfortunately, Patton's voice was stilled before it could be raised to protest the perfidy of our political establishment. On December 9, 1945, Patton and General Hobart Gay were backseat passengers in a military staff sedan speeding along the autobahn en route to a pheasant hunt. An army truck traveling in the opposite direction suddenly crossed their lane, creating the conditions for a head-on collision. Both drivers swerved to avoid a direct collision, but the side-swiping impact threw the general forward, striking his head on the sedan's interior dome light, and then whiplashing him back. Although both the driver and General Gay were uninjured, Patton suffered crushed vertebrae in his upper spinal column, leaving him paralyzed from the neck down and mortally wounded.

"This is a hell of a way for a soldier to die," protested Patton as he lay paralyzed in an Army hospital bed in Heidelberg.

For 12 days the indomitable 60-year-old general fought a rearguard action against death, valiantly battling an injury that would have killed most men within, at most, 72 hours. But on December 23rd the hero finally succumbed to pneumonia while in the company of his wife, Beatrice. "It is too dark; I mean too late," whispered the general as death came to claim him.

"He was buried in the drizzle of a fog-shrouded December morning on the day before Christmas in the American Military Cemetery at Hamm in Luxembourg," writes biographer Ladislas Farago. There he joined 5,076 other fallen Third Army heroes, whose honored remains repose beneath crosses and Stars of David. In death, as on the battlefield, Patton could be found amid his men. "The dead, most of whom had been killed fighting in the Battle of the Bulge, came from all of what were then the forty-eight states, from the District of Columbia, and from Alaska and Hawaii," records Farago.

Given Patton's bottomless courage, his voracious appetite for the written word, and his unyielding sense of honor, his legacy is perhaps best summarized in his favorite quotation from *Pilgrim's Progress*: " 'My sword I give to him that will succeed me in my pilgrimage, and my courage and skill to him that can get it. My works and scars I carry with me to be a witness for me that I have fought His battles who will now be my rewarder.' So he passed over and all the trumpets sounded for him on the other side." ∎

Natural leader: Draza Mihailovich's fearless gallantry endeared him to the Serbian people. Rescued by Mihailovich's Chetnik resistance after his bomber was shot down by Nazi fighters over Serbia, American airman Major Richard L. Felman recalled his first meeting with the Serb patriot: "The first time I saw him he was … surrounded by laughing children throwing flowers in his path."

General Draza Mihailovich was precisely the kind of man of whom Pericles spoke. An authentic hero of two world wars, Mihailovich became one of the greatest resistance fighters in history. Yet as we shall see, after years of struggle and sacrifice, he was betrayed by his allies and murdered by his enemies. Mihailovich was not honored after his death by any grand monuments, either in his own homeland or abroad. His only monument, thus far, is in the hearts of men, most especially in the hearts of his countrymen and in the hearts of 500 Americans whose lives he saved.

Draza Mihailovich was born in 1893 in the small town of Ivanytza, Serbia. Though his father devoted his life to teaching, Mihailovich himself decided on a career in his country's army and so entered the Serbian Military Academy in 1910. His plans for his formal education were soon disturbed, however, by a series of wars. Those wars, as it turned out, though they upset his plans, served his education in other ways. In the Serbo-Turkish War, the Serbo-Bulgarian War, and again in the First World War, Mi-

hailovich demonstrated both tremendous bravery in action and superior leadership capabilities. He was a natural-born leader of men and, consequently, rose during those war years from corporal to first lieutenant.

At the conclusion of the First World War, Mihailovich turned his attention once again to his formal education, studying, and always excelling, at both Yugoslav and French military schools. Within a few years he was promoted to staff officer and appointed professor of tactics at the Yugoslav Military Academy. In the 1930s, he served as military attaché at his country's embassy in Romania, and later as military attaché in Czechoslovakia.

After Hitler's rise to power, it was evident to all observers that Germany was determined to rearm and to resume a major role in European affairs. After the *Anschluss* with Austria in March 1938, the absorption of the Sudetenland in October 1938, and the occupation of the Czech portion of Czechoslovakia in March 1939, Germany was transformed into the most powerful nation in Europe. Even after the outbreak of war with Britain and

France, Germany's hegemonic position continued for several years and was confirmed by its lightning conquest of France in 1940.

The Three-Power Pact of September 1940 brought Germany, Italy, and Japan into a formidable military and diplomatic alliance. So dominant was Germany by that time that within six months the remaining central European countries, mindful of the realities of the moment, adhered to the pact as well. Hungary, Romania, Slovakia, and Bulgaria all hurried their diplomats to Berlin to sign. From the perspective of that period in history, these smaller nations had little choice. Like it or not, Germany was not only the military powerhouse of continental Europe, it was equally as robust economically. Moreover, the collapse of France seemed to indicate that Germany would retain its newly won position for a long time, maybe decades or centuries. Few observers in 1940, even the more astute, would have speculated that Germany would not continue to dominate the continent far into the future.

Yugoslavia's position in the late 1930s was particularly perilous. Since 1934 she had become, to a major extent, economically dependent on the Germans. From a strategic military standpoint, Yugoslavia had genuine reasons to feel threatened by her neighbor, Fascist Italy, and by that country's expansionist policies. In March 1941, therefore, Yugoslavia signed the Three-Power Pact, aligning herself with Germany. This move, though distasteful, seemed to her government and diplomats the only solution to an otherwise untenable political situation. However, those signatures on the Three-Power Pact produced an instantaneous and explosive reaction at home. Immediately, in all of the cities and towns of the country, huge crowds demonstrated against the policy, shouting the slogans, *Bolye rat nego pakt!* ("Better war than the pact!") and *Bolye grob, nego rob!* ("Better a grave than a slave!"). These sentiments were felt not only by the great mass of the people, but also by important military and political elements. Yugoslavia's

Mrs. Roosevelt
on Yugoslavia,
ed Mihailovich
hailovich led th
the country. In
ple, while dinin
sevelt at the Wh
the President to

After June
abruptly change
dination with t
Moscow. He de
tivities of Gene
perpetrated by
government-in-
goslavia rested
dent, constituti
by Mihailovich
rection of Russi
ic insisted, "wi
present racketee
East European
national republ
selves to the U
goslavia should
the Soviet Unio
stated, "are eag
tion.... If Sovie
plies — does oc
process. The Y
become a rep
Union...." Adar
Mihailovich o
States. Soon, c
same Commun
the radio. And,
in the eyes of tl
Tito's rose.

In Septembe
an article a
vich of dir
Germans. Thou
lous to anyone f
temperament, l
peated so often
Communists th
tain governmen
phisticated mer
bizarre atmosp
when "Uncle Jc
beloved humar
sian people and
celebrated as o

government was promptly overthrown and a more neutral-minded government installed.

Yugoslavia, however, was not destined to retain an independent, neutral existence. Fearing that Yugoslavia would allow itself to become a British base, Germany immediately attacked.

The Yugoslavs were certainly aware, when they overthrew the pro-German regime, that Hitler, so prone to fury, would react with deadly force. They knew also that in such a contest, Yugoslavia was like David facing Goliath and that, strategically speaking, her situation appeared hopeless. Finally, they knew that Yugoslavia would be alone in its fight. It would face, with absolute certainty, immense horrors, destruction, deaths, occupation, and loss of national freedom and independence. On the other hand, by defying Hitler, Yugoslavia would preserve its honor and preserve its inner, *spiritual* freedom.

In 1941, Yugoslavia's general staff adopted a plan wherein its armies were dispersed to the frontiers to contest every inch of territory. Mihailovich, who had authored a book on guerilla warfare, submitted a report advocating a radically different approach. In a face-to-face confrontation with Germany's motorized Panzer legions and her ultra-modern air force, Mihailovich reasoned, tiny Yugoslavia stood no chance. Her armies would be quickly overrun. The only possibility was to withdraw the armies from the frontiers, abandon the plains, and concentrate Yugoslavia's forces in the mountains where Germany's Panzers and Stukas would be useless. This, he reasoned, would neutralize at least some of Germany's huge advantage. In that way the nation could carry on its fight for independence, tie down the enemy for years, and cost the invader dearly.

Unfortunately for Yugoslavia, the generals ignored Mihailovich, who was then a mere colonel, and proceeded to deploy its units at the borders. As a result, Mihailovich's worst fears were realized. On April 6, 1941 German troops stormed the Yu-

goslav frontiers while simultaneously subjecting the capital, Belgrade, to devastating air attack, one that cost more than 17,000 civilian lives. Within one week the German army marched through Belgrade, and four days later the government, and a large portion of the Yugoslav army, surrendered.

However, other military units refused to recognize the order to lay down their arms and continued to fight German formations in pitched battles. Most of these units withdrew to the hills and soon came under the command of Mihailovich. To the government's order to capitulate, Mihailovich responded with these words: "Capitulation? I do not know what capitulation is. I have served in the army for many years, but I have never heard this word."

Instead of surrendering, Mihailovich raised the national flag above the mountaintop of Ravna Gora and announced to the world that the war against the occupiers of Yugoslavia would continue. This act inspired an uprising among the people of Serbia and Montenegro, causing additional problems for the thoroughly dumbfounded Germans. It was clear that, despite their defeat, the Yugoslavs were not overawed by German might and did

not regard themselves as a conquered people.

Within weeks, large portions of the more mountainous regions of Montenegro, Serbia, and Bosnia were under the de facto control of the Chetniks, the resistance armies of Mihailovich. In these areas, enemy troops could travel only in large numbers, and even then were frequently challenged. At no time and place could the enemy feel safe and secure.

The dauntless Chetnik force was the first serious armed resistance movement in Nazi-occupied Europe, taking a horrific toll on enemy occupation troops. In recognition of his astonishing abilities and accomplishments, the Yugoslav government-in-exile promoted Mihailovich to Major General in December 1941, to Minister of War and Lieutenant General in January 1942, and finally to full General and Deputy Commander-in-Chief in June 1942.

Meanwhile, the Germans were disconcerted by Mihailovich's unprecedented defiance of their power. The famed Blitzkrieg method of warfare, which had so effectively crushed Poland and France, proved useless in the mountainous terrain of the

Boldly defiant: The Serb people looked to Mihailovich to save their freedom from Nazi depravations. When the German conquest of Yugoslavia was nearly complete and he was ordered to capitulate, Mihailovich responded: "Capitulation? I do not know what capitulation is." Mihailovich's Chetnik force thereupon became the first serious armed resistance movement in Nazi-occupied Europe.

Balkan penin
massive scale
country, but tl
able because
Operation B
against Russia

It was deci
negotiate som
ment or truc
hailovich rece
then respond
wished peace
have it. His r
forward: "Th
evacuate my
be restored.
soldier remai
tinue to fight.

And so the
came a botton
macht, costin
German dead
ous historian
recognizes th
gle. John Tol
freedom fight
resistance
Throughout t
tains, in the
coast, in Serl
Montenegro,
— Mihailov
ready to attac
enemy would
of tranquility

The Germ
reprisals on z
50 civilians f
in ambush ar
The protrac
without respi
cuted, and c
the ground.
would not be
to the Germa
he announce
against them
for the pres
"Our fightin
based on ou
and on our u
ry of our Alli
dier killed o
shooting of

he met Dr. Sun Yat-sen and other future leaders of the Chinese freedom fight and heard their Western-inspired ideas on the need for a free, constitutional government in the Chinese homeland.

When revolution finally erupted, in October 1911, Chiang immediately returned to China, where his elite training proved a valuable asset to the revolutionary cause. His first feat was to lead his troops in the capture of the city of Hangchow, a stunning military victory. As a result of his military successes, Chiang was promoted rapidly, until he became Sun Yat-sen's right-hand man.

Unfortunately, the initial military successes were followed by overwhelming setbacks that saw the revolutionaries driven out of northern China, and their Kuomintang (National People's Party) outlawed. But Sun's revolutionaries were able to regroup in the south, where they established their capital at Canton.

As these events were unfolding, an-

other revolution was convulsing Russia. By 1918, the leaders of the newly formed Communist government in Moscow were already setting their sights on their next target: the subversion and conquest of China. Sensing opportunity in the Chinese conflict, Lenin's emissaries sought to draw Sun Yat-sen into the Communist camp. The Western-educated Chinese leader, afflicted with a certain degree of utopian idealism, was quite sympathetic with many of the stated goals of the Russian revolutionaries.

Chiang Kai-shek, however, was not so easily persuaded. Having been sent by Sun Yat-sen to Moscow to report on the Soviet system, he returned convinced of the malignity of the Russian Bolsheviks. As a result of his experiences with Bolshevism, he later wrote, "I became more convinced than ever that Soviet political institutions were instruments of tyranny and terror." Furthermore, he remarked that the Communists' "so-called interna-

> *"I became more convinced than ever that Soviet political institutions were instruments of tyranny and terror."*
>
> *— Chiang Kai-shek*

tionalism and World Revolution are nothing but Caesarism in another name, the better to hoodwink the outside world."

Unfortunately, Sun was not convinced of the Communists' ill intentions, and he allowed Lenin's handpicked agents, especially Michael Borodin, to continue their subversive activities in their capacity as "advisers" to the fledgling Chinese Republic.

With Sun Yat-sen's passing in 1925, Chiang Kai-shek inherited a government that still faced substantial opposition from various warlords in the unconquered northern China. From within, the Kuomintang was by then honeycombed with Communist intrigue, thanks to the tireless efforts of Borodin.

Nevertheless, in 1926 Chiang launched his "Northern Expedition," with the aim of unifying China under republican government. No sooner had he led his expeditionary forces north, than Borodin took advantage of his absence to stage a Communist coup d'etat in Canton.

Chiang, dismayed but undeterred, promptly returned to the south, where he overthrew the Communists, expelled Borodin and the other Soviet agents, and ousted Mao Tse-tung and his confederates from the Kuomintang. This stinging defeat was never forgotten by the Communists; from that day forward, Chiang Kai-shek was one of their most hated enemies.

Returning to the north, Chiang succeeded in bringing most of China under republican rule, although unrelenting resistance by certain of China's former

Chinese colossus: Chiang Kai-shek spent his entire life working for a free, united Chinese republic against a variety of enemies — home-grown warlords, the invading Japanese, Communist subversives, and duplicitous allies — who stopped at nothing in their attempts to thwart his noble plans.

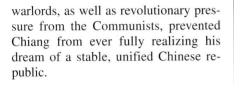
warlords, as well as revolutionary pressure from the Communists, prevented Chiang from ever fully realizing his dream of a stable, unified Chinese republic.

In the midst of these difficulties came one of the most important turning points in Chiang Kai-shek's life — his marriage to Mayling Soong in 1927. Mayling came from an extraordinary family, whose members included prominent political figures and financiers. Mayling, like her father and mother, was a devout Christian, a circumstance that led Mayling's family to oppose the match. Chiang, undaunted, finally managed to get an interview with Mayling's mother. He promised to seriously study Christianity, but refused to promise conversion except as a result of sincere belief. Because of Chiang's honesty, Mayling's mother gave her consent, and the couple was married in two separate ceremonies, Chinese and Christian.

Nor did Chiang Kai-shek forget his promise. He read the Bible conscientiously, and as a result, became a committed, lifelong Christian. Thereafter he made prayer and Bible study a daily priority, and his conduct, both public and private, was shaped by Christian values.

By 1930, the long and costly civil war in China was drawing to a close. The final months of fighting cost hundreds of thousands of lives, but by 1931 Chiang Kai-shek had succeeded in unifying China under the most enlightened government China had ever seen.

Chiang's government was based on three core tenets, the so-called "Three People's Principles," which had been first enunciated in 1905 by Sun Yat-sen. The principle of Nationalism called for a unified and independent China, free from crippling internal strife and foreign control. The principle of People's Sovereignty expressed the goal of constitutional government. The principle of People's Livelihood was the socialist doctrine that the government should assume responsibility for the well-being of its citizenry. Chiang was particularly concerned at the need for land redistribution,

a pet concern of socialists of every stripe. Regarding this third principle, Robert Welch, founder of the John Birch Society, remarked:

> [Chiang] sincerely believes in the responsibility of the state for [the people's] livelihood.... To that extent he is, in philosophy and action, a socialist today. To that extent he and this writer would categorically disagree … but … the marvel is not that Chiang became doctrinally a socialist, but that: 1) he has combined so much common sense, dependence on individual initiative, and true political liberalism, with … socialist dogma; and 2) that he has stood so firmly by the principle that socialism as a desirable end does not justify the use of barbaric means to achieve it or maintain it.

Moreover, in the historical context of militarism, despotism, and serfdom that have been the rule in China, and indeed all over Asia, for millennia, Chiang Kai-shek's enlightened views were nothing short of miraculous. For it is wise to remember that, unlike the American Founding Fathers, Chiang Kai-shek was not building on centuries-long currents of religious, political, and economic thought that had come to define the role of limited, constitutional government in relation to unalienable God-given rights.

For about nine years, from 1928 to 1937, Chiang Kai-shek worked to build China into a free and prosperous society. He built roads, encouraged literacy, and

Turning point: To gain the hand of Mayling Soong, the future Madame Chiang, in marriage, Chiang Kai-shek promised her parents to study Christianity, though he could not promise to convert. Keeping that promise after the wedding, Chiang studied the Bible conscientiously and became a lifelong Christian.

waged war on the rampant drug problem in China.

As it turned out, Chiang's dream of a free, unified, modern Chinese state was short-lived. With the onset of Japanese expansionism in the early 1930s, Chiang was confronted by a deadly external threat to Chinese independence. In 1931, Japanese forces occupied Manchuria. All through that decade, Japan expanded her territorial holdings into China from the northeast. Faced with continuing unrest, and ill-equipped to take on the modern Japanese military machine, Chiang stalled for time, refusing to give the Japanese a pretext to launch an all-out war.

In the meantime, the Communists, after being routed by Chiang's forces in the early 1930s, had established a base in remote northwestern China. They sowed vicious propaganda about Chiang and his government, saying that Chiang was only interested in fighting his fellow Chinese (i.e., the warlords and the Communists) and was unwilling to take on the encroaching Japanese imperialists. The Communists insisted, on the other hand, that they were willing and able to defend their homeland against the Japanese.

The propaganda took its toll on the Chinese military, including many officers, until, in late 1936, in an attempted coup d'etat, Chiang was taken captive at military headquarters in Sian by two of his top generals. In response to their demands, Chiang replied coldly that they had two choices only: kill him or release him. He refused to negotiate on any terms. After two weeks, his wife flew to Sian and confronted her husband's captors. Already wavering, they finally released Chiang and turned themselves over to him.

The following year, Japanese invasion forces poured into China, capturing Shanghai and Nanking. Chiang Kai-shek's Nationalist government was forced to retreat far inland to Chungking, where Chiang set up a provisional capital. Even so, Japanese bombers raided the city almost nonstop, while the Japanese armies consolidated their gains in northern China and conquered most of the southern coastal provinces.

The Communists exploited China's predicament by pledging military support for Chiang's government in fighting the Japanese, and then taking advantage of every opportunity to expand their own territorial control during the chaos.

By the time the U.S. entered the war, China had already been fighting the Japanese for four devastating years. Nevertheless, Chiang Kai-shek immediately threw in his lot with the United States, stating in a telegram to President Roosevelt the day after Japan's air raid on Pearl Harbor: "To our new common battle we offer all we are and all we have, to stand with you until the Pacific and the world are freed from the curse of brute force and endless perfidy."

China paid a terrible price for siding with the Allies. Her cities continued to take savage poundings from Japanese bombers, while her ill-equipped armies suffered devastating losses. Nevertheless, the valiant Chinese refused to surrender. By so doing, they rendered American forces in the Pacific theater a tremendous favor, keeping 1.5 million Japanese troops tied down on Chinese soil.

Unfortunately, the U.S. failed to reciprocate Chiang's loyalty. While America poured resources into the war in Europe, China was virtually ignored. To make matters worse, General Joseph ("Vinegar Joe") Stilwell was made Chiang Kai-shek's chief of staff. An early prototype of the self-serving, careerist politician-cum-military officer that now dominates the upper echelons of the American military, Stilwell made every effort to undermine Chiang Kai-shek's authority. He diverted supplies from China to Burma, and pressured Chiang to concede to Communist demands. In the words of Patrick Hurley, former U.S. ambassador to China: "The record of General Stilwell in China is irrevocably coupled in history with the conspiracy to overthrow the Nationalist Goverment of China, and to set up in its place a Communist regime — and all this movement was part of … the Communist cell or apparatus that existed at the time in the Government in Washington."

Time of trouble: Madame Chiang (left) inspects damage inflicted by Japanese bombs. The Chinese military was no match for the Imperial Japanese invaders and Chiang's Nationalist government was forced to retreat far inland to Chungking. Meanwhile, as Japanese bombers raided Chinese cities, the Communists under Mao Tse-tung pledged to help resist Japan but nevertheless worked to subvert the Nationalist government at every opportunity.

The crowning insult came when Stilwell persuaded FDR to authorize the replacement of Chiang Kai-shek as military chief of staff with Stilwell himself. Stilwell smugly delivered FDR's order to Chiang Kai-shek in person. Chiang, however, was not cowed, and demanded Stilwell's replacement. For once, the American government backed down. Yet for the most part, the history of Sino-American relations during and immediately after the war is a sorry litany of Communist-inspired efforts to destroy Chiang's Nationalist government, and to appease and build up his Communist enemies.

As WWII drew to a close, the Russian Communists finally declared war on Japan and invaded Manchuria. Vast caches of Japanese weapons were seized and sent to the Chinese Communists. Following the war, aid which Congress voted to send to Chiang to fight the Communists was repeatedly delayed — or stymied altogether — by an American Department of State dominated by Communists and Communist sympathizers. One can only wonder at Chiang Kai-shek's emotions when he came to realize that, after fighting the Oriental despotism of the Manchus, Japanese militarism, and Communist subversion, his most decisive enemies were the Americans, whom he had trusted, admired, and to whom he had faithfully pledged his allegiance during the war. It is to his everlasting credit that Chiang, who had ample cause for bitterness if ever anyone had, remained both a friend of the U.S. and a dedicated Christian to the end of his life.

In the end, realizing that a Communist takeover was unavoidable, Chiang managed to salvage what he could of the Republic of China. In 1948, in fulfillment of another of Chiang's dreams, the first country-wide free elections in China's history were held. At that time, Chiang tried to step down as China's leader, but the Chinese people elected him President for a six-year term by an overwhelming margin. It was a fortuitous event: Shortly thereafter, the Nationalists, under the leadership of Chiang Kai-shek, were

Corbis

Oriental oasis: The Chiang Kai-shek Memorial in Taipei, Taiwan, is a fitting monument to China's greatest 20th century hero. But Chiang's greatest monument is undoubtedly the oasis of freedom and prosperity he created on Taiwan — an oasis that stands in stark contrast to the despotism and misery that still exist in Mainland China.

forced to retreat to the island of Formosa, the one part of China that the Communists had been unable to dominate.

The exodus itself was a heroic effort: Tens of thousands of Nationalists sailed across the treacherous Strait of Formosa in overcrowded boats, many of them leaving behind their belongings, family, and friends. They were destitute and heartbroken, and began their new lives on the tropical island living in misery and poverty. But in a very short time, they transformed Formosa, now usually called Taiwan, into one of the social and economic marvels of the 20th century.

Though densely populated, Taiwan is graced with towering mountains, dense tropical rainforests, rugged and beautiful seacoasts, and is famous for its abundance and variety of butterflies and wild orchids. Unlike most other tropical countries, the water is safe to drink everywhere. Diseases such as malaria and typhoid were eradicated long ago. Compared to the sweltering, gritty poverty of other parts of tropical Asia, Taiwan is clean, orderly, and completely modern. In stark contrast with the brooding colossus across the Strait, Tai-

wan is a happy and colorful society, and its citizens enjoy a standard of living found in very few places elsewhere in Asia.

All of this came as a result of Chiang Kai-shek's labors. While Mao Tse-tung's "agrarian reformers" were slaughtering tens of millions of their countrymen during the Cultural Revolution, Chiang and his followers were holding free elections and granting political and economic freedoms to the industrious Taiwanese. Chiang never relinquished his goal of a unified, republican China, but he died in 1975 with his dream unrealized.

Had he lived to see it, Chiang would doubtless have been dismayed at America's final betrayal of Taiwan, when, in 1979, the U.S. granted diplomatic recognition to the Communist Mainland, and turned its back on its loyal allies in Taipei. When this writer lived in Taiwan in the 1980s, the American embassy compound in downtown Taipei had been left completely undisturbed, overgrown with luxuriant tropical vegetation. This, I was told, was to send a message to America: When you decide to return, we have saved your place.

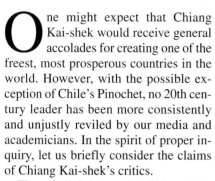
One might expect that Chiang Kai-shek would receive general accolades for creating one of the freest, most prosperous countries in the world. However, with the possible exception of Chile's Pinochet, no 20th century leader has been more consistently and unjustly reviled by our media and academicians. In the spirit of proper inquiry, let us briefly consider the claims of Chiang Kai-shek's critics.

First of all, it is true that Chiang Kai-shek was a military strongman of sorts, at first. He was capable of decisive military action against his enemies, which his critics have been eager to point out. In 1927 during the Northern Expedition, for example, certain of Chiang's troops, left in Nanking, were persuaded by Communists to loot the city and commit various atrocities, including the murder of several foreigners. After taking full responsibility for the outrages, Chiang marched back to the city, and rounded up and executed those responsible. Immediately afterward, upon hearing that the Communists were planning a similar uprising in Shanghai, he placed the city under martial law and arrested and executed sizeable numbers of Communists and their fellow-travelers. Naturally enough, Chiang's implacable, left-wing detractors have seized upon such incidents to unfairly portray him as a bloodthirsty military despot.

Left unsaid are such mitigating facts as Chiang's own cultural tradition, which often dictated that decisive, ruthless moves against opponents were necessary for mere survival. Moreover, the Shanghai incident occurred before Chiang's conversion to Christianity. In his later years, his faith in God prompted him to practice mercy, as when he implored his countrymen, in the spirit of Christian forgiveness, to refrain from exacting revenge on the Japanese in China after the end of World War II. Finally, in comparison to his predecessors the Manchus, his rivals the warlords, and his brutal Communist successors on the Mainland, Chiang Kai-shek was a model of restraint, integrity, and enlightenment.

The libertarian will note that, in the final analysis, Chiang Kai-shek was still a socialist, and therefore cannot qualify as a true champion of freedom. The basis of this claim is, as we have already seen, correct: Chiang believed all his life in the responsibility of the state to nurture its citizens. Once established on Taiwan, he embarked on a thorough program of land reform, which, though very fair-minded, was nonetheless redistributionist. While permitting a wide range of freedoms, the government of Taiwan still maintained certain draconian measures, especially during the period of martial law. These included restrictions on the right of assembly and some of the world's most severe gun-control laws. For all his enlightenment, Chiang Kai-shek always retained strands of beliefs stemming from his authoritarian cultural heritage.

But if we judge the totality of the man, Chiang's virtues and achievements loom very large over his faults — especially considering the Orient's lack of a centuries-old tradition of freedom and individual worth. Regarding the glittering island of freedom and prosperity off China's southeast coast, we may search in vain for its equal elsewhere in Asia. From the pseudo-Marxist regimes that have kept the peoples of India and Indonesia in ignorance and poverty, to brutal military juntas in Burma and the Philippines, to the appalling human suffering inflicted by Communist regimes in Korea, China, and much of Southeast Asia, most of Asia's political history in this century has been a pageant of tragedy and oppression.

Against this backdrop of tyranny and despair throughout the majority of Asia, the life and achievements of Chiang Kai-shek are nothing short of miraculous. He was, quite simply, the father of a free, modern republic. He achieved this in the space of only about three decades, leading a backward, impoverished people ruled by oppressive medieval satraps into a modern, prosperous republic of laws and an unimagined degree of freedom. ■

Spanish Savior

Whatever his faults, Francisco Franco stood bravely against totalitarianism, saving Spain and hastening Axis defeat.

by William Norman Grigg

Few figures of the 20th century have been as relentlessly maligned as Francisco Franco y Bahamonde, who ruled as Spain's *Caudillo* (supreme leader) from 1939 until his death in 1975. Franco's death was celebrated with vulgar, vindictive glee in the obituary columns of Establishment publications that had treated the passing of Communist mass murderers with respectful solemnity.

Newsweek's obituary denounced what it called Franco's "relentless cruelty" and insisted that his regime was "a throwback to the age of Hitler and Mussolini and, as such, [is] a painful embarrassment to the rest of Europe." Upon the Generalissimo's death, concluded the magazine, "Liberals throughout Western Europe breathed a sigh of relief that the world's most durable fascist dictator has been removed from their midst."

Franco's obituary in the *New York Times* accused him of turning Spain "into a totalitarian dictatorship of the right as ingrown and intolerant as the most rigid Communist dictatorships of the left." (It is only in the context of such strained attempts to create moral symmetry, of course, that the *Times* would ever criticize, albeit obliquely, "Communist dictatorships of the left.")

When Red Chinese Premier Chou En-lai, one of the century's most accomplished Communist mass murderers, died a few months after Franco, the same Establishment media organs waxed lyrical in hymning his memory. "An intellectual who was also a man of action, Chou possessed grace, charm, tact and grit," cooed *Newsweek*. "Once dashingly handsome with smoldering black eyes, slim expressive hands and aristocratic mien, he remained physically impressive into his later years and radiated an unmistakable attraction." The *New York Times* extolled Chou as a "great Chinese leader" and designated him "one of the more far-sighted statesmen of the 20th century." Commentator Max Lerner, all but weeping into his typewriter, lamented in his syn-

Courage under fire: The man who would save Spain from both the Nazis and the Communists began a military career as a young officer in Morocco where he distinguished himself by his bravery and conduct. He was justly rewarded: At the age of 20 he was promoted to Captain and by the age of 24 he was the youngest Major in the Spanish Army.

dicated column that "Chou En-lai's death removes a giant figure from the world scene, and impoverishes every people, because while he was a Marxist revolutionary he was also basically a moderate and a realist...."

Obviously, the custodians of "respectable" opinion did not object to dictatorship in principle; what they found objectionable in Franco was not his authoritarianism, but rather the fact that he was an *anti-Communist* ruler. According to the Establishment-approved caricature, Franco was a fascist tyrant who seized power from Spain's democratic

government with the help of Nazi Germany and Fascist Italy. After mercilessly purging his political opponents, Franco imposed an oppressive, puritanical regime upon Spain, reversing decades of social progress — or so runs the common indictment.

In fact, under Franco's rule, Spain experienced its first prolonged period of domestic peace and stability in centuries. As a result, Spain — a nation that had been in an apparently irreversible decline since the 17th century, and was teetering on the brink of totalitarianism in 1936 — enjoyed dramatic economic progress: Between 1960 and 1975, per-capita income in Spain rose nearly 900 percent. Just as importantly, despite drastic measures imposed by Franco to deal with a Soviet-organized revolutionary movement, individual freedom enjoyed by Spanish citizens consistently expanded during Franco's rule.

"Franco was never a fascist or had the smallest belief in any kind of Utopia or system," comments British historian Paul Johnson. A resolute believer in the crown, the Church, and the *Patria*, Franco was prompted to participate in the July 1936 coup by his desire to turn back "the invasion by post-Christian totalitarian culture," which was embodied in the Soviet-sponsored "Popular Front" that was on the verge of taking power.

The so-called "Spanish Civil War," which is more properly considered a Soviet-directed war of subversion, claimed the lives of more than 200,000 Spaniards and left more than one million crippled (the battlefield carnage of the war produced innovative techniques for surgery and blood transfusions). Malnutrition and disease plagued Spain for years after the war's end. Revolutionary figures such as Lenin and Hitler exploited the tragedy of war-ravaged nations to begin the process of creating the total state. Franco, however, was not an ideologue, and he used his power to restore Spain's traditional institutions.

Upon achieving victory in 1939, Paul Johnson observes, "Franco determined to end the destructive process of corruption

> *"Franco determined to end the destructive process of corruption by amputating the agonized limb of Spanish collectivism."*
> *— British historian Paul Johnson*

by amputating the agonized limb of Spanish collectivism." Once the Communist-led forces were defeated, Franco de-Communized Spain's institutions, much as the Allies de-Nazified Germany after World War II. Franco's methods were admittedly harsh; he was dealing, as we will shortly see, with utterly depraved and vicious criminals who had committed unspeakable crimes. But as Johnson notes, Franco's campaign to de-Communize Spain "was not a Leninstyle massacre by classes: the Law of Political Responsibilities of 9 February 1939 dealt with responsibility for crimes on an individual basis.... Strictly speaking, there was no death penalty for political offenses as such."

Franco declared in a December 1939 speech that his intention was "to liquidate the hatred and passions left us by our past war." Those who had been imprisoned for crimes against Christian Spain were urged to seek redemption "through work accompanied by repentance and penitence." While some might object to the medieval overtones of this statement, it is reasonable to believe that Franco's neo-medievalism was preferable to the plague of totalitarianism and total war that was raging through most of the world.

Just as important as Franco's victory over the Communists was his insistence on keeping Spain neutral during World War II. Franco's Nationalists received assistance from Germany and Italy in their war against the Soviet-supported Popular Front, and without the help of German and Italian planes and pilots it is almost certain that the Nationalists would have lost. But Hitler and Mussolini had their own designs for the Iberian peninsula and Northern Africa, and

they expected Franco to express his gratitude by eagerly enlisting in the Axis cause. Franco would confound this expectation.

Franco defined his approach to foreign policy as one of *habil prudencia* — "skillful prudence." As British historian Brian Crozier observes, at the end of the civil war in 1939, Franco told his erstwhile Italian allies, "We need a period of peace of at least five years." Although Franco recognized the role of Germany and Italy in his victory, "he was unwilling to allow Spain to become a satellite of Germany or Italy," Crozier writes. In 1938, with victory in the civil war far from certain, the Nationalists had refused to sign a secret treaty of friendship with Nazi Germany, which, notes Crozier, "would have tied Spanish foreign policy to that of the Nazis after victory."

Crozier points out that "Hitler was less interested in helping Franco win than in prolonging the Civil War for Germany's advantage" — something that the Spanish leader was sufficiently perceptive to understand. Franco's own inclination, on the other hand, was to turn "to the democracies for economic succor, and [move] away from Germany," but this desire was impeded, in large measure, by "the indignantly anti-Franco sentiments that dominated public opinion in Britain, France, and the United States." Franco's chief foreign policy objective was "to preserve Spain's independence and territorial integrity and keep out of the impending European war."

Many of those who condemn Franco for taking assistance from Germany and Italy have not considered how European history might have developed had a Soviet-dominated regime been in place in 1939 when Hitler and Stalin entered into their non-aggression pact. "It would have been a tragedy for America and the rest

of the world if Franco had lost the war with the Communists," Monaco-based historian/adventurer Hilaire du Berrier — the sole surviving pilot of the Spanish Civil War — remarked to THE NEW AMERICAN. "It would have been a catastrophe for the West if Franco had joined the war on the side of the Axis after Hitler conquered France and joined his pact with the Soviet Union. Franco looked out for Spain's interests first, but by doing so

Hitler thwarted: Franco, who "was never a fascist" according to historian Paul Johnson, received help from Germany and Italy during the Spanish Civil War, but harbored no illusions about the Fascists and Nazis. After an October 1940 meeting during which Hitler tried to make Franco commit to the Triple Alliance between Germany, Italy, and Japan, the German despot left "angry and frustrated" according to British historian Brian Crozier.

he was actually one of our best allies — not only by actively opposing the Communists, but also by refusing to help the Axis seize Gibraltar and seal off the Mediterranean."

When Franco met Hitler in the border town of Hendaya in October 1940, the result was "the most infuriating hours of Hitler's life," according to Crozier. "Hitler met Franco with two objectives in mind: to bring Spain into the Triple Alliance, and to gain the *Caudillo's* assent to German plans for an assault on Gibraltar. The *Caudillo*, for his part, came to the meeting with a single negative, but onerous, objective of avoiding all precise commitments of any kind. It is clear that Franco left Hendaya satisfied and relieved; and

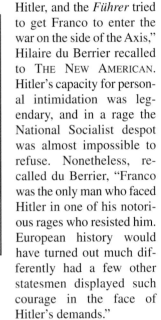

Hitler, angry and frustrated."

The *Führer* later famously remarked that he would rather have his teeth pulled than endure another confrontation such as he had with Franco. The episode was perhaps even more taxing to the Spanish *Caudillo*, who after all was not negotiating with Hitler from a position of military or material strength. "Franco said to many of his advisers that the hardest battle he ever fought was when he faced Hitler, and the *Führer* tried to get Franco to enter the war on the side of the Axis," Hilaire du Berrier recalled to THE NEW AMERICAN. Hitler's capacity for personal intimidation was legendary, and in a rage the National Socialist despot was almost impossible to refuse. Nonetheless, recalled du Berrier, "Franco was the only man who faced Hitler in one of his notorious rages who resisted him. European history would have turned out much differently had a few other statesmen displayed such courage in the face of Hitler's demands."

Franco's determination to keep Spain disentangled from the European war eventually led Hitler to regret his decision to support the Nationalists in the civil war. Author and historian Erik von Kuehnelt-Leddihn, who covered the Spanish Civil War as a young journalist, observes that "for military, but above all for ideological reasons, Hitler greatly regretted having given aid to Franco, whom he sincerely detested. Too late he discovered, when he met them in France, his deep affinity for Red Spaniards, whom he ironically planned to use as allies at some future date."

Just as frustrating to Hitler, no doubt, was Franco's determination to protect Jews from the Third Reich. When the Civil War erupted in Spain, observes Kuehnelt-Leddihn, "the Spanish Jews, most notably those living in northern

Accomplished leader: Franco's achievements were not limited to thwarting the plans of the Nazis and Communists. Generally forgotten, but no less significant, is the economic progress made by Spain under his rule. From 1960 to 1975, Spain's per capita income rose nearly 900 percent.

Morocco … sided with the Right." This was a wise choice: Under Franco, Spain's "consulates and embassies throughout Europe began to issue passports to Jews of Spanish descent.... An estimated forty to sixty thousand passports were granted, which accords to 'Franco Spain,' after the Vatican, title as the greatest protector of Jews" during World War II.

Little in Franco's family background suggested that he would one day become a world historical figure. He was a product of what today would be called a "dysfunctional" home. His father, Nicolas Franco Salgado-Araujo, was a minor naval official stationed in El Ferrol, a small town in Spain's northwestern Galicia region. Franco's father, notes Paul Preston's re-

lentlessly critical biography *Franco*, was "a bad-tempered authoritarian who easily lost control of himself when contradicted." Nor was that authoritarian temper wedded to sound moral values: "Marriage had only briefly diminished the number and length of [Nicolas'] card games and drinking sessions at the officers' club." After the birth of Francisco's sister Paz in 1903, Nicolas "returned to his bachelor habits," conducting numerous extramarital affairs and eventually contracting a sham marriage to another woman.

In addition to his morally dissolute personal life, notes Preston, Franco's father was politically "a liberal, sympathetic to freemasonry and critical of the Catholic Church." Franco's brothers emulated his father's politics; this was particularly true of his younger brother Ramón, who would earn notoriety as an aviator — he was the first flier to cross the south Atlantic — and political radical. (While Ramón Franco initially applauded Communist and anarchist atrocities against the Catholic Church, he eventually joined Franco's Nationalists; he died while flying a bombing mission in October 1938.) Although the young Franco would occasionally retreat into a "deep sulk" as a reaction to his father's abusive behavior, he was a loyal and obedient son. After his military exploits in Spanish North Africa earned him celebrity status, Franco tactfully refused to publicize his family's problems. When, as Spain's *Caudillo*, he was confronted by an intrusive question about his father's infidelity, he tersely conceded the reality of his father's weaknesses and transgres-

sions, but insisted that "they never diminished his paternal authority."

Franco obviously took seriously the biblical commandment to honor his father, even when his father's behavior was substantially less than honorable. However, Franco consciously strove to avoid both his father's vices and his politics. Notes Preston, "Franco's own lifelong avoidance of drink, gambling, and women bore testimony to a determination to create an existence which was the antithesis of his father's life."

It was much easier for Franco to honor his mother, Pilar Bahamonde, who is described by Preston as "politically conservative and a deeply pious Catholic." "Francisco was much more deeply attached to his mother than were either of his brothers," continues Preston. "He regularly accompanied her to communion and was a pious child. He cried when he made his first communion. When on leave in El Ferrol, the adult Francisco would never fail to fulfill any religious duty for fear of upsetting his mother."

After her husband abandoned her, Doña Pilar constantly wore black. The desertion left a lasting impression upon young Franco as well. The adult Franco would be the most uxorious of husbands to his wife, Carmen, and a devoted father to his daughter, who was also named Carmen (and given the nickname *Muñeca,* or "doll").

As a young man, Franco eschewed the vices that had entranced his wayward father. Even after Franco became "a leader with almost unlimited power," wrote commentator Holmes Alexander in 1970, "he never bothered to accumulate the fortunes and mistresses and dissipated habits so often associated with the terrible name of dictator."

The Franco family had a centuries-long tradition of service in the Spanish Navy, and young Francisco had aspired to continue the tradition. However, in the aftermath of Spain's defeat in the 1898 Spanish-American war — in which the badly outclassed Spanish Navy had acquitted itself very well — the Spanish government entered a period of retrenchment, and new admissions to the Naval Academy were suspended at just the time Francisco sought to enroll. In August 1907, the 14-year-old Franco, determined to pursue a military career, packed his worldly possessions in a single slender suitcase and traveled to Toledo to enroll in the Alcazar Infantry College.

The future Generalissimo cut an unimpressive figure: He was short, so thin that his childhood friends handed him the nickname *Cerillito* ("Little Matchstick"), and possessed a reedy, high-pitched voice. During his three years in military school, Franco would undergo a constant barrage of taunts, pranks, and petty humiliations on account of his size and background, and also because he had no taste for the gamier diversions — such as drinking and womanizing — that many of his classmates preferred.

The Toledo academy emphasized "discipline, military history, and moral virtue," rather than modern military theory, writes Preston; cadets were prepared to display "bravery in the face of the enemy, unquestioning faith in military regulations, [and] absolute obedience and loyalty to superior officers."

Franco graduated with honors in 1910. "The year was significant," comments biographer Alan Lloyd. "In Morocco, the last theater of Spanish colonial operations, Spain's oldest enemies were honing their daggers and charging their long guns." The Moorish tribesmen who inhabited "the Rif" were emboldened by Spain's defeat in 1898. Franco requested a posting to Morocco in Northern Africa, where Spain was embroiled in a protracted — and dubious — colonial conflict that in some ways approximated America's experience in Vietnam. For many in Spain's military command, observes Paul Preston, "the hypocritical politicians were playing a double game" with Spanish troops assigned to Morocco, "demanding of the soldiers cheap victories while remaining determined not to be seen sinking resources into a colonial war."

When Franco arrived in Morocco as a Second Lieutenant in 1912, he was greet-

ed by a Spanish force that was crippled by inefficiency, ravaged by disease, badly equipped, and burdened with poor morale. He was assigned command over a group of Moroccan conscripts whose loyalty was suspect; Franco spent "more than one sleepless night on guard rather than chance having his throat cut by his own troops," recalls Lloyd. For three years, Franco led his troops on a series of grinding, unglamorous campaigns, using what spare time he had to study topography, military theory, and combat psychology. At the age of 20, he was promoted to Captain.

As Franco increased in rank, his reputation grew — in large measure because of his uncanny composure in combat. Preston — who, it must be remembered, is a determined critic of Franco — refers to Franco's "apparent imperturbability under fire" and his unflagging "optimism and determination" as a military leader, and recounts how in the heat of battle Franco was "cold and serene in his risk-taking rather than recklessly brave."

Although his obvious ambition alienated some of his superiors, Franco was immensely popular with his soldiers "because of his methodical thoroughness and his insistence on always leading assaults himself."

Franco's determination to lead from the front nearly cost him his life during a June 1916 engagement with Moroccan guerillas in El Biutz. The guerillas, who commanded the high ground, planned to send a group of tribesmen down the back of the hill to sweep behind the embattled Spanish forces and catch them in a deadly cross-fire. Franco was part of a frontal assault up the slope. When the company commander was badly wounded, Franco took command. "With men dropping all around him," Preston records, "[Franco] broke through the enemy encirclement and played a significant role in the fall of El Biutz." However, he was shot in the stomach — an almost invariably lethal wound in the African theater. Miraculously, the bullet missed all of Franco's vital organs — by a fraction of an inch in any direction. It

is little wonder that Franco's Moroccan troops came to believe that he possessed *Baraka*, a mystical quality of divine protection.

Following his heroism at El Biutz, Franco became, at age 24, the youngest Major in the Spanish Army. Accounts of Franco's exploits in Morocco were published in Spanish newspapers, and the young Major's modest celebrity was useful in courting Carmen — the popular daughter of prominent parents who looked dimly upon Franco because of his unremarkable family background. Francisco and Carmen became engaged in 1920, but duty intervened to delay the marriage: Franco was chosen to return to Morocco to be second-in-command of the newly formed Spanish Foreign Legion.

As had been the case when he first arrived in Morocco, Franco's new command was as dangerous to him as it was to the enemy. The Legion was largely composed of thieves, murderers, and other criminals for whom military service was an alternative to imprisonment — or execution. In such company, Preston wrote, "Franco was to show a merciless readiness to impose his power over men physically bigger and harder than himself, compensating for his size with an unnerving coldness." Once again Franco served with distinction, becoming, at 33, Europe's youngest general — the youngest since Napoleon.

Franco's service in Africa would play a decisive role in his decision to participate in the 1936 coup. The *Africanistas* — Spaniards who had served in the thankless Moroccan campaigns — were a distinctive group in the Spanish military, in terms of personal attitudes and alliances forged under fire. As a group, the *Africanistas* believed that Spain's institutions were being subverted from within, and that separatist forces threatened not only to deprive their nation of its few remaining colonial possessions, but also to rend asunder the *Patria* herself.

As bloody revolutions erupted in Mexico, Russia, Germany, and elsewhere, many in the Spanish military became convinced that decisive action may even-

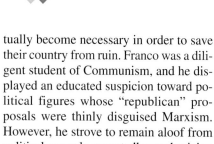

tually become necessary in order to save their country from ruin. Franco was a diligent student of Communism, and he displayed an educated suspicion toward political figures whose "republican" proposals were thinly disguised Marxism. However, he strove to remain aloof from political quarrels, repeatedly emphasizing that "a soldier serves Spain and not a particular regime," and that Spain needed soldiers who were committed to the nation, rather than to a political movement. It was only when he became convinced that Spain confronted a mortal danger that Franco decided to mount a coup.

After King Alfonso XIII was deposed in 1931 and the "Second Republic" was declared, Spanish politics became terminally polarized. In May 1931, the militant Left celebrated its ascendancy by putting churches to the torch in Madrid, Malaga, Seville, Cadiz, and Alicante. By 1934, Spanish socialist leader Francisco Largo Caballero — known as "the Spanish Lenin" — was touring the country "prescribing the dictatorship of the proletariat as a cure for Spain's ailments," Alan Lloyd recalls, while terrorists of both the radical left and the Fascist-supported "right" prepared for war. When a republican government of the right came to power, "Spain's Socialists no longer contented themselves with parliamentary opposition, but veered toward open revolt." Largo Caballero told Mallory Browne of the *Christian Science Monitor* that "evolutionary progress" was no longer possible, and that (in Lloyd's words) "Socialist leaders were almost unanimous in favoring a rebellion."

As Spain lurched toward elections in 1936, street violence between political factions escalated into assassination. In anticipation of the nation's descent into anarchy, the Soviet-supported Popular Front began to organize for a reign of terror. With the guidance and support of Comintern agents, Spanish revolutionaries established "repressive commissions with unlimited authority for the realization of arrests, requisitions and assassinations"; these organs were referred to as *Checas* — a Spanish transliteration of "Cheka," the name given to the original

Soviet secret police by Vladimir Lenin and Feliks Dzherzhinsky. Scores of *Checas* honeycombed every major Spanish city, and "Revolutionary Committees" tasked with exporting terror to the countryside were organized in country districts.

On July 18, 1936, convinced that his beloved *Patria* was descending into anarchy and eventually into Soviet-style tyranny, Franco flew from the Canary Islands to Spanish Morocco, where he took charge of a long-simmering coup against the Republic. Thus began a conflict that would be, for the international Left, "the Crusade of Crusades, a far more sacred cause than either World War I or World War II," observes Kuehnelt-Leddihn. Franco's Nationalists were fighting to restore Spain's traditional Christian order; the Soviet-inspired and Comintern-directed "Loyalists" of the Popular Front — including the notorious "Abraham Lincoln Brigade" organized by Communists in the U.S. — were propelled by an utterly depraved hatred of Christian society, as their depredations clearly illustrated.

As part of the "Loyalist" war effort, writes Alan Lloyd, "gangs of revolutionaries roamed the country burning churches, torturing and murdering clerics, [and] wantonly terrorizing the bourgeoisie and the upper classes. In a little over a month, an estimated 75,000 people would [meet] a senseless death at the hands of promiscuous and ignorant killers...." Kuehnelt-Leddihn reports that Spanish Communists butchered at least 6,000 priests, friars, and nuns. Some of the nuns, he recalls, were "publicly undressed, raped, slaughtered, and exhibited on a butcher's hook."

Nor did Communist cruelty spare the mortal remains of those who had already perished. Kuehnelt-Leddihn recalls a visit he made to the city of Huesca, which endured a two-year siege conducted by Marxist "Loyalist" forces. Since the "forces of progress, democracy, and enlightenment could not take Huesca, they vented their spleen on the dead. The vulgarities, the obscenities — the corpses torn out of their graves and assembled in obscene postures — left an unforgettable impression; they were appalling witness to the noble spirit so enthusiastically supported by the American and British left."

The "Loyalist" campaign was "an orgy of rape, sadism, and unspeakable obscenities, all perpetrated by our friend the Common Man," summarizes Kuehnelt-

Leddihn. Recalling the orgy of anti-Christian violence that took place during the French Revolution's reign of terror — particularly the savage onslaught against the Christians of Le Vendee — Kuehnelt-Leddihn concludes that the "Loyalists ... showed themselves faithful disciples of de Sade and the Bluecoats in the Vendee." He also asserts that the "horrors that took place in the Congo were anticipated in this war." This refers to the UN's suppression of Katanga, a former province of the Congo that declared its independence from the Soviet-installed Communist regime of Patrice Lumumba and created a peaceful, multi-ethnic society under the leadership of Moise Tshombe, a pro-Western, Christian anti-Communist. The UN punished Katanga by deploying (with U.S. assistance)

blue-helmeted "peacekeepers" who emulated the bestial behavior of the Soviet-sponsored "Loyalist" forces in Spain.

For all of his faults, Francisco Franco understood the nature of Communism and resisted its advance with skill and courage. His leadership helped save Spain from the fate that has befallen so many tragic countries in this bloody century; his resistance to Hitler's demands played a key role in the eventual defeat of the Third Reich. By offering sanctuary to Spain's Jews, he saved thousands who otherwise would have perished in the Holocaust. Clearly, Franco deserves a prominent place among this century's outstanding champions of human liberty.

"Franco had his share of faults, of

course, and he made plenty of important mistakes," concedes Hilaire du Berrier. "He was sometimes extreme in his methods, and he could be cruel, but then it should be remembered that he was from a military tradition in which war was seen as applied cruelty. He tended to overestimate his own indispensability, but unlike genuine despots he provided for orderly succession by restoring the monarchy and appointing Juan Carlos to succeed him in 1969. His devotion to Catholicism was admirable, but it sometimes lapsed into religious bigotry. But whatever his faults, down at the fundamental level, he was perhaps our greatest ally. If he had not stood firm against both the Communists and the Nazis, the world quite literally may have been doomed." ∎

Portugal's Protector

Dr. António de Oliveira Salazar's reluctant yet faithful public service gave his homeland 40 years of stability and growth.

by Fr. James Thornton

António de Oliveira Salazar, Prime Minister of Portugal from 1932 to 1968, was one of the most extraordinary men of our age. Austere, cultured, self-effacing, indifferent to public adulation, and more scholar than politician or government functionary, Salazar rose to high position in Portugal only with reluctance, after spending a night in prayer, seeking guidance from God. His place as a true hero of the 20th century is assured, since he delivered his country from anarchy and totalitarianism, giving it 40 years of stability and growth, and made significant contributions to the slowing of the disintegration of Christian civilization.

Salazar was born April 28, 1889 in the village of Vimieiro, only a few miles north of Coimbra, one of the great university towns of Portugal. His father, António de Oliveira, owner of a small farm, was noted for his loving devotion to his family, while his mother, Maria do Resgate Salazar, was an intelligent and intensely practical woman, and very religious in her outlook. Both parents were by nature tradition-minded, members of the poor but conservative peasant class.

Young Salazar attended local schools and, at age 11, entered a religious seminary, as was the custom for brighter Portuguese boys in the predominantly Catholic country. From there he was admitted to the ancient University of Coimbra, where he centered his studies on law, political science, and economics, receiving his bachelor's degree in 1914 and doctorate in political economics in 1918.

In 1910, shortly after Salazar began his university studies, Portugal was convulsed by a revolution of ultra-left political factions which overthrew the constitutional monarchy and established a democratic republic, somewhat on the model of the French revolutionary republics. That revolution was the offspring not only of the atheistic left, but of violently anti-religious, secret societies that had conspired for several centuries

ineptitude of the politicians — and of inflation, economic stagnation, falling standards of living, and unemployment — that there could be no question of going back. The rewards of Salazar's frugality were not long in coming. Though a poor country, Portugal remained largely immune from the world economic depression of the '30s. The external and internal national debts were drastically reduced. The country returned to the gold standard in 1931, making Portugal's currency, the escudo, one of the hardest currencies in Europe.

The National Savings Bank, the *Caixa Geral de Depositos*, whose lending capital had previously been absorbed by government deficits, was reorganized and thereafter the amount of bank resources that could be lent to government was limited by law to 22 percent, opening the way for private borrowing and economic development. During the first six years of the Salazar program, confidence in national institutions rose to such heights that deposits in the *Caixa* increased dramatically. Salazar's popularity increased too; he was the man of ideas, *practical* ideas, and he dominated the course of events from the moment he became Finance Minister.

The conspirators against Christian Portugal — the revolutionary republicans, socialists, and Communists — had not disappeared, however. In 1931 a united front of the old, discredited parties staged an uprising in Lisbon in which 40 people died. It failed miserably since the people of Portugal had no desire to return to the anarchy of the past. The following year, President Carmona decided to formalize that which was already, informally, a reality. On July 5, 1932, Dr. Salazar was sworn in as Prime Minister of Portugal, an office he would hold for the next 36 years. Portugal had been made economically secure, but economics are not the sole basis of life. Portugal required something more; it required a social and political renewal that would permeate the whole of national life.

A few months after he became Prime Minister, Salazar published a draft of a constitution, which, he believed, would bring stability to Portugal, mend the tears in the national fabric, and prevent a return to the radicalism and irreligion that had brought so much unhappiness. In March of the following year a national plebiscite gave the new constitution overwhelming approval. It was from that time that the Salazar era in Portugal came to be called the *Estado Novo*, literally the "New State," but perhaps better translated as "New-Style Government," the new distinguished from the old by its honesty, integrity, responsibility, and patriotism.

Article V of the Constitution of 1933 defined the *Estado Novo* as "a unitary and corporative republic, founded on the equality of its citizens before the law, on the free access of all classes to the benefits of civilization, and on the participation of all the elements that make up the nation in the administrative life and in the enactment of its laws." As Michael Derrick writes, "the word 'Corporative' means that the nation is regarded as an organic whole, and not as an accidental agglomeration of individuals," as liberal theory would have it.

Economically, the *Estado Novo* proposed a "corporative" system. It is useful before we proceed further to explore this concept. First, it must be emphasized that "corporativism" is distinct from the "corporate state" of Mussolini's Fascist Italy. Corporativism is compatible with Christianity, especially Christian social teaching, while Fascist corporatism, founded on an exaggerated glorification of the state, possessed a decidedly pagan flavor. As Derrick points out, Italian Fascism created a *State Corporatism*, where, in contrast, Dr. Salazar — rejecting statism in all its forms — proposed a *Corporativism of Association*. This means that the corporative institutions of Salazar's Portugal were self-governing, while in Italy the corresponding institutions were organs of the government and the Fascist Party, under the direct control of Mussolini and his ministers. To Mussolini the power of government was theoretically limitless, but for Dr. Salazar the limits of power were strictly circumscribed by law, both statutory and moral.

Why did Dr. Salazar seek this economic path and not turn instead to *laissez-faire* capitalism? Let us seek to define our terms carefully before we attempt to answer that question. We have become accustomed, especially since the days of the Cold War, to think in terms of the dichotomy "capitalism versus socialism" or "capitalism versus Communism." Capitalism is a word we have been taught to consider synonymous with personal freedom and private ownership of property, and we forget that personal freedom and private ownership existed long before modern capitalism was developed. What we call "capitalism" Dr. Salazar would have called "private enterprise" and agreed that it indeed signifies economic freedom.

However, the predatory, monopolistic, internationalistic kind of capitalism, the sort that knows no national loyalties and respects no national boundaries, and is based especially on the machinations of international high finance and on brutal competition, Salazar opposed. It is private in a sense, but it permits private ownership to pass into the hands of a tiny minority who then use economic power to control and manipulate government and society, thereby augmenting their own power and control both politically and economically. Derrick notes that private ownership of property was "a fundamental fact in the Portugal of Salazar." The right to own, he says, is fundamental to human existence, and was "defined as fundamental at the beginning of the Constitution [of 1933].... It is a right that has been denied equally by Capitalism and by Socialism, which is the logical conclusion of Capitalism. Capitalism means the concentration of ownership in the hands of a few, and therefore denies men the natural right of ownership; Socialism seeks to remedy the state of affairs so produced by withdrawing ownership even from the few. Salazar would restore ownership to many."

Interestingly, viewed from this standpoint, monopolistic capitalism and socialism are actually similar entities. And one may add that the American experience in the 20th century seems to confirm

No one ca
or the power
tency, or of a
and impartial
processes. At
was being pil
"world comm
China maint
the largest en
so much as tl
at the UN de
ment.

Huma
mom
tion
September 19
to the Red Cr
fering from
hematoma. It
al weeks befo
en, but had fo
nessed it to m
eration was p
clot but left tl
ly impaired.
upon hearing
tion, announe
"served the n
unflagging de
years," but wa

The new g
Professor Ma
of the *Estado*
tugal as a gov
dent of the Co
tor of Lisbon l
er capacities.
declared: "Th
tomed itself t
nius; from to
government by
tano, although
ideas, allowec
ization. Salaz
in retirement,
1970.

Professor C
man, and dec
Salazar progr
heartedly beli
ilant as his pr
around him to
derstanding c

this, since transnational capitalism and Big Government have entered into an enduring alliance for the economic socialization of America and the other Western "democracies."

Family life received notable recognition in the Constitution of the *Estado Novo*. The entire third section of the Constitution concerned itself with the role of the family in Portuguese life. The family was lauded as the "source and development" of the Portuguese people, and the government committed to its protection. Moreover, the family was seen "as the primary foundation of education and of social discipline and harmony, and as a fundamental of political and administrative order...."

Article XIV required both national and local government authorities to encourage the establishment of separate homes under healthy conditions, to protect maternity, and to establish taxation in accordance with the legitimate expenses of the family, promoting too the adoption of the family wage. It also mandated that authorities assist parents in the discharge of their duty of instructing and educating their children and take all effective precautions to guard against the corruption of morals. Derrick comments that "to define constitutionally that taxation must consider preeminently the necessity of providing the family with adequate means of subsistence is an excellent application of the principle that the State exists for society, and not society for the State." Obviously, under such a constitution, abortion, pornography, anti-family propaganda, and the like were strictly prohibited (as they once were in America).

Salazar's views on education, codified in the new Constitution, are enlightening. "The family, and not the State-owned and compulsory school, is the natural milieu of the [Portuguese] child," explains Derrick, and "... every child is bound to receive at least an elementary education. But every parent is free to decide whether his child shall receive that education at home, in a private school, or in a State school; and the home is considered the normal place."

In short, Dr. Salazar's *Estado Novo* sought to constitute society in such a manner as to be immune from the blandishments of class war and Communism. Portugal was a tinderbox of social jealousies and class hatreds under the old regime. Salazar strove to replace all of that with the perception that all classes were Portuguese first and foremost, all were necessary to a healthy society, and all must work together to create a nation of order, justice, and freedom. Author Hugh Kay, in his book *Salazar and Modern Portugal*, comments that Salazar saw the nation as "a family which achieves its aims and solves its disputes at a *round* table, not an aggregate of conflicting interests seeking a compromise through tensions *across* the table." Yet, in all of this Salazar was a cautious man, the opposite of an ideologue, proceeding with his plans slowly. He was loath to upset traditional patterns of life or to plunge his people into some unexpected vortex.

Very soon after Salazar's assumption of duties as head of government, grave international crises began to shake Europe to its foundations. Had the government of Portugal been in the hands of a man less insightful, less patient, and perhaps more impetuous and prone to adventurism, the Portuguese people might have been thrust into the cauldron of revolution, war, and catastrophe. The wisdom of Dr. Salazar, however, repeatedly saved his nation from the blood-soaked tragedies into which most of the other nations of Europe had immersed themselves.

The first of these external crises was the Spanish Civil War. From the very beginning of this conflict, which was in truth a struggle to the death between Stalin's world-menacing Bolshevist terror, on the one hand, and the Christian Spain of General Franco on the other, Dr. Salazar made very plain where his sympathies rested. While so much of the world was beguiled by gibberish about Spanish "democracy," the Portuguese Prime Minister remained cognizant of the mortal peril that his nation, and even the world, faced should General Franco fail

"We do not ask for much, only an understanding and consciousness of your country and of national unity; of the family ... of authority ... of the spiritual values of life ... of the sacred nature of religion — that is what is essential in the mental and moral foundation of a citizen of the Estado Novo.*"*

— Dr. Salazar

to win. Salazar had, after all, read the words of Francisco Largo Caballero, Prime Minister of the Spanish Republic, in which the Spanish Communist boasted: "A union of Iberian Soviet republics — that is our aim. The Iberian peninsula will again be one country. Portugal will come in, peaceably we hope, but by force if necessary.... Lenin declared Spain would be the second Soviet Republic in Europe. Lenin's prophecy will come true. I shall be the second Lenin who shall make it come true."

Despite pressure from England and France to remain neutral in the Spanish conflict, Salazar reckoned it a matter of life and death that the war end in victory for Franco; the choice was simply Franco or the abyss. Moreover, from the standpoint of the world, Salazar understood that if Stalin established a base encompassing the whole of the Iberian peninsula, he would control access to the Mediterranean and threaten shipping routes far into the Atlantic. One can only speculate how changed the map of the world might be today had Franco failed.

The outbreak of World War II, coming immediately on the heels of the Spanish Civil War, was the next crisis faced by Salazar. Portugal celebrated the 790th anniversary of its alliance with England in 1937. Dr. Salazar, who actively disliked the regime of Adolf Hitler, decided at the outbreak of war in 1939 that Portugal would strive for three objectives: to remain out of active participation in the

conflict; to
ways possibl
honor and so
middle years
assault on th
pressed hope
the Soviet Ur
but that the t
one another s
nificant fact
Readers ma
Herbert Hoo
larly at the ti

Salazar ne
could prevail
Britain. Afte
spring of 194
sors sought
German dire
many had wo
to be tempte
was not beat
buttress Spai
keeping the N
shipping.

Critics hav
tinuing to tra
portantly for
tities of wolf
manufacture
one of the fe
tugal, one wh
dance there th
However, as
allies, if he di
Axis, Germa
over nearly
continent, wo
Salazar there
arranged that
ly larger sup

F or a de
Portug
level
the 1960s, tro
horizon, this
tions. With i
ipation in tha
of the Frencl
gian empires
sures to go th
pendence to
Salazar re

Chile's Champion of Liberty

General Augusto Pinochet was targeted for persecution for successfully defending his homeland from a vicious Marxist tyranny.

by William F. Jasper

Newsmakers

Accurding to the collective wisdom of the Washington political classes, the media "experts," and the self-anointed champions of human rights, a great new day has dawned for the "rule of law." One of the most vicious villains of all time, they say, has been arrested and now awaits his day before the bar of justice. The verdict is already foreordained, it would seem, and virtually unanimous. Charles Manson, Adolf Hitler, Joseph Stalin, Pol Pot, and Jack the Ripper each appears to have more defenders in his corner than does this "arch-criminal."

We are speaking, of course, of General Augusto Pinochet Ugarte, former President of Chile and, since his arrest on October 16, 1998, a prisoner of the Labor Government of British Prime Minister Tony Blair. He was arrested and detained in response to a warrant issued by Spanish Judge Baltasar Garzon, a Socialist Party militant who has used his "investigative" powers to pursue targets singled out by the relentless hounds of the global "human rights" network.

It matters not, say the voices of virtue, that General Pinochet had traveled to England under diplomatic immunity, both as a former sovereign head of state and in his current capacity as senator. Or that eminent Spanish and British jurists have pointed out that Spain has no jurisdiction

This article was written in August 1999, while General Pinochet was being held under house arrest in England and suffering the daily abuse of a noisy, militant, international "human rights" choir. Except for one other entry (Dan Smoot) in our "20th Century Heroes" series, this tribute is unique in that it is about a still-living person. Because of the ongoing nature of this story and the magnitude and intensity of the global campaign against General Pinochet this story differs in style, tone, and length from the other hero entries. General Pinochet was released from his captivity in England on March 2, 2000 and allowed to return to Chile, but the international campaign to prosecute and persecute him for alleged crimes continues.

Marxism and mayhem: Salvador Allende practices with a submachine gun. Once elected, Allende used a 14,000-strong army of Red mercenaries to turn Chile into a Communist dictatorship.

over, and Garzon no authority to seek extradition for, the crimes alleged against the former Chilean strongman. Nor does it matter to the professional compassion lobby that the 83-year-old Senator Pinochet is ill and was arrested on his sickbed while recuperating from back surgery at a private British clinic. These and many other important considerations are of no moment to the shrill, international, anti-Pinochet chorus. This man, they shriek incessantly, is a "bloody dictator" who "overthrew the legitimate, democratically elected government of President Salvador Allende," and then unleashed "a systematic reign of terror."

According to reports by various anti-Pinochet activists, the Chilean strongman is guilty of the torture, murder, and/or disappearance of some three thousand persons during his 17-year rule, from 1973 to 1990. Very serious charges. And worthy of righteous outrage — if true. But really, does it take a certified geopolitical genius to recognize that there is something terribly wrong with this picture?

Shouldn't any reasonable, fair-minded person be asking: "Why is there such a blatantly disproportionate allotment of wrath focused on this man? And why such intensity and depth of feeling on the part of his detractors?" After all, by world standards today, General Pinochet, it must be admitted (even by his harshest critics) does not qualify even for entry-level status to the rogues' gallery of butchers and terrorists who enjoy worldwide approbation and honor. Fidel Castro, Hun Sen, Yasir Arafat, Nelson Mandela, Mikhail Gorbachev, Boris Yeltsin, and Red China butchers Li Peng and Jiang Zemin all know they have little to fear from the "human rights" phonies who prattle ceaselessly about Chile's uniquely odious record.

Even as Spanish authorities sought to extradite Pinochet, Spain was playing host to Cuba's Castro at the Ibero-American Summit in Oporto. Comrade Fidel's Stalinist legacy includes an estimated one million refugees and tens of thousands of political prisoners rotting in his brutal jails. Survivors of those hell holes, like Armando Valladarez and Anthony Bryant, testify that sadistic torture is routine and systemic throughout the Cuban gulag. More than 60,000 of Castro's victims have drowned fleeing his "workers paradise." According to Cuban scholar Dr. Armando Lago, Castro's regime has executed an estimated 30,000 opponents.

The "human rights" hypocrisy of the "liberal" political elite is shared (and is made politically acceptable) by the "liberal" media elite. A study of media reporting on human rights more than two decades ago found that in 1976 the *Washington Post* ran nine human rights articles on Cambodia, four on Cuba, one on North Korea — and 58 on Chile. The *New York Times* conditioned its readers with four human rights stories on Cambodia, three on Cuba, none on North Korea, and 66 on Chile! The same kind of grotesque imbalance held true for much of the rest of the media. And the same holds true today.

The incredible double standard operating here is candidly explained by Willy Meyer, a parliamentary spokesman for

The Communists, the Marxist Left, and the one-world internationalists hate Pinochet not only because he led one of the few counter-revolutions that succeeded in ousting a Communist regime, but also because he is a Christian patriot who stands for everything they oppose.

Izquerida Unida (United Left), Spain's renamed Communist Party. "We do not consider that Fidel Castro is a dictator," says Meyer. "We respect the Marxist-Leninist legality by whose definition political persecution, torture, and disappearances cannot exist in Cuba." "We are dividing the world between good guys and bad guys," Comrade Meyer declared. "There is a vacuum in the international enforcement of human rights and we realize that whoever seizes the initiative to punish violators wins the high ground."

Unfortunately, such candor is all too rare among the fanatical "Get Pinochet" crowd. But it is easy to see that Meyer's explanation neatly fits the transparent double standard that is applied to Pinochet and all others "on the right." A fair assessment of the facts in the case of Augusto Pinochet will reveal that the current round of demonization is a continuation of the furious smear campaign launched against Señor Pinochet in 1973 when he and the Chilean military overthrew the Marxist regime of Salvador Allende. He has never been forgiven by the Communists or the international Marxist left for that heroic act, or for saving the economy that Allende had ruined and turning it into an economic showcase. For the past 26 years, the same international network of Communist and Marxist-Left individuals and organizations — the Institute for Policy Studies, the Washington Office on Latin America,

Amnesty International, Human Rights Watch, et al — and their political and media allies, has relentlessly attacked Pinochet and his remarkable achievements. They are the force behind the incredible black propaganda and disinformation offensive aimed at Señor Pinochet.

The truth, in short, is this:

• Salvador Allende and his Marxist-Communist coalition party *Unidad Popular*, employing massive electoral fraud and with financial backing from the Soviet Union, barely squeaked out a plurality of 36 percent in Chile's 1970 presidential elections.

• With an army of some 14,000 foreign Communists, Allende began to transform Chile into a totalitarian dictatorship.

• Allende's administration was thoroughly packed with Cubans, Soviets, and other international Communists.

• In short order, the Allende forces had looted the treasury, destroyed the economy, illegally expropriated thousands of private farms, homes, and businesses, and unleashed a wave of terror.

• Chile's judiciary and legislature, as well as prominent leaders of all sectors of Chilean society, repeatedly condemned Allende's actions and called upon the military to intervene.

• The Pinochet-led coup was supported overwhelmingly by the Chilean people, who also voted to approve the new constitution offered by the junta.

• Documents and arms captured when Allende was overthrown on September 11, 1973, proved that Allende was planning to stage his own coup on September 19th, and to slaughter his opposition.

• The international Communist apparatus has continued an unceasing war of terrorism, subversion, and propaganda against Pinochet's Chile ever since.

• The Pinochet junta reacted with remarkable restraint toward its violent opponents.

• The Pinochet junta has never received credit for the peace and freedom it delivered to the Chilean people, or for the marvelous economic and social reforms it accomplished.

• President Pinochet, as he promised, voluntarily stepped down from power, re-

turning the reins of government to civilian control, after establishing stability, security, and constitutional reform.

Now, let us expand on the above points. General Pinochet's accusers always begin with the charge that his military junta overthrew the "democratically elected" government of President Allende. This seems to offer proof, right from the outset, of an autocratic, dictatorial bent that lends credibility to later, more ugly, charges. Some of the Allende champions will admit that their hero was "Marxist" (which carries a warmer, fuzzier, less threatening ring than "Communist"), but all of his camp followers deny that he intended to turn Chile into a Cuban-style dictatorship.

But Salvador Allende was no fuzzy "social reform" Marxist. His *Unidad Popular* and his government were filled with hard-core Communist revolutionaries like Luis Fernandez Oña, Orlando Letelier, Luis Corvalan, Daniel Vergara, Pedro Vuskovic, Jacques Conchol, Carlos Altamirano, Pablo Neruda, Hernan del Canto, Volodia Teitelboim, Eduardo Paredes, Carlos Toro, Valenti Rossi, Clodomiro Almeyda Medina, and Alfredo Joignant (to name but a few). Señor Oña is particularly noteworthy, inasmuch as he not only was the second in command of Cuba's military intelligence, "G-2," but was Allende's son-in-law, married

to the President's daughter, Beatriz Allende. Oña had been Castro's intelligence liaison to Che Guevara in Bolivia. It was Comrade Oña who organized Allende's personal Praetorian Guard, known as GAP, *Grupo de Amigos del Presidente* (Group of Friends of the President). Oña placed this group of armed thugs under the control of Max Joel Marambio, who was trained in Cuba.

Senator Luis Corvalan was secretary-general of Chile's Communist Party and one of Allende's closest allies. Like Allende, he was no social reformer. As a disciplined, Moscow-controlled Red he counseled Allende against the rash actions advocated by some of the hothead revolutionaries with itchy trigger fingers. "We need time to prepare ourselves for the exigencies of a civil war," he warned.

One of the preparations involved obtaining funding from foreign Communist Parties. After the coup, a "Dear Comrade" letter of March 21, 1973 from Communist Party official Antonio Benedicto in Spain to Senator Corvalan was found. Benedicto was reporting on the progress of his negotiations for Allende for loans from the Communist Parties of France and Spain. He informed Corvalan that the best prospects for major loans might be through Interagra, the cash-rich export organization of the French Union of Agricultural Cooperatives, "chaired by comrade Jean Doumeng." Benedicto noted

Red unrest: In 1973, thousands of foreign Communist agitators coordinated violent street demonstrations with a murderous terror campaign and policies promulgated by Allende's Marxist regime.

that "Interagra is known as 'The Party Cashbox' because it is controlled by the French CP [Communist Party]." Comrade Benedicto opined to Corvalan that "it would be possible to obtain loans in the course of this year for about 150 million dollars, in France and Spain alone."

Cuban-trained Eduardo Paredes was the first to head the Investigations Department (ID), Chile's analog to the FBI, under Allende. Photos show Paredes instructing Allende in guerrilla warfare and the firing of automatic weapons. On April 11, 1972, Paredes returned to Chile from one of his frequent trips to Cuba. He brought with him 13 large crates that he refused to open for Chilean Customs officials. He insisted they contained only art objects, cigars, and mango-flavored ice-cream — all gifts from the Cuban people. After Allende was deposed, a huge arsenal of weapons was discovered in Allende's residence — along with a bill of lading for the Cuban crates. The ice cream and cigars turned out to be rifles and machine guns.

Paredes' assistant director of Investigations was Communist Party stalwart Carlos Toro. It was Paredes and Toro who headed the "investigations" of the terrorist group known as the People's Organized Vanguard (VOP), responsible for the assassination of former Vice President Edmundo Perez Zujovic and the murder of numerous civilians and policemen. It did not escape the notice of many observers that whenever the ID captured VOP members, the assassins invariably ended up corpses before they could reveal who was the brains behind their campaign of terror; some evidence indicates it was either Paredes or Toro — or both men — who were covering their trail by liquidating their own liquidators.

Senator Carlos Altamirano, secretary-general of the Socialist Party, was another Allende sweetheart. The Chilean Socialist Party, it should be noted, was even more radical than the Communist Party — and far less disciplined. They were for

armed revolution — now! On August 7, 1973, a group of Communist sailors aboard the cruiser *Latorre* and the destroyer *Blanco* were arrested for a conspiracy to mutiny and assassinate their officers. The sailors were associated with MIR (Movement of the Revolutionary Left), a Maoist group committed to revolutionary violence. Most outrageous was the discovery that two of Allende's top congressional allies, Altamirano and Oscar Garreton, were ringleaders in the

Biding his time: As Army Commander in Chief, General Pinochet quietly planned the overthrow of Allende (right).

conspiracy. Altamirano defiantly admitted that he had conspired to instigate the mutiny and said he would do it again to "defend" the Allende regime.

Senator Volodia Teitelboim, another key Allende supporter, was a member of the Communist Party Central Committee and a regular propagandist for the Chilean CP during the Allende years over Radio Moscow. Allende's foreign minister, Clodomiro Almeyda Medina, a self-described Maoist, befriended every Red regime and facilitated the transformation of Santiago into an international Mecca for terrorists and Marxists of every hue.

Such were the "democratic" elements who helped bring Allende to power. But they did not fly their true colors so openly when they were pushing the Allende ticket in 1970. Like most politicians, they carried the banner of moderation when campaigning before

mainstream voters. Even so, they managed to snooker only 36 percent of the electorate. Actually, it was significantly lower than that since the Allende forces had engaged in ballot stuffing and other "irregular" practices. Violations of the election laws escalated sharply under Allende's rule. According to the March 1973 report of a commission chaired by Jaime del Valle Alliende, dean of the faculty of law at the Catholic University of Chile, Allende's *Unidad Popular* (UP) perpetrated massive electoral fraud in the March 1973 parliamentary elections. "This monstrous machinery aimed at destroying the genuine expression of majorities continues in force," said del Valle in a telecast on the university's Channel 13 (which Allende subsequently shut down). "Having discovered the easy road to fraud," the distinguished Dean of Law charged, "it is reasonable to assume that after the last election the volume of fraud has increased much more than we have seen.... Chilean men and women: Our nation is the victim of infamy."

But Allende's infamy in the 1970 election fraud was but a foretaste of more and bigger crimes to come. With only a plurality of 36 percent (and fraudulent at that), Allende needed the support of the majority Christian Democrat Party, so that Congress would ratify his relative victory and confirm him as president of the republic. In order to obtain the Christian Democrats' support and allay their concerns about the heavy presence of Communists and other Marxist elements in his *Unidad Popular*, he signed — and publicly announced his complete agreement with — a Statute of Constitutional Guarantees. This constitutional amendment reaffirmed freedom of the press, education, electoral process, and the non-involvement of the military in political matters. In typical Leninist fashion, however, he quickly showed that he considered his promise no more than a pie crust — meant to be broken.

In an interview with the French Communist writer Regis Debray, published in *Punto Final* on March 16, 1971, Allende cynically confessed that his agreement to accept the Statute was merely "a tactical necessity." Moreover, he said, "At that time the main thing was to take over the government." He told his followers, "Santiago will be painted red with blood if I am not ratified as President." However, "President" Allende proceeded to paint Santiago red with blood even after he was ratified. In typical Communist style, he wasted no time in grabbing power — and exercising it, lethally. His armed GAP thugs were just the start.

Award-winning journalist James R. Whelan, one of the few genuine U.S. experts on Chile, in his perceptive book, *Allende: Death of a Marxist Dream* (1981) aptly described GAP as a "Praetorian Guard of private gunslingers." Whelan observed: "Their trademarks were Fiat 125 automobiles (blue), submachineguns, and bullyboy manners. They had no precedent in Chilean history, and no place in Chilean law. The Law of Internal Security prohibited the existence of armed forces in Chile other than the army, navy, air force, Corps of Carabineros, and Gendarmerie of Prisons. So, too, did Article 22 of the Constitution."

F idel Castro landed in Chile in November 1971 and, with Allende's enthusiastic blessing, toured the country for 25 days, giving revolutionary speeches in favor of the Allende regime and pledging his support for the revolution. That's the only kind of promise Red Fidel always makes good on. Castro's number three man at the Cuban embassy in Santiago (which had swollen incredibly to 1,500 persons) was Juan Carreto Ibanez, a member of Cuba's G-2, who headed the Latin American Liberation Movement and ran a guerrilla training center in Santiago.

On July 29, 1973, Castro dispatched Carlos Rafael Rodriguez, his number two man as deputy prime minister, and Manuel Pineiro, chief of the Cuban secret service, on an unannounced mission to Santiago. In a letter he sent with them, Castro said the pretext of their visit would be to discuss plans for the upcoming meeting of the so-called non-aligned countries, but: "the real purpose is to find out, from you, the situation, and offer you, as always, our willingness to cooperate in the face of the difficulties and angers blocking and threatening the process of making Chile Socialist."

Besides sending hundreds of his best agents, Castro had already established his "willingness to cooperate" by providing Allende with enough rifles, pistols, machine guns, and other weapons to arm more than 20,000 guerrillas. In addition to the international terrorist brigades who flooded into Chile, the bulk of Allende's guerrilla army of conquest was recruited from the *poblaciones*, the insta-slums, created by Allende's policies.

O nly five months after the Allende claque took office, daily reports from all over the country exploded with news of expropriations of farms, empty lots, buildings, and factories — both by official action, and by the criminal acts of armed, revolutionary thugs. Under the guidance of Communist cadres, who were usually supplied with government funds, food, and other provisions, unemployed peasants and laborers were recruited to build huge slum settlements that grew into a double-tiered cordon around Santiago. These *poblaciones*, also known as *callampas* (mushrooms), sprouted overnight on the peripheries of large cities. These "Red Zones," controlled by Allende's Soviet/Cuban-directed cadres, became off-limits to the police, military, and other constitutionally authorized authorities. The purpose of this plan was unmistakably clear: The Allende forces were preparing to launch a full scale civil war, and the armed-and-occupied *poblaciones* were vital to their pincer strategy.

Many of the *poblaciones* recruits were destitute peasants who had been forced to come to the cities after having been evicted from their farms by Allende's Communist "agrarian reform" programs. Dr. Susan Huck, who visited Chile a year after the overthrow of Allende, wrote in the November 1974 *American Opinion* (a predecessor of THE NEW AMERICAN) that "by September of 1973, over 5,800 farms had been expropriated, giving the Marxists control of sixty percent of all irrigated land in the country and thirty percent of the unirrigated arable land. By replacing farmers with Marxist ignoramuses, only nineteen percent of the arable land under government control was even planted."

Time after time, rural property owners, like their urban counterparts, attempted to fight these illegal actions in the courts. And, time after time, Chile's judicial officers, recognizing the illegal, unconstitutional, and immoral nature of the expropriations, ruled in favor of those whose property had been taken. That did not matter to Allende and his worldwide supporters, who prattled incessantly about their pretended reverence for the "rule of law." Angelo Codevilla, professor of international relations at Boston University, told THE NEW AMERICAN that "Pinochet's critics, and the American media in general, have studiously ignored the hard fact that the Allende regime illegally ignored, violated, and refused to enforce more than 7,000 court rulings. His was a totally lawless government."

Dr. Huck, on her return from Chile, noted that "not a single land title was given to any landless peasants during the entire Allende regime. That part of 'land reform' was total eyewash, as it is in every Marxist country." The results of Allende's agrarian program were entirely predictable. Chief among those results were food shortages. Which then gave Allende an excuse to impose rationing. Dr. Huck reported that "food production plunged and the bill for food imports … soared from $100 million annually to $650 million. The Reds had managed to cut wheat production by a whopping fifty percent in one year. When the junta took over, it confronted a truly hair-raising situation — four days' grain supply, and barely enough money in the Treasury to pay for two days' food imports!"

President Pinochet, in the important book, *The Crucial Day: September 11, 1973*, an extensive interview with the General-President, recounts how his experience with food shortages and rationing in a previous socialist administration had played a key role in the development of his political consciousness, and prepared him for what was to come under Allende. When the election of 1946 brought Gabriel Gonzalez Videla to power, then-Captain Pinochet and his fellow officers were not overly concerned because, as he put it, "we officers looked on political strife as an activity peculiar to the civilian population and wholly irrelevant to our profession." "Nevertheless," he noted, "in those days we could not help noticing that wherever we went people had only one central topic of conversation: It was always the fact that Señor Gabriel Gonzalez Videla had been elected President thanks to the communist vote and that his victory with the help of such partners would mean every kind of disturbance in Chile."

Pinochet initially dismissed such talk as mere political squabbling by those who had lost the election. Soon, however, he found these warnings and predictions completely accurate. Within a few months of Videla's inauguration, his socialist policies had created shortages and rationing. The people began to experience difficulty in obtaining basic food staples — bread, flour, cooking oil, meat, fish, milk, sugar — as well as other goods. Chileans were introduced to a standard feature of socialism: the rationing queue. Recalls General Pinochet: "In the mornings long lines of people would form before the stores, particularly the bakeries. Initially these queues of men, women, and children would start to form during daylight hours, but after a few weeks they could be seen from the earliest hours of dawn. They also became longer each day, so that in order to obtain bread or other staples, some people had to wait all night before the store. This anxiety over obtaining provisions became daily more intense...."

Captain Pinochet quickly realized that shortages and rationing provided a pathway to power for unprincipled politicians and outright subversives. "Obviously the stomach, that is to say food rationing, is a means for men to be easily subjected," Pinochet noted, "and also a basic princi-

ple of communist tactics...." Pinochet was particularly struck by the discovery that the Communists (and their Marxist allies), while professing great compassion for the plight of the workers and the poor, were themselves not only living high on the hog, but doing everything within their power to increase the suffering of Chile's most destitute classes.

As Communist-inspired demonstrations and violence escalated, the government was forced, in October 1947, to employ the constitutionally provided Emergency Area decree to avoid complete social breakdown and civil war. Pinochet and other military commanders were given orders to arrest the Communist leaders and agitators. After arresting Communist Angel Veas, the government-appointed *Intendente* of the Tarapaca area, Pinochet made an interesting discovery: "Warehouses controlled by the Intendente were found bursting with cartons of canned food, cans of oil, flour, pasta, and a thousand other items. I was to see the same thing happen again during the Unidad Popular [Allende] government."

He recognized the Communist program well, observing: "One of the most well-known and traditional tactics of Marxism is to stop the improvement of a people's welfare by any means ... and promote from the beginning any destructive distribution of capital, facing away from economic reality, until growing poverty is brought about, even chaos, if possible, arising from uncontrolled inflation and leading eventually to the annihilation of private economic activities."

The Allende socialists did indeed use the insidious weapon of inflation to add to their program of planned chaos, wiping out personal savings and earnings with the power of the printing press. Lieutenant Colonel Patrick J. Ryan (USMC), in a 1976 monograph for the American Chilean Council, provided this summary: "Upon its October 1970 stand down, the Frei Government turned over an excess of US $343 million in international reserves to the Allende Government. Less than three years later, in September 1973, Chile had a deficit of more than $300 million, or a net loss of ap-

proximately US $650 million. The Allende Government's officially acknowledged rate of inflation was 508%. Independent economists pegged the figure closer to 700% — either way, one of the highest inflation rates in the history of the world."

It will not surprise those familiar with the Communist origins and collectivist history of the United Nations to learn that much of Allende's socialist program was designed and implemented by professional UN apparatchiks. British journalist Robert Moss wrote in *Chile's Marxist Experiment* (1973): "It is significant that the majority of the members of Chile's new class of Marxist technocrats — headed by Pedro Vuskovic [Minister of Economics] ... and Gonzalo Martner, who took over the state planning agency, ODEPLAN — had worked for the [UN] Economic Commission on Latin America, or the [UN] Food and Agriculture Organization, or some other of the U.N.'s technical agencies."

"The role of economic planning was in their eyes not confined to increasing production ... or improving the general standard of living," said Moss. " It was part of the process of creating a socialist revolution. Within this perspective, they were willing to shrug off the appalling economic consequences of their program.... It became ... clear that their whole economic strategy was concerned with power, not with productivity, efficiency, or even any novel experiment in socialism."

Allende's transparent lust for power was well recognized in Chile by the time of the 1973 coup. On August 23, 1973 the Chamber of Deputies, the equivalent of our House of Representatives, adopted a resolution charging: "It is a fact that the present Government of the Republic [the Allende administration], from its inception, has been bent on conquering total power, with the evident purpose of submitting all individuals to the strictest economic and political control by the State, thus achieving the establishment of a totalitarian system, absolutely contrary to the representative democratic system prescribed by the Constitution."

Earlier that month, on August 8th, the General Council of Chile's Bar Association issued a declaration charging that Allende's egregious violations of the Constitution threatened "collapse of the rule

purpose of the reports was to identify those who were to be liquidated.

Another find was a Communist Party document of June 30, 1973, intended for the inner core of the Communist hierar-

have stopped with those select targets. Opposition to the Allende program was so widespread and vigorous, and Allende was so determined and pitiless, that a Communist-style bloodbath and a savage civil war seemed certain. In the final months of his reign, Chile was virtually paralyzed, as truckers, transportation workers, business owners, and professional groups went on strike.

Like all Marxists, Allende claimed that his policies were being carried out in the name of, and for the benefit of, "the people." But it was "the people" who rose up to throw him out, and who implored the military to save them from his oppression. It was the women who sparked the growing demonstrations of popular op-

of law," and asserting that the "obvious fracturing of our legal structure can no longer be tolerated." Still earlier, on May 26, 1973, Chile's Supreme Court issued a unanimous resolution denouncing the Allende regime's "disruption of the legality of the nation" by its failure to uphold judicial decisions.

The total ruthlessness of the Allende drive for power was not fully realized until after he was overthrown. Then numerous documents were discovered revealing the bloodbath he and his foreign controllers had planned for Chile.

Chile's Senate had voted in November 1972 to remove Alfredo Joignant, an extreme radical of the Socialist Party, as mayor of Santiago because of "repeated violations of the Constitution." Not to be deterred, Allende appointed Joignant head of the Investigations Department, which was gradually transformed into a Gestapo.

In Joignant's office safe were found a number of incriminating secret reports. The reports had been made by Joignant's Communist agents who had infiltrated the military and the police, with extensive details about individual officers, including the personality and political leanings of each, his home, family, usual schedule, and routes followed daily. The

chy. It stated: "In case of confrontation [civil war], a group belonging to the Communist Party which is highly specialized *will physically eliminate the opposition leaders*." (Emphasis in original.)

It also revealed the Reds' plan of destruction against the common people of Chile: "The objective of storing candles, matches, foodstuffs, kerosene, etc., will be exclusively for the survival of the militants since in case of confrontation *electricity and water plants will be destroyed*." (Emphasis in the original.)

But the big find was a secret plan with the code name, "Plan Z," found in the presidential palace in the office safe of Daniel Vergara, Under Secretary of the Interior. Plan Z provided detailed instructions for the intended massacre of a large percentage of Chile's officer corps, who would be gathered in Cousino Park on September 19th for an annual military celebration and review. Some 600 politicians, journalists, and conservative leaders were also slated for elimination.

However, if the Allende forces had prevailed, the bloodletting would not

Red regime's end: La Moneda, Chile's Ministry of Defense headquarters **(top)**, where Salvador Allende's Communist cadres bunkered down at the start of the Pinochet-led coup. After being hit with a few well-placed rockets **(above)**, most of the Reds surrendered and Allende committed suicide.

position with their famous "march of the empty pots." Chilean women by the thousands took to the streets, armed only with empty pots and pans as noisemakers, to march in defense of their homes, their families, their children, and their security — all of which were being trampled into dust by the Allendeites. Popular outrage against Allende intensified when his thugs — wielding stones, clubs, chains, and bottles — viciously attacked the women.

It was at this crucial juncture, when utter disaster, despotism, and bloody civil war threatened, that Augusto Pinochet and the military saved Chile. But don't take *our* word for it. One week

Rebuilding: After the coup, Pinochet (second from left) moved quickly to restore order in Chile. He was supported and praised in this effort by three former presidents of Chile, leaders of Chile's judiciary, parliament, and military, and the overwhelming majority of the Chilean people.

after the coup, on September 18th, three former Presidents of Chile — Gabriel Gonzalez Videla, Jorge Alessandri Rodriguez, and Eduardo Frei Montalva — attended a ceremony at the Church of National Gratitude to say exactly that. Former President Videla said: "I have no words to thank the Armed Forces for having freed us from the clutches of Marxism." Moreover, he added, "they have saved us … because the totalitarian apparatus that was prepared to destroy us has been itself destroyed." According to President Frei, "The military has saved Chile and all of us.... A civil war was being well-prepared by the Marxists. And that is what the world does not know, refuses to know." This statement came from no right-winger, but a politician who was himself a Marxist!

The story of how Augusto Pinochet saved Chile is an inspiring story of dauntless courage, faith, and honor. General Pinochet himself credits God with the success of the relatively bloodless coup, pointing to the many turns of "fate" that not only saved him and his fellow plotters from exposure and certain death, but also time and again opened doors for them, while closing doors for their enemies. Following the pattern of all Communist dictatorships, Allende had instituted an extensive spy network. So the greatest

danger was that plans for the coup would be discovered before Pinochet could coordinate with the other Armed Services and deploy the Army units for a rapid, decisive blow that would oust the Allende forces without sparking a prolonged and bloody civil war.

On the morning of September 11, 1973, Pinochet's forces surrounded Allende in La Moneda, the fortress-like Ministry of Defense in Santiago. After the Air Force delivered a few well-aimed rockets into the building, the once-swaggering bullyboy revolutionaries surrendered. All except Allende, that is, who committed suicide — ironically, with a machine gun that had been given to him as a present and bearing this engraved salutation on a gold plate: "To my good friend Salvador Allende. Fidel Castro."

The general's persuasive attributions to Divine Providence notwithstanding, much of the credit for the success of the coup must be given to Pinochet himself, for his brilliant strategy, methodical planning, prudent selection of officers, discretion, and cool courage under pressure. The best accounts of the coup and the events leading up to it are to be found in *Allende: Death of a Marxist Dream*, by James Whelan, and *The Crucial Day* by Editorial Renaciamento. Unfortunately, neither book is now in print.

eneral Pinochet says that he felt the military vocation since childhood. "Quite possibly," he says, "the tales of heroic deeds and similar subjects, followed by reading the History of Chile, gradually impressed my spirit deeply with the value of the service of arms. Anyway, since I was a child I had the idea that the goal of my life should be to become an Army officer and to devote my life to the career of arms."

After four years of strict military instruction and rigid discipline, he left the Military Academy in 1936 as an infantry *alferez* — a commissioned officer of the lowest rank in the Chilean Army. His staunch anti-Communist convictions developed from both personal experience and intense study over a 20-year period, beginning in 1948.

"My rejection of Marxists-Leninists arose from my knowledge of their doctrine," he explained in *The Crucial Day*. "I first came in contact with it when I was in charge of the communists relegated to Pisagua in January and part of February 1948, and later when I was Delegate for the Chief of the Emergency Area in the Schwager coal-mining district. There I also had to [deal] with communists, their doctrine and methods, and went into the concept of scientific socialism. In my reading I noted with concern how Marxism contributes to alter the moral principles that should uphold the society, until such principles are destroyed, in order to replace them with the ideological shibboleths of communism."

Pinochet understood the nature of the enemy he was facing, as far too few political and military leaders have. Again, from *The Crucial Day*:

The better I knew these relegates as I listened to their arguments, while I progressed simultaneously in reading Marx and Engels, a conception totally different from what we had thought of the Communist Party began to take shape before me. It was not just another party. There was a great and very profound difference. The way they analysed the different subjects revealed a system that upset everything and left no faith or belief standing. How right His Holiness [Pope] Pius XI was when he said this doctrine was "intrinsically perverse." I confess that from that moment I felt a profound desire to go into these concepts and study them to find out their purposes, because I was much concerned that such pernicious and contaminating ideas should continue to be disseminated in Chile.

At the end of 1953 Pinochet was appointed professor at Chile's War College, and while teaching he enrolled in the law school at the University of Chile. "I think the greatest benefit to me from having been a law student," he recalled years later, "was that I went deeper into subjects I had known only in passing. With real pleasure I studied Roman Law, Economics, Constitutional History, Constitutional Law."

In early 1960 Pinochet was promoted to Lieutenant Colonel, and at the end of the year was designated commander of an infantry regiment. At the end of 1963 he was appointed assistant director of the War College. In 1968 Pinochet was appointed chief of staff at the Headquarters of the Second Army Division in Santiago. Before the end of the year, he was promoted to Brigadier General and given command of the Sixth Army Division, the position he held when Allende came to power on September 4, 1970.

As a vocal anti-Communist, Pinochet expected his military career to come to an abrupt end under the new regime. "My fate did not take the course I imagined that day," he later recalled. "Apparently Allende mistook me for General Manuel Pinochet [no relation] as he had done several times before, and I, remembering the tactics they use, kept quiet and acted with caution." In January 1971 Pinochet was promoted to the rank of Major General, and the following year was appointed Chief of the Army General Staff. Then through a further series of quirks of fate, he was named Acting Commander in Chief of the Army, and, finally, Commander in Chief of the Army.

Contrary to the black propaganda which holds that General Pinochet is a "ruthless, iron-fisted dictator," an honest survey of the facts shows that he reacted with heroic restraint against the traitors and foreign intruders who sought to deliver Chile into totalitarian hands. He offered Allende safe passage from the country. Allende refused, preferring suicide. Those who accepted Pinochet's offer found he kept his word. Considering the egregious nature of the crimes they had committed and the vengeance they had planned for Chile, the thousands of foreigners who were deported received incredibly soft treatment. Likewise the Chilean citizens who were imprisoned for their treasonous acts. Many of these "martyrs" were soon

Ruthless Red: Orlando Letelier, one of Allende's top officials, was a darling of the U.S. media and Insider political establishment. He was also a ruthless Soviet-Cuban agent.

sprung from jail, thanks to the intervention of Henry Kissinger and similar pressure from other American Insiders of the pro-Marxist, pro-world government Council on Foreign Relations (CFR).

It was Kissinger's intercession, for instance, that brought about the release of Orlando Letelier, who served the Allende regime in a variety of posts, including ambassador to the United States and Minister of Defense. He also served the Soviet Union and Cuba, as an agent of influence for the KGB and the DGI. When Letelier was murdered by a car bomb in Washington, DC in 1976, he was catapulted to special sainthood status in the Communist martyrology by the CFR-dominated U.S. media. A recent Associ-

ated Press article referred to Letelier only as "a former Chilean ambassador opposed to Pinochet." Likewise, in a recent *Washington Post* op-ed, Kenneth Roth (CFR) of Human Rights Watch called him "a former foreign minister and Pinochet critic."

That is lying by omission, like referring to Mafia kingpin John Gotti as merely an Italian-American with a pizza delivery business. Letelier was killed just as he was preparing to head for Cuba — with a briefcase full of incriminating documents. Those "Letelier Papers" revealed a great deal about Soviet espionage-disinformation-strategic deception operations in America and the amazing network of professional radicals, politicians, government officials, and journalists who were (and in many cases, still are) aiding these operations. Letelier operated principally through the Institute for Policy Studies (IPS), a Marxist front for Soviet-Cuban intelligence, and the IPS spin-off known as the Transnational Institute.

The contents of Letelier's briefcase showed not only that he was regularly receiving and disbursing funds from Soviet and Cuban intelligence services, but that he also had good contacts on Capitol Hill and in the Executive Branch. His contacts included Senators Ted Kennedy, George McGovern, Hubert Humphrey, and James Abourezk; Representatives John Conyers, Bella Abzug, George Miller, and Toby Moffett; Assistant Secretary of State William D. Rogers (CFR); and Sol Linowitz (CFR), then head of the Ford Foundation-sponsored Commission on United States-Latin American Relations, and later head of "our" negotiating team for the treacherous Carter-Torrijos treaties on the Panama Canal.

Without an understanding of this ongoing network, it is impossible for Americans to understand the forces and motives behind the current campaign to get Pinochet. Take Peter Kornbluh, for instance, who heads a private (but official-sounding) outfit called the National Security Archive, which is described by the Associated Press as "a private group that works to preserve and open government records on national security matters." Kornbluh has received a lot of attention lately for publicizing documents released by the Clinton administration purporting to show President Pinochet's culpability for various crimes with which he has been charged. (We have reviewed many of those documents and have seen no such proof therein.) What no one in the media has bothered to point out is that Kornbluh is a veteran apparatchik from the IPS-Letelier network. It was IPS fellow Kornbluh who arranged the crucial meeting between the Sandinista junta leaders and Senators John Kerry and Tom Harkin, just eight hours before the congressional vote on aid to the Contras. The senators' trip provided a huge propaganda coup that is credited with stopping the aid.

Working with Comrade Kornbluh then was Reed Brody (CFR), a former New York Assistant Attorney General and member of the pro-Communist National Lawyers Guild. He is the author of the 1985 "Brody Report," which was published by the radical Washington Office on Latin America (WOLA), one of the IPS network affiliates, as a propaganda gift to the Communist Sandinista regime in Managua. Brody now works with the above-mentioned Kenneth Roth at Human Rights Watch, which is a leading player in the "Get Pinochet" gang. Although he is often quoted by the major media, his left-wing pedigree and work for the Sandinista thugocracy is never mentioned.

The governments of the United States, England, and Spain, which are aiding this campaign, are populated with alumni from the old IPS/Communist network. The most notorious of the IPS veterans in the Clinton camp are Anthony Lake (CFR) and Morton Halperin (CFR), both of whom played key roles during the Carter administration's "human rights" attacks on anti-Communist governments. Another Carter retread is IPS cadre David L. Aaron (CFR), a Marxist who worked with Letelier. He has been holding various posts in the Clinton regime, such as ambassador to the Organization for Economic Cooperation and Development. Then there's Karl F. Inderfurth (CFR), a former staff member of Senator Frank Church's Select Committee on Intelligence, who was "briefed" by Communist agent Letelier in Letelier's home on multiple occasions and used this Soviet-supplied disinformation in attacks on U.S. intelligence. He was appointed by Clinton to the U.S. mission to the UN.

Over in England, in the Socialist regime of Tony Blair, it's a similar story. Blair's Interior Minister, Jack Straw, who was a central player in the decision to arrest Pinochet, was a Marxist student agitator in the 1970s who organized demonstrations against Pinochet. Blair's trade and industry minister Peter Mandelson is another whose motives and connections should be questioned. As Martin Argostegui pointed out in *Insight* magazine, some of the British press has revealed that "Mandelson, while chairman of the British Youth Council during his university years, organized a delegation to attend the 1978 Communist Youth Festival in Cuba, whose main acts were repudiating Pinochet while supporting Castro — even while the Cuban regime was filling concentration camps, sending troops to garrison Soviet proxy states, and supporting terrorists throughout Latin America."

Mr. Blair's government, which has seen fit to free IRA terrorists convicted of murder, torture, and terrorism, is singularly obsessed with aiding the international Marxist Left in its persecution of Pinochet, even denying him permission to receive Holy Communion on Christmas, and subjecting him to humiliating restrictions and round-the-clock surveillance in relatively tight living quarters (not the "12-bedroom mansion" often reported in the press). "Look, it's no secret that most of these leaders [in the campaign against Pinochet] smoked dope together and demonstrated together in the 1960s and '70s," Professor Angelo Codevilla told THE NEW AMERICAN. "What is this about? It's not about human rights, that's for sure," noted Codevilla. "It's about using the color of law and pseudo-judicial proceedings for

"I would like to be remembered as a man who served his country, who served Chile throughout his entire life on this earth. And what he did was always done thinking about the welfare of Chile, and never sacrificing his tradition to hand it over to other countries."
— General Augusto Pinochet

private vengeance and for advancing an ideological agenda."

The Communists, the Marxist Left, and the one-world internationalists hate Pinochet not only because he led one of the few counter-revolutions that succeeded in ousting a Communist regime, but also because he is a Christian patriot who stands for everything they oppose. They also despise him because he has so thoroughly exposed the bankruptcy — economic, political, social, and moral — of socialism with his free-market reforms. In just a few years, the Pinochet junta transformed the devastated Chilean economy (collapsing under triple-digit inflation, wage and price controls, food shortages, rationing, nationalized industries, collectivized agriculture, expropriated properties, etc.) into a thriving, prosperous nation.

Under the guidance of economists schooled at the University of Chicago by Professor Milton Friedman, the junta scrapped the entire structure of stifling statist controls that had been put in place by Allende. Import tariffs of 100 percent were reduced to ten percent and subsidies were dramatically slashed or abolished. Over 200 businesses were returned to their rightful owners.

Chile's export base was diversified and the country's traditional reliance on copper exports declined from 80 percent to under 40 percent. Foreign investment laws were liberalized, which, together with its other reforms, gave Chile the most favorable investment climate in South America. Foreign capital flooded in and domestic savings and investment soared. Taxes were cut and government spending was drastically reduced. Wage and price controls, innumerable regulations, and union "closed shop" rules were all abolished. Social security was privatized, and hundreds of thousands of government bureaucrats and workers went back to work in the private sector.

Professor Angelo Codevilla wrote, in the November/December 1993 issue of *Foreign Affairs*:

> Between 1970 and 1990 Chile changed dramatically. In 1970, when Eduardo Frei transferred the presidency to Salvador Allende, Chile had enjoyed six years as the beneficiary of worldwide prosperity and record prices for its copper exports. Chile was the second largest recipient of foreign aid per capita. Yet only half the homes in the country had inside bathrooms. In 1990, after Pinochet — despite 16 years as an international pariah and the target of trade boycotts, disinvestment and foreign aid cutoffs — about nine out of ten Chilean homes had them.

Moreover, Codevilla noted:

> After Frei, 82.2 babies per thousand died in infancy. After Pinochet, that figure fell to 17. Reduced infant mortality plus better nutrition and sanitation increased life expectancy from 63.6 years in 1970 to 71.8 in 1990. In 1973 the Chilean government had 650,000 employees. By 1989 the Chilean people had only 157,871 central government employees to support and to obey. By 1992 polls showed that people of all classes rated their satisfaction with bureaucracy as 5.2 out of 7.

By 1980, the Pinochet government had drawn up a remarkable constitution similar to our own which was approved by 68 percent of the voters. "Chile's reformers," wrote Angelo Codevilla, "tried to think of as many ways as possible, tiny steps along with big ones, to reduce political patronage and to remove government from the majority of people's lives while maintaining a safety net for the poorest." The constitution, he noted, "attempted to outlaw pork-barrel politics by making it as difficult as possible for laws to benefit or disadvantage specific sectors, activities, or geographic zones. It requires the congress, whenever it passes a spending bill, to specify from where the money will come."

And what of Chile's military, so viciously reviled by the U.S. media? "To its credit," said Codevilla, "the Chilean military did not try to become a new ruling class. No former member of the military government followed the U.S. practice of going into business as a lobbyist, or the Latin American practice of getting a government franchise for a particular business. Moreover, the military government never tried to build a political party or movement that would support it."

Perhaps Pinochet's most important contribution to Chile's "miraculous turnabout" was the privatization of that country's Social Security system. Under the compulsory, government-run Social Security system, Chilean workers paid up to 25 percent of their earnings, yet the system was broke. The new privatized system, enacted in 1980, continued to pay the elderly who had become dependent on the government system, while allowing every worker the freedom to opt out with a private pension savings account (PSA). Under the new system, each worker is required to contribute at least ten percent of his earnings (of his first $25,000) to his PSA, which is his personal private property. These contributions are invested in capital markets through private investment managers.

"During the first month, 25 percent of Chilean workers ... opted out of the government-run system," Jose Pinera, a principal architect of the system, reported in the July 1997 issue of *The Freeman*. "By the end of the first year, 70 percent of Chilean workers chose to open tax-deferred pension savings accounts. By the end of the second year, 90 percent had."

In July 1999, the Cato Institute released the most recent study on Chile's pension system, authored by L. Jacobo Rodriguez, assistant director of the Institute's Project on Global Economic Liberty. Mr. Rodriguez writes: "Today, more than 95 percent of Chilean workers have

Promise kept: In March 1998, Pinochet retired, as he had promised to do, from his long and faithful command of Chile's military.

their own pension savings accounts; assets have grown to over $34 billion, or about 42 percent of gross domestic product; and the average real rate of return has been approximately 11.3 percent per year, which has allowed workers to retire with better and more secure pensions."

"Chilean Social Security reform under Pinochet," Mr. Rodriguez told THE NEW AMERICAN, "by any measure, has been an astounding success." Nobel Prize-winning economist Milton Friedman agrees. His memoirs, *Two Lucky People*, written with his wife, Rose, and published last year, deal extensively with the Chilean reforms. The Pinochet government, he told THE NEW AMERICAN, "should be receiving praise and appreciation from the rest of the world for throwing off socialism and demonstrating how free markets and limited government lead to greater personal freedom and prosperity." Instead, he noted, General Pinochet has been under relentless attack for 26 years. The current persecution, he believes, is "outrageous, absolutely outrageous."

But what of all those charges of murder, torture, and disappearances? That's just it; so far they are only *charges*. And considering the sources of those charges (as we have already noted) there are very good reasons for skepticism. As has happened so often in the past with disinformation operations against a besieged "right-wing" government, the U.S. and European press have been treating the "human rights" charges as *fact* before they have been verified.

Undoubtedly, some people were murdered and tortured, and some disappeared. That began under Allende. And after his regime was overthrown in 1973, the terrorist war against Chile continued. In 1984 alone, there were 735 terrorist bombings. Responsibility for most of these acts was claimed by the Manuel Rodriguez Patriotic Front (MRPF), created by the Chilean Communist Party and supported by Cuba, Nicaragua, Libya, East Germany, and the Soviet Union. Many Chilean officials have been assassinated by these terrorists, and Pinochet

himself has been the target of several assassination attempts. On September 7, 1986 President Pinochet and his 10-year-old grandson narrowly escaped death when their motorcade was ambushed by terrorists armed with automatic rifles, rocket launchers, bazookas, and grenades. Five members of Pinochet's police and military escort were killed and 11 were wounded in the attack.

Chile has been the target of a sustained, murderous, international terrorist

Reuters

campaign — for nearly 30 years. When terrorists are killed in clashes with the police or armed forces, their identities are often unknown. In which case, the corpses may be put on public display so that relatives may claim them. When no one claims them, they are buried as "unknowns." This undoubtedly accounts for some of the "disappeareds." In any ongoing, bitter, desperate war of this type, extralegal retribution and retaliation is almost inevitable. Individual private citizens, private militias, or military or police units may take the law into their own hands, sometimes to avenge the murder of their relatives or fellow officers. And their aggression may be directed not only at actual terrorists, but at those whom they suspect of aiding the terrorists. However, we have seen no evidence to sustain the charges that Pinochet ordered, knew

of, or approved of, any plan for the use of murder or torture against his political opponents.

It is remarkable that those who are the harshest critics of Pinochet for his use of force against a real terrorist threat to his nation, are more than willing to excuse President Clinton's abuse of lethal force at Waco against people — including women and children — who were, under even the most wild surmise, only a *potential* threat. The same Pinochet haters support Bill Clinton's demands for vast new police-state powers, supposedly to combat terrorism. Yet we in the United States have never experienced anything close to the level of terrorism that has been visited upon Chile.

Nevertheless, President Pinochet, true to his word, voluntarily stepped down from power after reestablishing order, justice, security, prosperity, and the rule of law in his country. In 1988, in obedience to a national plebiscite, he called elections for a return to civilian rule, even though he had the full backing of the military and sufficient popular support to maintain his junta's control. How rare such an occurrence has been in history.

General Pinochet is a deeply religious man, a devout Roman Catholic who, reportedly, prays the Rosary daily and, when possible, attends daily Mass and receives Holy Communion. He is also a devoted family man, still "very much" in love, he says, with his wife of 56 years, and always ready to play with his adoring grandchildren and great grandchildren.

In an interview with the *London Telegraph*, General Pinochet was asked how he would like to be remembered. He answered: "I would like to be remembered as a man who served his country, who served Chile throughout his entire life on this earth. And what he did was always done thinking about the welfare of Chile, and never sacrificing his tradition to hand it over to other countries."

And, surely, that *is* how he will be remembered by millions of his countrymen who recognize the tremendous debt they owe to this heroic patriot. ∎

The Statesman

Regardless of the political risks or the unpopularity of the cause, Senator Robert A. Taft chose principle over pragmatism.

by Steve Bonta

We are tempted to view history as a succession of great occurrences, epoch-making cataclysms like Pearl Harbor and the assassination of President Kennedy, that suddenly and irrevocably reroute the course of human events. But in reality, the bulk of history turns on smaller things, the apparently insignificant, even anonymous, victories and defeats, the initiatives seized and the opportunities squandered. These episodes are seldom spectacular or widely appreciated in their time, but hindsight inevitably traces their real impact.

Such an episode was the Republican Convention in 1952, when a popular, charismatic general, Dwight D. Eisenhower, wrested the Republican presidential nomination from the outspoken, unapologetically conservative senator from Ohio, Robert Taft. It is impossible to gauge how history might have turned had Taft received the nomination instead, and had gone on to win the Presidency.

Many modern conservatives and Americanists peg the Eisenhower nomination as the pivotal event that led to the exclusion of the pre-WW II Old Right from the Republican mainstream. Indeed, except for the Goldwater campaign more than a decade later, the dominant political culture among modern Republicans has been the diluted, internationalist, selectively constitutionalist dogma of the neo-conservatives. But it was not always so.

Robert Alphonso Taft, born in Cincinnati in 1889, was destined to lead if any man ever was. His father, William Howard Taft, was the only man ever to be both a U.S. President and Chief Justice of the Supreme Court. Like his father, Robert Taft was educated at Yale, where he graduated at the top of his class. He then studied at Harvard Law, where he received the highest marks of any student in 15 years. Yet despite his extraordinary potential, Robert Taft turned down job prospects in Washington and returned to

Ohio, apparently feeling little inclination to follow in his father's distinguished footsteps. He married college sweetheart Martha Bowers, and settled down to a modest family life and quiet career with a Cincinnati law firm.

But Taft's anonymity would not endure. Alarmed at the radical political agenda of the so-called "progressives," and stirred by momentous events in Europe such as world war and the Russian revolution, Taft soon became heavily involved in local and state politics.

Throughout his life, Taft's detractors found fault with his public persona. His manner was too blunt, they said, his demeanor too distant. He lacked the unctuous warmth of the natural politician, but he compensated with uncommon character assets. He was a man of unwavering convictions and personal courage, as he would show over and over again during his political career. He never used profanity and was a faithful, devoted husband. He was physically unimposing, to the delight of his caricaturists, standing just over six feet, with large ears, prominent upper teeth, and rapidly receding hair. But his considerable mental powers, especially his memory, as well as his immense legal erudition, made him a persuasive speaker and debater.

In 1920, Taft was elected to the Ohio House of Representatives. Ten years later, he was elected to the Ohio State Senate, where he served a single term before suffering defeat in 1932. During his years in Ohio state government, he worked tirelessly to reduce taxes, while earning a reputation as a capable leader and organizer and a dependably loyal Republican partisan.

In 1938, after several years in the private sector, Robert Taft launched an improbable campaign for the United States Senate. He competed for the Republican primary nomination against the popular, charismatic Arthur Day, who enjoyed the support of much of the Republican establishment. Taft, by contrast, was blunt, undiplomatic, not too gregarious, and viewed with narrow suspicion by many party insiders. Nevertheless, he campaigned feverishly and his efforts paid off. After defeating Day in the primary, he won another upset against the Democratic incumbent, becoming the new Republican senator from Ohio.

Like many of his Republican comrades-at-arms, Taft was driven by a desire to oppose the socialist excesses of President Franklin D. Roosevelt's New Deal. Taft, in company with many conservatives of the day, was horrified by Roo-

William Howard Taft, Robert's father, was the only man ever to be both a U.S. President and Chief Justice of the Supreme Court.

sevelt's naked power grabs, from the confiscation of gold to the flagrantly unconstitutional National Recovery Act. In Washington, however, he discovered a Republican Party adrift. Shell-shocked by Roosevelt's political juggernaut, many Republicans had abandoned their opposition to the New Deal, choosing instead to follow public passions rather than defend the genuine public interest. Of the period Russell Kirk wrote: "The 'liberal' or anti-Taft element of the Republican party acted upon the assumption that the New Deal was irrevocable. Concessions, therefore, must be made to public opinion, made with the best face possible.... Victory at the polls, rather than the defense or vindication of principles, seemed to most of the liberal Republicans the object of their party. In some

matters, it might be possible to outbid the New Dealers; in most, to offer nearly as much as Roosevelt offered."

Taft, by contrast, understood that political parties must be united in the defense of great principles, even at the expense of immediate partisan self-interest. Great parties, according to Tocqueville, "are those which cling to principles rather than to their consequences, to general and not to special cases, to ideas and not to men." And Kirk affirmed that "the party which abides by principle must be willing to go out of office, or to abstain from taking office, if the price of power is the sacrifice of that party's reason for existence. And the party's leaders must be ready ... to oppose elements of their own party when some abandon those principles and thereby harm the national interest." Taft believed in these ideals and, more importantly, did not hesitate to act upon them. Throughout his distinguished, decades-long Senate career, he labored to restore the Republican Party to its former stature as the party of principled, Americanist, constitutional conservatism. For his leadership in the fight for the soul of the Republican Party and his dependability in standing for principle, regardless of the political risk, he earned the nickname "Mr. Republican."

Like many pre-WW II conservatives, Robert Taft was staunchly opposed to military interventionism abroad. He resisted calls for American involvement in the European war. Even after Pearl Harbor made war inevitable, his support for America's role in the conflict was tempered by anxiety over wartime statism:

In our efforts to protect the freedom of this country against aggression from without ... we must constantly be on guard against the suppression of freedom in the United States itself.... No President has ever had as much power at the beginning of a war as has President Roosevelt, and no Congress has ever been as liberal in the granting of additional powers to the executive as has the present Congress in the last six months.... There is every reason to believe that many officials of the administration are using the war as an excuse for the extension in domestic affairs of a lot of unsound [policies] which they could not get Congress to approve in peace.

Over and over during the war years, Taft warned his colleagues and Americans generally of the deadly internal perils to freedom created by the wartime emergency. War, he understood, was at least the equal of economic hardship in providing fertile ground for totalitarianism to take root.

As soon as the war had concluded, it was Taft who led his congressional colleagues to abolish most of the oppressive emergency powers that the Executive branch had hoped to enjoy in perpetuity. Taft also firmly opposed the peacetime draft throughout his Senate career, believing it to be a form of involuntary servitude.

In the postwar years, Taft reached the peak of his abilities. Besides being known and respected far and wide for his integrity, he mastered the art of politics. No longer an inexperienced junior senator, he became the torchbearer for his par-

ty. His prominence did not lure him into the ranks of the invertebrate compromisers and handwringers who so typically populate the echelons of party leadership; from such he remained aloof when co-operation meant compromise on principle. Taft seldom hesitated to speak his mind, even on issues that made the country-clubbers squirm.

Perhaps no truer measure of the man has been recorded than his speech, given at Kenyon College in October 1946, in which he expressed his opposition to the trials of Nazi leaders at Nuremberg. In those tumultuous months, when America was still mourning her war dead, when retribution was almost universally favored, Taft took a hugely unpopular position. The trials were illegal under American law, he averred, because they violated "the fundamental principle of American law that a man cannot be tried under an *ex post facto* statute.... In these trials we have accepted the Russian idea of the purpose of trials — government policy and not justice — with little relation to Anglo-Saxon heritage. By clothing policy in the forms of legal procedure, we may discredit the whole idea of justice in Europe for years to come." Moreover, he observed, "about

"Fundamentally, the ultimate purpose of our foreign policy must be to protect the liberty of the people of the United States. War should never be undertaken, or seriously risked, except to protect American liberty."

— Senator Robert A. Taft

this whole judgment there is a spirit of vengeance, and vengeance is seldom justice. The hanging of the eleven men convicted will be a blot on the American record which we shall long regret."

Taft's remarks provoked a predictable uproar. His enemies filled the papers and airwaves with ululations of opportunistic outrage, while his fellow Republicans scurried for political cover. Taft was portrayed as a Nazi sympathizer and a cold-hearted elitist who defended the Nazis but opposed the "social" justice of the New Deal. A parade of politicians, editorialists, and legal experts went on record to defend the legality of the Nuremberg tribunals. The Toledo *Blade* sneered, "On this issue, as on so many others, Senator Taft shows that he has a wonderful mind which knows practically everything and understands practically nothing." The Cleveland *Plain Dealer* admitted that Taft "may be technically correct," but turning "loose on the world the worst gang of cutthroats in history … would have failed to give the world that great principle … that planning and waging aggressive war is definitely a crime against humanity."

The Republican Party leadership, of course, was chiefly concerned with repercussions at the polls the following month. As events turned out, though, their worries were baseless: The expected electoral catastrophe failed to materialize, and the furor soon died down.

Taft's principled defense of legal justice, even for abominated mass murderers, was a timely corrective for a country

Franklin Roosevelt: The Father of the American Welfare State, his excesses were opposed by Taft.

Taft-Hartley: The two lawmakers coauthored landmark legislation to curb excessive union power.

only recently emerged from Roosevelt's de facto wartime dictatorship. It was also a warning of things to come — the nasty, long-term consequences of a victor's justice meted out in the flush of emotionally charged national euphoria.

For Taft was right in cautioning against the precedent that was set by allowing political policy to masquerade as legal justice. In our day, aggressive internationalists use the Nuremberg trials and other "war crimes" tribunals to justify a supranational world court for trying offenders for United Nations-defined "crimes against humanity." In keeping with the spirit of international socialist ideologues, justice against "international offenders" is applied selectively, according to policy directives, rather than the impartial demands of justice. Alleged Serbian war criminals are hunted down, apprehended, and bundled off to The Hague without any semblance of due process, while "former" Communist mass murderers in Eastern Europe luxuriate in retirement villas or reinvent themselves as moderate socialists. Former anti-Communist strongmen like Pinochet are hounded and persecuted, while current dictators like Fidel Castro travel to the free world with impunity. And saddest of all, justice for "war criminals" continues to have an unequal claim on victors and the vanquished.

Robert Taft could not have foreseen all of the pernicious consequences of Nuremberg. But his unflinching stand on the Nazi trials became perhaps his best-known act of statesmanship, the ultimate touchstone of the character of a man utterly incapable of embracing expediency at the cost of a burning principle.

For most of his political career, Taft was concerned about the excessive power and coercive methods of unions. Because of government intervention, he believed, the balance of power between unions and corporate management had been severely weighted in favor of the unions and needed correction. The Taft-Hartley Act of 1947, which Taft coauthored with Representative Fred Hartley, sought to do just that. The bill, which was passed over President Harry S. Truman's veto, prohibited unions from forcing workers to become union members, from compelling employers to pay for work not performed, and from engaging in strikes intended to force an employer or self-employed individual to join the union.

For his principled stand, Taft was tarred as an enemy of the workers and Taft-Hartley was labeled a "slave-labor bill." Yet no one defended the rights of workers more passionately than Taft, when principle obliged. In 1946, when President Truman tried to forcibly conscript striking railway workers, it was Taft who led the Senate to vote down Truman's emergency measure — scant

hours after the House, in a fit of short-sighted hysteria, had passed it by an overwhelming majority. Taft, ever consistent in his defense of legal justice, was just as dismayed by dictatorial action against unions as by the abuses the unions themselves perpetrated.

Just as he had proven his ability to lead a principled opposition against Truman on domestic issues, Taft was to show himself equally capable of opposing the administration's actions abroad. In the era of post-war Communist expansion and mealy-mouthed Western accommodationism, a strong voice was sorely needed to articulate alternatives to Truman's policies of appeasement. Robert Taft was that voice. In *A Foreign Policy for Americans*, the only book he ever authored, Taft reminded Americans of some of the common-sense principles of foreign policy that were being abandoned in favor of postwar internationalist "engagement." "Fundamentally," he cautioned, "the ultimate purpose of our foreign policy must be to protect the liberty of the people of the United States. War should never be undertaken, or seriously risked, except to protect American liberty." He decried the imbecility of waging war to promote "democracy," arguing that "… the forcing of any special brand of freedom and democracy on a people, whether they want it or not, by the brute force of war will be a denial of those very democratic principles which we are striving to advance."

Taft was alarmed at President Truman's willingness to usurp from Congress the power to authorize war. "In the long run," he advised, "the question which the country must decide involves vitally not only the freedom of the people of the United States but the peace of the people of the United States…. If in the great field of foreign policy the President has the arbitrary and unlimited powers he now claims, then there is an end to freedom in the United States not only in the foreign field but in the great realm of domestic activity which necessarily follows any foreign commitments." Taft believed that military conflicts would occur more frequently if the President were given unlimited power to start wars, because "[history] shows that arbitrary rulers are more inclined to favor war than are the people at any time."

To his credit, Taft correctly perceived how the West had created the Communist menace in Europe by unnecessarily conceding huge swaths of territory to the Red Army. He excoriated American policy in the Far East, where deliberately treacherous policies, cooked up in a State Department honeycombed with Communists and Communist sympathizers, sought to undermine the free, anti-Communist governments of Chiang Kai-shek in China and Syngman Rhee in Korea. Most importantly, he warned of the subtler effects of Communism at home, of the growing acceptance of Communism as merely another strain of humanitarian idealism, consistent with Western egalitarian thinking. Such naïveté, Taft warned, was perilous, since Communism "denies every principle of Americanism. It denies liberty.... It denies religion. It denies God Himself.... It is hard to find any philosophy which is more the antithesis of American principles."

Despite his unflinching opposition to Communism, Taft was no warmonger. He insisted that the battle against Communism would have to be won in the hearts of men. War, he pointed out, "far from establishing liberty throughout the world, has actually encouraged and built up the development of dictatorships and has only restored liberty in limited areas at the cost of untold hardship, of human suffering, of death and destruction beyond the conception of our fathers."

In his later years, Taft became a strong opponent of the United Nations. As a young man, he had supported the League of Nations; and in 1945 he even voted for the UN charter, believing the UN to be an honest effort to create a forum for international understanding and conflict resolution. Before long, though, he came to understand that he and his colleagues had been tricked. "The U.N. has become a trap," he warned. "Let's go it alone."

By 1952, Robert Taft, the best-known and most widely respected Republican in Congress, was the GOP's obvious choice for its presidential standard-bearer. His candidacy had been considered before, to be sure, but never ringingly endorsed by an appreciable segment of party insiders. In 1940, he was pushed aside by the vapid Wendell Willkie, and in 1948 by the mushy moderate and consummate Eastern establishmentarian Thomas Dewey. With the embarrassing defeat of several successive centrist party insiders, the conditions seemed ripe for Mr. Republican to finally lead his party back to the White House.

The Taft campaign got off to a roaring start, snowballing through the southern and midwestern states, and also attracting wide support in certain populous eastern states such as Pennsylvania and Michigan. After two decades of depression, war, and exponential growth of federal government power, huge numbers of American voters were apparently ready to elect leadership that could be relied upon to roll back the gargantuan excesses of the federal welfare/warfare state.

The liberal, internationalist wing of the Republican Party, however, had no intention of serving up the White House to a man opposed to America's new globalist policies. Taft was an open critic of myriad planks of the emerging house of world order — including the United Nations, the International Monetary Fund and the World Bank, and NATO — putting him at odds with the globalist agendas of Wall Street, much of official Washington, and the Eastern Establishment dynasties.

The Establishment found its champion in popular war hero Dwight Eisenhower.

General Eisenhower, a political weathercock, was neither politically well-informed nor encumbered by deep-seated convictions. He was not even unambiguously Republican. Portrayed as a political neophyte, he was in fact a canny manipulator. With feigned reluctance, he accepted the mantle of standard-bearer for the Eastern Establishment, and set about sabotaging the Taft campaign.

With the indispensable support of America's power elite, the Eisenhower campaign took national electoral politics to new lows. Determined to win at any cost, it launched massive PR campaigns in a number of crucial states, including New Jersey and Texas, to persuade Democrats to vote in Republican primaries. Leaflets were circulated advising Democrats of their responsibility to join forces with Republican moderates to keep the "extremist" Taft from securing the nomination. Major newspapers, led by the *New York Times*, trumpeted the specious claim that "Taft can't win," encouraging voters to choose the security of expedience over the risk of principle.

Despite the skulduggery of the Eisenhower camp, the race for the nomination was still a close heat when the Republican National Convention convened in Chicago in July of 1952. It had been so far an epic contest — the people's choice

Politician vs. statesman: Skulduggery on behalf of Eisenhower cost Taft the '52 GOP nomination.

versus the Establishment's man, the thoughtful, straight-talking legal scholar and policy expert versus the charismatic, shallow, media-manufactured mythic hero. In essence, the Statesman versus the Politician.

But at the convention, the adepts of long-knife, below-the-belt parliamentarianism carried the day for Eisenhower. With a backdrop of choreographed street demonstrations and convention-hall campaign chorusing, Eisenhower's ham-fisted surrogates pushed through last-minute procedural modifications designed to handicap the Taft delegates. The convention handed the nomination to Eisenhower, and in doing so the Republican Party decisively repudiated the pre-WW II constitutionalist, non-interventionist conservatism of the Old Right. The dogma that replaced it — the aristocratic, internationalist, halftone "conservatism" of Eisenhower, Buckley, Nixon, and the "country-club" set in general — has, with the exception of the Goldwater campaign, owned the Republican party ever since.

Taft, gracious in defeat, mended fences with Eisenhower and gave him his full support. Even when

John F. Kennedy (right), in *Profiles in Courage*, lauded Taft's courage in condemning the Nuremberg Trials **(above)**. "[W]e are not concerned today with the question of whether Taft was right or wrong...," JFK wrote. "What is noteworthy is the illustration ... of Taft's unhesitating courage in standing against the flow of public opinion for a cause he believed to be right."

Eisenhower refused to give Taft a Cabinet position, the Republican senator bore no ill will. In January of 1953, Taft became Senate Floor Leader. Despite his defeat in Chicago, Mr. Republican showed no sign of flagging.

But in May of 1953, Robert Taft began experiencing severe hip and leg pains. He was soon diagnosed with cancer, although the extent of the disease was not immediately determined. By early June, however, his doctors had found tumors throughout his body. Robert Taft was fighting his last battle. Ever reticent about personal problems, Taft concealed the nature of his illness to all but his immediate family. He resigned in mid-June as Senate Floor Leader and drew up his will. A little over a month later, on the last day of July 1953, Robert Taft passed away at the age of 63.

In death, his was a character that invited praise even from those who had been his bitterest foes. His old adversary Harry Truman said: "He and I did not agree on public policy, but he knew where I stood and I knew where he stood. We need intellectually honest men like Senator Taft." Herbert Hoover called him "more nearly the irreplaceable man in American life than we have seen in three generations." A few years after Taft's death, he was elected, along with John C. Calhoun, Daniel Webster, Henry Clay, and Robert La Follette Sr., to the Senate Hall of Fame. The committee that elected them stated that they had all transcended party and state lines and "left a permanent mark on our nation's history and brought distinction to the Senate."

But far beyond the hermetic precincts of the nation's capital, it was in the country's heartland where Taft would be most sorely missed. For he was a champion not only of liberty and justice, but of the interests of the grassroots con-

stituency that had elected and re-elected him. No silver-tongued, Bryan-esque populist popinjay, Robert Taft, in standing for equal justice, decency, and liberty under the Constitution, tapped into a deep vein of popular respect for integrity that no populist demagogue could ever reach. He returned a measure of dignity to a once-principled Republican Party. After his passing, in the words of one eulogist, there remained only "a faceless, slinking thing, bearing only the name Republican, a name indeed which President Eisenhower hardly has mentioned since he was elected under its label."

Taft was above all things a lover of liberty, one of a very few such men to have attained high political office in America this century. "Liberty," he once said, "is freedom of speech and of the press ... but it is much more. It is the freedom of the individual to choose his own work and his life occupation, to spend his earnings as he desires to spend them, to choose the place where he desires to live.... It is the freedom of the local community to work out its own salvation, when it has the power to do so. It is the freedom of cities, of counties, of school districts; the freedom to educate one's children as one thinks best. It is the freedom of thought and experiment in academic institutions. It is the freedom of men in industry to run their business as they think best, so long as they do not interfere with the rights of others to do the same."

We shall never know how history might have been altered had Robert Taft followed his father's footsteps into the White House. In retrospect, his finest moment was his refusal to stoop to his opponent's level in the race for the 1952 Republican nomination. He might have improved his chances by lowering himself to trench-warfare tactics, but his great soul would have been forever compromised. As John F. Kennedy would later record in his *Profiles in Courage*, "Senator Robert A. Taft of Ohio was never President of the United States. Therein lies his personal tragedy. And therein lies his national greatness." ∎

Faith, Courage, Character

Faith, as the Holy Bible instructs us, is "the substance of things hoped for, the evidence of things not seen." Many of those to whom God gave the gift of faith have been called upon to endure the "trial of cruel mockings and scourgings … [and] of bonds and imprisonment."

During his ministry, Hungary's Jozsef Cardinal Mindszenty endured torture, persecution, humiliation, defamation, and imprisonment at the hands of both the Nazis and the Communists, but remained an undaunted witness for Christ and champion of liberty.

John Birch, a Baptist missionary born to missionary parents in India, was a missionary in China when he was thrust into World War II as an intelligence officer for General Claire Chennault's "Flying Tigers." Birch, in the words of a comrade in arms, was "absolutely fearless, completely unselfish, [and] never [thought] … of his personal discomfort or danger." Another officer extolled him as "the most brilliant, finest, most able, bravest officer I ever met." His abbreviated life — cut short by Communist assassins — illustrates that through faith even the most "common" man is capable of uncommon courage and achievements.

Aviator Charles Lindbergh captured the world's imagination with his intrepid trans-Atlantic airplane voyage in 1927. He was also among those who pioneered rocket science, jet propulsion, and biomedical research. Striving to keep America out of World War II, Lindbergh became a leader of the America First Committee — and volunteered to fly combat missions in the Pacific after Pearl Harbor propelled our nation into the war. Throughout his life, Lindbergh displayed the personal courage and independence of mind that were keys to our nation's greatness.

If "character" is the aggregate of small acts of integrity performed quietly and without recognition, Ezra Taft Benson would epitomize the term. A product of a pious, farm-community upbringing, Benson was a leader in the field of agriculture, eventually serving as Secretary of Agriculture under President Dwight Eisenhower. An opponent of socialist controls over America's farmers, Benson was subjected to torrential abuse and invective from Marxists inside and outside the federal government. As a religious leader, Benson offered devoted service to "Jesus Christ, the Redeemer of the World." As an exponent of Americanism, Benson championed the U.S. Constitution and forcefully condemned collectivism in all its pernicious varieties.

Born into slavery and unfathomable poverty, Booker T. Washington rose to commanding heights on the strength of his integrity, industry, and insatiable appetite for learning. The first widely recognized leader of black Americans, Washington embodied the virtues through which emancipated blacks could take advantage of the blessing of living in America. The "legacy of slavery" notwithstanding, Washington wrote, blacks in America "are in a stronger and more hopeful condition … than is true of an equal number of black people in any other portion of the globe." Washington founded Alabama's Tuskegee Institute as a means of helping other blacks equip themselves for life as free and responsible men and women.

The Cardinal's Cross

The Communist torturers could not conquer the abiding faith of Hungary's Jozsef Cardinal Mindszenty.

by John F. McManus

Srtega Photos

I t is an elementary truth that, if no one opposes evil, evil will triumph. History provides numerous examples of unforgettable courage exhibited by individuals who would not compromise or keep silent in the face of iniquity. In the post-World War II era, there were and continue to be many heroes who resisted the evil known as Communism. Perhaps no one has more typified indomitable will in the face of Red brutality than Hungary's Jozsef Cardinal Mindszenty.

During the years Mindszenty was languishing in a Communist prison, a movie entitled *The Prisoner* was shown throughout the West. Reputed to have told his story, it attracted large audiences partly because famed actor Alec Guinness played the leading role. But, if the scriptwriters intended to present Mindszenty's ordeal, they failed almost completely. The film glossed over the reality of the injustices endured by its subject and showed not a glimpse of the torture he suffered. Mindszenty himself would later comment that "the only thing it had in common with events in Hungary is the presence of a cardinal."

After he was released to the West in 1971, Mindszenty told his story in a book entitled *Memoirs* (1974). Much of what follows is drawn from its pages. In the preface, he stated:

The reader is entitled to ask whether I am telling everything. My answer is: I mean to tell everything and shall preserve silence only when it is required by decency, by manly and priestly honor. But I am not speaking out now to harvest the fruits of my sufferings and wounds. I am publishing all this only so that the world may see what fate communism has in store for mankind. I want to show that communism does not respect the dignity of man; I shall describe my cross only in order to direct the world's eyes to Hungary's cross and that of her Church.

The man who became known to the world as Jozsef Mindszenty was born Jozsef Pehm on March 29, 1892 in Mindszent, Hungary. During World War II, Nazi occupiers urged Hungarians of German descent to discard their Hungarian names and readopt German names. In a small act of defiance, Father Joszef Pehm did the opposite, changing his German name to reflect the Hungarian community where he had been born and where his parents still lived.

Mindszent, Hungary: the future cardinal changed his name to that of his birthplace in an act of defiance against the Nazis.

The future cardinal graduated from the seminary in Szombathely in 1915. His first assignment as a priest took him to nearby Felsopaty. Two years later, he was transferred to Zalaegerszeg where his abhorrence for socialism and Communism soon brought him into conflict with the local authorities.

When World War I ended in 1918, the constitutional monarchy was replaced by a revolutionary socialist government led by Count Michael Karolyi. Mindszenty immediately used the newspaper he presided over to publish sharp criticism of the Karolyi regime. For this he was arrested in February 1919, held for ten days, and then released but forbidden to return to his parish in Zalaegerszeg. When he attempted to return, he was again held prisoner.

In March 1919, Karolyi turned the government over to a Communist uprising led by the notorious Bela Kun. Executions and terror became the routine, and Communist authorities ordered Mindszenty to leave the country. Instead, he escaped to his parents' home in Mindszent, where he stayed until the extremely bloody but short-lived Communist rule ended in August 1919.

When it was safe to do so, Mindszenty returned to Zalaegerszeg and was named pastor of its church late in 1919 at the unusually young age of 27. Bishop Janos Mikes responded to the young priest's misgivings about accepting the assignment at such a young age by assuring him that his youth was "a fault that would diminish from day to day." Mindszenty plunged into his duties, and in only a few years the fruits of his labor included a newspaper and publishing company, numerous new churches and schools, even homes for the aged. By 1922 he was named a titular abbot, and by 1937 he was designated a papal prelate with the title of monsignor.

In March 1944, his happy and fruitful 25 years in Zalaegerszeg came to an end when Pope Pius XII named him bishop of Veszprem, a large county in western Hungary. He arrived at his new home on March 29, 1944, only 10 days after the Nazis had completely occupied Hungary. In obedience to Hitler's decrees, the Nazi puppet government ordered the confinement of Jews in ghettos. But the Hungarian bishops, including Mindszenty, vigorously protested in a statement in part reminiscent of the American Declaration of Independence:

> When innate rights, such as the right to life, human dignity, personal freedom, the free exercise of religion, freedom of work, livelihood, property, etc., or rights acquired by legal means, are unjustly prejudiced either by individuals, by associations, or even by the representatives of the government, the Hungarian bishops, as is their duty, raise their protesting voices and point out that these rights are conferred not by individuals, not by associations, not even by representatives of the government, but by God Himself.

It is beyond doubt that this intervention saved most of the Jews of Budapest from Nazi extermination. The Nazi commissioner of Jewish affairs angrily commented, "Unfortunately the clergy of all ranks have taken first place in the efforts to save the Jews. They justify their activities by appealing to the commandment to love one's neighbors."

Patriotic Hungarians attempted to form a resistance to Nazi occupation in late 1944, but the Nazis arrested resistance leader Milkos Horthy and installed Nazi collaborator Ferenc Szalasi as the head of their puppet government. These were perilous times for Hungary, a period when the Nazi invaders had already arrived and Soviet Communists were on its doorstep. Mindszenty described the situation: "From the West the brown peril threatened us; and from the east, the red."

As the Communist forces advanced, tens of thousands fled to the West. Aware of what was coming to his diocese, Mindszenty hid chalices and vestments in his parents' home. He watched in dismay as the pro-Nazi Hungarian Arrow Cross Party arose to aid Hitler's forces. He organized a petition campaign seeking to keep Veszprem and the rest of western Hungary out of any war zone. But when he presented it to Arrow Cross leaders, they arrested and incarcerated him in Sopron along with 25 other priests and seminarians.

Eventually, the Nazi collaborators moved these captives to a monastery and placed them under house arrest. Here, in March 1945, Mindszenty found himself beset upon by several friends, including a naïve bishop who believed the foreign broadcasts claiming that Soviet Communism had changed and was no longer a threat to the church or the people. These well-meaning friends entreated Mindszenty to escape from the Nazis and flee to the east where Soviet forces were advancing.

But Mindszenty had studied papal encyclicals, especially the 1937 letter of Pope Pius XI condemning atheistic Communism. He had also read the works of domestic and foreign Communists, and he had never forgotten a passage in Lenin's message to Gorki: "Every concept of God is an unspeakable business, an abominable expression of self-contempt." He had no intention of asking refuge from any adherent to Leninism.

The Communists arrived in Sopron on Easter Sunday 1945, and Mindszenty was permitted to return to his post in Zalaegerszeg. The new occupiers had raped, pillaged, and destroyed nearly everything in their wake as they swept across Hungary from the east. But now they sought to put on a friendly face. A proclamation from the Soviet high command declared: "Hungarians, the Red Army calls upon you to remain where you are and continue your peaceable work. The clergy and the faithful can carry on the exercise of their religion unhindered."

Mindszenty knew that "unhindered" meant that the exercise of religion would eventually be confined to church services alone and that all church-led cultural, educational, social, and charitable activity would be restricted and eventually eliminated. In time, this is exactly what happened. One way the Communists did this was to require licenses to publish newspapers. Feigning a paper shortage, the Communist regime licensed only two Catholic weeklies — yet Red agents were publishing 24 daily newspapers, five weeklies, and several magazines.

The Communist-led government also decreed that political parties must henceforth receive permits to operate. The Hungarian Christian Party, which had enjoyed a strong and beneficial influence between the two world wars, was denied a permit. Conversely, the Communists approved a small faction of "progressive Catholics," a group none of the bishops would support. The Communists published an attack on St. Stephen (the patron saint of the nation), mandated the teaching of Marxism in the schools, and converted Catholic youth groups into Marxist young people's organizations.

After the defeat of Nazi Germany in May 1945, Soviet forces continued to occupy Hungary, just as they remained in place elsewhere in Eastern and Central Europe. The Soviets set up a government run by Hungarian Communists, most of whom had spent the war years in Russia training for such an opportunity.

In September 1945, Pope Pius XII appointed Mindszenty to fill the vacant post of Archbishop of Esztergom, which carried with it the title of Primate of Hungary. Historically, the primate (the first among the bishops in a nation) had served as the second highest political official in Hungary. In the past, if a king violated the constitution, it was the duty of the primate to rebuke him. The Communist leaders, anxious to appear friendly, sent congratulations to Mindszenty on his appointment. The archbishop responded: "Many thanks for your congratulations. The highest constitutional authority of the country stands ready to serve his native land." His message did not endear him to the Red leaders, who soon realized they could not afford to leave Mindszenty in his position.

Prior to the November 1945 national elections, the new Primate issued a pastoral letter that was read in all the Catholic churches throughout the nation and also reached many Protestant congregations. After recounting some of the crimes of the Communist post-war government, Mindszenty stated: "[W]e can no longer keep silent. We must publicly declare that no Christian voter can support a party that rules by violence and oppression and that tramples underfoot all natural laws and human rights." He implored the people "to vote only for those candidates who represent law, morality, order, and justice. Vote only for men strong enough to hold to their beliefs no matter what the cost. Do not yield to threats, the less people resist violence, the stronger it grows."

Partly as a result of this message, the Church-favored Smallholders Party de-

feated the Communists by a vote of 58 percent to 17 percent. But after the election, the Smallholders Party was beguiled into forming a coalition government with the Communists, setting the stage of complete Communist control.

Fearing that the worst was still to come as the Communists tightened their grip, Mindszenty rallied the people religiously with radio addresses and printed exhortations. In early 1946, swarms of the faithful filled the churches and a huge throng greeted him in the capital city of Budapest. But within that assemblage, Communist *agents provocateurs* joyously shouted the name of the leader of the

Years of peril: As World War II drew to a close, the Nazi troops in Hungary were replaced by Communist troops. Mindszenty opposed them both.

pro-Nazi Arrow Cross Party. Their purpose was clear: supply a pretext for eventual arrests and suppression of the church for its supposed pro-Nazism.

In February 1946, Pope Pius XII named Mindszenty and 31 other bishops worldwide as Cardinals of the Catholic Church. Scheduled to go to Rome for the ceremony, Mindszenty was initially unable to secure a passport. But one was quickly provided when the Communists realized that Mindszenty's absence would reflect badly on them, and Mindszenty arrived in Rome a day late.

During 1946 and 1947, the government increased its harassment of the church and its leader. Phony charges against the Catholic schools and youth organizations forced Mindszenty to issue formal protests

"[N]o Christian voter can support a party that rules by violence … that tramples underfoot all natural laws and human rights.… [V]ote only for those candidates who represent law, morality, order, and justice. Vote only for men strong enough to hold to their beliefs no matter what the cost."

— Cardinal Mindszenty

to the government. His stand won the support of numerous Protestant leaders including Calvinist Bishop Laszlo Ravasz. The more the authorities targeted what they didn't completely control, the more they realized that Mindszenty was their chief enemy. He knew it too, and he responded by increasing his visibility throughout the nation and by rallying the people spiritually.

On the political front, representatives of the Smallholders Party and some patriotic army officers were arrested and accused of fomenting an anti-state conspiracy. Several of them soon "confessed" to having participated in the bogus conspiracy, providing the excuse for additional Smallholders Party leaders to be rounded up and removed from their posts. Others fled the country. In a matter of weeks, the Communists had succeeded in smashing their once-influential political opposition and had become dominant in parliament.

With the government effectively in their hands, the Communists enacted a new electoral law enabling them to control the 1947 national elections. Under the guise of legality, the Communists denied many opponents the right to vote, eased the way for their own cadres to vote numerous times, employed forged registration cards, and stationed their Political Police at polling places. Not surprisingly, the so-called elections converted the national parliament into a docile tool of Communism.

Mindszenty responded to the growing peril by organizing more religious rallies. Early in September 1947, his call for the people to visit Catholic shrines was answered by 1,768,000. Before the month ended, he led 100,000 at one gathering and 120,000 at another. In October, he addressed an afternoon assemblage of 150,000 young people in Budapest, and 90,000 workers turned out that same evening. Another rally the next day turned out 250,000. A few days later, 200,000 Catholic parents joined him in the main square of Budapest. In *Memoirs*, Mindszenty reported that although the Communists didn't dare prohibit these ceremonies outright, they soon reduced the number of trains transporting people to them, denied access to public address systems, and began the insidious process of banning public meetings because of phony concerns about possible epidemics.

In April 1948, the government's Minister of Religion and Education offered his plan to nationalize the nation's schools. Mindszenty's protest was ignored, and 4,885 schools, of which 3,148 belonged to the Catholic Church, were brought under government control.

During this period Communism's Iron Curtain had not yet completely closed Hungary's borders. Mindszenty diligently informed the Catholic press worldwide about the tragic events in his nation, and this caused the Communists both inside and outside Hungary to intensify their efforts to discredit him. In *Memoirs* Mindszenty related details of this escalating campaign:

The attacks on me and the slanders directed against me continued throughout the summer of 1948. In the autumn, as an immediate preliminary to my arrest, a new campaign was launched under the slogan: "We will annihilate Mindszentyism! The well-being of the Hungarian people and peace between the Church and state depend on it." School children and factory workers were ordered into the streets to demonstrate against me. Communist agents led demonstrators to my epis-

copal palace and demanded that the bishops help remove me, "the obstinate and politically short-sighted" cardinal-primate from his position as the head of the Church.

On November 19th, the authorities arrested Mindszenty's secretary, Dr. András Zakar. A few days later, former allies of the cardinal visited him and urged him to acquiesce in the takeover by the Communist Party because, they claimed, Communism was no longer an enemy of religion. He not only condemned this lie, he denounced Communism as an "atheistic ideology" in a published reply. He then prepared for his arrest. In *Memoirs* he recalled: "I declared that even in prison I would never voluntarily abdicate or make a 'confession' of any kind of wrongdoing. If, subsequently, such a confession should nevertheless be produced, it would have to be regarded as either forged or the consequence of torture and the shattering of my personality."

His last conference of bishops met at his Esztergom residence on December 16th. He asked his confreres not to sign any concordat with the state and told them never to accept any pay from the government because "in an atheistic state a church that is not independent can only play the part of a slave." One week later, a long column of police cars arrived; several top government officials ransacked his residence and claimed to have found incriminating documents.

The day after Christmas, another column of cars appeared at the cardinal's residence. Police Colonel Decsi, leading a contingent of 80 police officers, found Mindszenty at prayer and announced, "We have come to arrest you." Asked to produce a warrant, one of the officers snarled, "We don't need anything like that."

Taken directly to the notorious 60 Andrassy Street, the cardinal knew what was in store for him. The building had previously been used by the Gestapo for torturing and terrorizing prisoners. Ordinary citizens who happened to pass by feared the structure so greatly that they regularly gave it as wide a berth as possible. Inside were Hungarian torturers who had been trained by Soviet experts. In *Memoirs*, Mindszenty recounted his introduction to Andrassy Street: "… I was led to a cold room on the ground floor, where a sizable crowd had gathered to watch my clothes being changed. The police major and a lame secret policeman grabbed me and pulled off my gown, while the bystanders bleated with laughter, and finally stripped me of my underwear. I was given a wide, particolored, Oriental clown's outfit. Several of the onlookers danced around me, and the major bellowed: 'You dog, how long we have been waiting for this moment....'"

The humiliation was bad enough. Then came interminable interrogations when he was told to confess, among other falsehoods, that he had been collaborating with Americans to intervene in Hungary's affairs. He denied the charges, prompting Colonel Decsi's hissing reply, "Remember this: The defendants here have to make a confession in the form we want." Decsi then turned the prisoner over to guards who led him to a torture chamber. The cardinal described the beginning of his ordeal:

... a massively built lieutenant entered. "I was a partisan," he said. His language was Hungarian, but not his savage, hate-filled face. I turned away; he drew back, but suddenly came charging at me and kicked me with all his might. Both of us fell against the wall. Laughing diabolically, he exclaimed: "This is the happiest moment in my life." The words were unnecessary; I could read his feelings in his distorted, sadistic features.

The major returned and the partisan was sent out again. The major produced a rubber truncheon, forced me to the floor, and began beating me, first only on the soles of my feet, but then raining blows on my whole body. In the corridor and in the adjacent rooms raucous laughter

of sadistic delight accompanied the blows.... [T]he major was soon breathing heavily, but he did not slacken his blows. In spite of the exertions, the beatings obviously gave him sheer pleasure.

I clenched my teeth, but did not succeed in remaining wholly mute. And so I whimpered softly from pain. Then I lost consciousness, and came to only after water had been splashed on me. I was then lifted and laid on the couch. How long this ordeal lasted, I cannot say. My watch had been taken away, and if I

Solitary suffering: Outfitted in a black suit by Communist authorities, Mindszenty was displayed in a mock trial following weeks of imprisonment and torture. His "crime"? Consistent opposition to Communism.

had had one, I would scarcely have been able to read the numerals. I thought about the fate and feelings of innumerable honest Hungarian girls, nuns and mothers who had been raped....

Then I was dressed and taken back to interrogation. Once more, my signature was demanded. I refused it again.... Furious, Decsi ordered: "Take him back." And once more I was beaten. For the third time they demanded my signature — without success. For the third time they tried to thrash it out of me with the rubber truncheon.... And once more I was told: "Here the police decide what is confessed, not the defendant."

This treatment continued for 39 days! It included beatings, sleepless nights, drugged food, and various forms of humiliation. His prayer book had been taken from him, and when guards surmised that he was praying, additional punishment was administered. Attempting to maintain his senses, he refused to eat. He explained in *Memoirs*: "I had no doubt that the food was prepared in Andrassy Street and that stupefying drugs would be mixed with it to numb the will. I had previously heard how strong men were broken in this place. It was public knowledge that two sorts of drugs were employed. One loosened the tongue; the other made him totally apathetic."

But hunger eventually forced him to eat something, and the authorities were able to drug the man their tortures couldn't break. After weeks of beatings, sleeplessness, drugs, and various indescribable deprivations, Mindszenty recalled: "My powers of resistance gradually faded. Apathy and indifference grew. More and more the boundaries between true and false, reality and unreality, seemed blurred to me. I became insecure in my judgment. Day and night my alleged 'sins' had been hammered into me, and now I myself began to think that somehow I might very well be guilty.... My shaken nervous system weakened the resistance of my mind, clouded my memory, undermined my self-confidence, unhinged my will — in short undid all the capacities that are most human in man."

The horror he was subjected to continued to take its toll. After weeks of such constant inhumanities, he noted that his memory faded to the point that what happened to him "after the end of the second week of detention, January 10-24, 1949, remains in my memory only in fragmentary form." He described this period as living "in a kind of twilight state." Finally, the physical abuse lessened and, as the authorities prepared him for his February 3rd trial, no torture was inflicted for two days.

The cardinal was amazed when he was given a black suit to wear at the trial. Then, he was stunned to find that he was one of seven "conspirators" facing Communist-style justice. Ludicrously labeled the "general staff of a worldwide conspiracy," the seven included his secretary and a monk whose health battered and the medical care he needed wasn't forthcoming. His mother was allowed three short visits, each accompanied by a police lieutenant who listened to their every word. But the cardinal at least had the consolation of being able to say Mass each day. He was enabled to do so by several guards who, at great risk to

Uprising: In 1956, freedom fighters temporarily liberated Hungary, freeing Mindszenty from Red captivity. When Soviet troops retook Budapest, Mindszenty took refuge in the American embassy — his home for the next 15 years.

had obviously been shattered. Mindszenty himself was charged with treason, misuse of foreign currency, and conspiracy against the government and the people. A letter he had never written was read into the proceedings. In part, it stated, "I voluntarily confess that I did in fact commit the offenses with which I am charged."

Kalman Kiczko, his government-appointed defense attorney, refused to allow the cardinal to mention any of the tortures he had suffered. Photos taken during the trial show a gaunt figure in a black suit staring blankly, almost hypnotically, from the prisoner's dock. Mindszenty's recollection of the event was that "the police, the prosecution, the judge, and the counsel for the defense were collaborating."

The trial lasted for only three days and, to the surprise of no one, each of the defendants was found guilty. Mindszenty's sentence, the most severe given to any of the "conspirators," was life imprisonment. Taken immediately to Kobanya Prison, he was confined to a filthy hospital room for the next seven months. While he endured no more beatings, drugs, and sleepless nights, his body was

themselves, sneaked small quantities of bread and wine into his room. In time, even this "privilege" was suppressed.

In September 1949, the authorities moved the emaciated prelate to a Budapest penitentiary where he languished for the next five years. Wherever they put him, his condition amounted to solitary confinement. Though there were other prisoners, contact was forbidden. He commented: "The greatest torment in prison is the monotony, which sooner or later shatters the nervous system and wears the soul thin, for it is monotony that seems to have no possible end."

The years passed but the health he had once enjoyed did not return. By 1954, his pre-prison weight of 170 pounds had fallen to 97 pounds. His eyesight had begun to fail; he suffered dizzy spells; and his condition deteriorated so greatly that he was placed in a prison hospital for an entire year. The authorities didn't want him to die while imprisoned, so they nursed him back to a semblance of good health.

In July 1955, the authorities moved him to Puspokszentlaszlo in southern Hungary. Again his mother was permitted to visit, a great consolation to both of them. When winter came, he was moved again, this time to Felsopeteny in the far northern part of Hungary.

Another true measure of the man emerged when two clergymen, Archbishop Grosz and Father Toth, attempted to persuade Mindszenty to accept a pardon. The cardinal knew that Grosz had sought his own release by negotiating with the Communists. As a result, the "peace priests" who had collaborated with the regime and formerly slandered Grosz had become Grosz's admirers. The government then spread the word via its newspapers that Mindszenty was about to be pardoned and released "at his request." But the indomitable cardinal told Grosz and Toth that he "wanted not mercy but justice." He recounted in *Memoirs*, "If I asked for clemency, I thought, I would have to be ready to meet my adversaries' conditions," which he knew he could not do. Instead, he sent a letter to the minister of justice proposing conditions for a general amnesty. His letter received no answer.

On October 23, 1956, Hungary erupted in revolution. News almost immediately reached the castle where Mindszenty was being held. The guards ordered him to prepare to leave for Budapest claiming that they wanted to "protect him" from the joyous throngs who were dancing in the streets of the nearby town and shouting his name. Mindszenty knew that he needed no such protection. Finally, after four days, the people bypassed the guards and freed him. A detachment of uniformed Hungarian patriots arrived and arranged to take him to Budapest.

As he prepared to leave, large numbers of ordinary people flocked to the castle to see for themselves that Soviet armored cars had not carried him off to some other prison. He wrote: "The Protestants came, with sincere joy, led by their pastor; they were followed by the Catholic minorities and the Baptists; young men, girls, old men."

He arrived in Budapest on October 31st. After meeting with several of his

bishops, he immediately dissolved the "peace priest" movement that had collaborated with the Red regime. In his radio address to the nation on November 3rd, he called for forgiveness and urged no recriminations for those who had carried out the Communists' will. But he was unaware that a betrayal of the brave freedom fighters was already underway.

One of the more dastardly acts of treachery ever performed by the U.S. government was bared by Representative Michael Feighan (D-OH) four years later. His report appears in the *Congressional Record* for August 31, 1960:

You will recall the revolution broke out on October 23, 1956, and that by October 28, the Hungarian patriots had rid their country of the Russian oppressors. A revolutionary regime took over and there was a political hiatus for five days.

Then the State Department, allegedly concerned about the delicate feelings of Communist dictator Tito, sent him the following cable assurances of our national intentions in the late afternoon of Friday, November 2, 1956: "The Government of the United States does not look with favor upon governments unfriendly to the Soviet Union on the borders of the Soviet Union."

It was no accident or misjudgment of consequences which led the imperial Russian Army to reinvade Hungary at 4 a.m. on the morning of November 4, 1956. The cabled message to Tito was the go-ahead signal to the Russians because any American school boy knows that Tito is Moscow's Trojan Horse.

The U.S. not only failed to send promised aid to the freedom fighters while assuring the Soviets that our nation would not intervene, our nation's State Department blocked plans of Spain's Francisco Franco and West Germany's Konrad Adenauer to aid the courageous Hungarians.

When the Soviet tanks and troops reappeared in Budapest, Mindszenty rushed by auto to the parliament building and learned that the leaders of the uprising had already been arrested. In addition, Soviet forces had sealed off the city and had even confiscated the automobile that had brought him there only a few hours earlier. The cardinal and his aide sped on foot to the American Embassy and were welcomed by the U.S. ambassador, who immediately cabled Washington for permission to grant the two men refuge. Within 30 minutes, permission arrived from President Dwight Eisenhower himself. A grateful Joszef Mindszenty, at the time unaware of what else the U.S. government had done, sent a message of gratitude to Eisenhower.

For the next 15 years, the cardinal resided in the American Embassy, his presence there a symbol of hope for the betrayed Hungarian people. In many ways he was still a prisoner, and his situation made it impossible for him to officiate at the funeral of his mother, who passed away in 1960. The Communists kept a round-the-clock vigil outside the embassy to guarantee that he would not flee or find his way into interior Hungary to stimulate another uprising.

Before long, the Communist regime forced the reinstatement of the "peace priests" and reestablished its hated Bureau for Church Affairs. Mindszenty commented about these developments: "In many respects the situation of the Church was worse than it had been in the years before the uprising."

In 1963 and again in 1965, Austria's Cardinal Konig visited and, following instructions from Popes John XXIII and Paul VI, offered Mindszenty a post in the Vatican. Hungary's primate replied that he would accede to such a request only if it "meant furthering the liberty of the Church," thereby effectively declining the invitations.

By 1971, Paul VI's emissary, Msgr. Jozsef Zagon, brought Mindszenty word of the pope's desire that he leave Hungary. But Mindszenty objected chiefly on the grounds "that I did not want to abandon my flock and the church in their difficult situation" and did want "to end my life in my native land." He warned that the Communists would use any change in his situation to their advantage.

He wrote to President Nixon, whose speedy response made known the U.S. government's desire to have him depart the embassy. He then decided to comply with the pope's wishes, having expressed to him in a letter his willingness to "subordinate [his] own destiny to the interests of the Church." He left the embassy on September 29, 1971, and was transported by automobile across the Hungarian-Austrian border. Through the car window, he was able to view the Iron Curtain, a sight that both shocked and saddened him. He was then flown to Rome, where he was brought to the pope.

Only a few days later, he read in the Vatican newspaper *Osservatore Romano*

Roads to Rome: Cardinal Mindszenty departed Budapest in 1971 for the Vatican, where the living symbol of Hungarian freedom met Pope Paul VI.

that his departure from Hungary had removed an obstacle to better relations between church and state in Hungary. The Vatican, he later concluded, "was not paying any attention to the specific terms I had formulated in Budapest" — to insure that the Communist regime would not benefit from his departure. By mid-

October, his willingness to go to Vienna and live at the Hungarian seminary known as the Pazmaneum was accepted. Before he left, Paul VI assured him in person: "You are and remain archbishop of Esztergom and primate of Hungary. Continue working, and if you have difficulties, always turn trustfully to us."

During 1972, the cardinal traveled throughout Europe visiting with ethnic Hungarians. In all of his speeches, sermons, and radio addresses, he focused on the untenable situation of the church in Hungary and of the nation itself. It didn't take long for the Communist regime in Budapest to protest to the Vatican and demand that he be silenced. Of what then transpired, he wrote:

These protests were received in the Vatican, and on October 10, 1972 — in the thirteenth month of my exile — I was informed by the papal nuncio in Vienna that the Holy See in the summer of 1971 had given the Hungarian Communist Government a pledge that while I was abroad I would not do or say anything that could possibly displease that government. I replied that in the negotiations conducted from June 25 to June 28, 1971, between the Holy Father's personal emissary and myself there had been no mention of any such pledge. Had I known about any guarantee of this sort, I would have been so shocked that I would have asked the Holy Father to rescind all the arrangements that had been made in conjunction with my departure from Hungary. After all, the fact was widely known that I had wanted to remain in the midst of my suffering people and to die in my native land. I asked the nuncio to inform the appropriate Vatican authorities that a sinister silence already prevailed within Hungary and that I shrank from the thought of having to keep silent in the free world as well.

On November 1, 1973, Mindszenty was asked by the pope to resign his post as archbishop of Esztergom and primate of Hungary. He responded by stating that, "because of the present condition of the Catholic Church in Hungary," he could not abdicate. He told of his fear that "my abdication, and the subsequent occupation of the post of primate of Hungary by a churchman who would be chosen with the consent of the Bureau of Religious Affairs, would contribute to legitimizing the present catastrophic ecclesiastical conditions in Hungary."

Yet, on the very date of the 25th anniversary of his arrest by the Communists, Mindszenty received a letter from Paul VI informing him that the post of

Faith: The weapon tyrants cannot overcome.

archbishop of Esztergom had been declared vacant. Then, on February 5, 1974, the 25th anniversary of his show trial, the announcement of his removal appeared in the press. In profound sorrow, Mindszenty issued a correction through his office:

A number of news agencies have transmitted the Vatican decision in such a way as to imply that Joszef Cardinal Mindszenty has voluntarily retired.... In the interests of truth Cardinal Mindszenty has authorized

his office to issue the following statement:

Cardinal Mindszenty has not abdicated his office as archbishop nor his dignity as primate of Hungary. The decision was taken by the Holy See alone.

After long and conscientious consideration, the cardinal has justified his attitude on this question as follows:

1. Hungary and the Catholic Church of Hungary are not free.

2. The leadership of the Hungarian dioceses is in the hands of a church administration built and controlled by the communist regime.

3. Not a single archbishop or apostolic administrator is in a position to alter the composition or the functioning of the above-mentioned church administration.

4. The regime decides who is to occupy ecclesiastical positions and for how long. Furthermore, the regime also decides what persons the bishops will be allowed to consecrate as priests.

5. The freedom of conscience and religion guaranteed by the Constitution is in practice suppressed. "Optional" religious instruction has been banned from the schools in the cities and the larger towns....

6. The appointment of bishops or apostolic administrators without the elimination of the above-mentioned abuses does not solve the problems of the Hungarian Church. The installation of "peace priests" in important ecclesiastical posts has shaken the confidence of loyal priests and lay Catholics in the highest administration of the Church. In these grave circumstances Cardinal Mindszenty cannot abdicate.

For his last line in *Memoirs*, Mindszenty stated that he had "arrived at complete and total exile." The cardinal passed away on May 6, 1975. His remains were initially interred at a shrine in Austria, but were transferred to Hungary in 1991. The cardinal had returned home. ∎

Soldier-Missionary

John Birch, fortified by Christian virtue, fought and died in an effort to liberate, in body and soul, China's oppressed masses.

by Steve Bonta

In April 1942, America had been at war more than four months. The long, bloody campaign across the islands of the Pacific lay ahead. Imperial Japan had wrested Singapore from the British, and had expanded her dominions across the Philippines, southeast Asia, the East Indies, New Guinea, and deep into the Chinese mainland. Yet, late in April of that momentous year, a squadron of American bombers, led by Jimmy Doolittle, flew into the heart of this vast empire to conduct an unexpected raid on Tokyo.

The purpose behind Doolittle's daring raid was primarily psychological; it was to show the Japanese that they were not invulnerable on their island fortress, and that, sooner or later, the war would be brought to their doorstep. Doolittle and his men were well aware of the risks of what was potentially a suicide mission. After dropping their payloads they would simply have nowhere to go, except inland over occupied China. They therefore planned to fly westward until their fuel ran out and then bail out, hoping not to fall into enemy hands.

For several crews, the mission turned out badly. Some were captured by the Japanese, and a few perished. Colonel Doolittle and his crew were more fortunate; after bailing out, they were rescued by sympathetic Chinese and smuggled by river into Chekiang Province.

Several days after the raid, at a tiny village somewhere in Chekiang, a curious figure was eating dinner. Tall, spare, and dressed in coolie clothes, he ate native fare uncomplainingly. He spoke Mandarin Chinese with near-native fluency, and was known to the locals as Pai Shang-wei. Yet he was an American, a young Baptist missionary named John Birch.

While Birch was eating, he was approached by a Chinese man who sat at his table unbidden. At length, the local quietly asked the American missionary to follow him outside. After making sure they were unobserved, he led Birch to a sampan

moored inconspicuously on the riverbank nearby. Indicating the boat, the anonymous Chinese simply said, "Americans," and left the scene.

Birch boarded the sampan and knocked on the door, calling, "Anybody in there? Anybody who can speak English?" The group of Americans hiding inside the boat hesitated. Was this a ruse? At length, convinced by Birch's authentic southern drawl that he could not be Japanese, they invited him in. Once inside the cramped boat, Birch found Colonel Doolittle and

out protest, confident that, in some small way, he was aiding the cause of righteousness among the oppressed Chinese, a people he had come to love and respect.

John Birch, despite being a red-blooded American boy, seemed to be linked by destiny to Asia. He was born in India in 1918, the oldest son of George and Ethel Birch who, like their son two decades later, were missionaries. When John was only two and a half years old, though, his father's health forced

China in 1940.

Arriving in Shanghai, Birch began intensive study of Mandarin Chinese, for which he displayed an uncommon aptitude. After six months of training, he was assigned to Hangchow, where he proselytized tirelessly. Hangchow at the time was outside the Japanese occupation zone, so Birch was left alone by the Japanese until the attack on Pearl Harbor. On the very first day of U.S. involvement in the war, however, the Japanese sent a delegation to Hangchow to arrest him, forcing John Birch to flee into the interior.

Unfortunately, he now found himself cut off from contact with the outside world, his funds rapidly dwindling. Finding that no bank would cash his traveler's checks, Birch lived on his meager savings until April 1942, when, against all odds, he finally managed to cash his traveler's checks at Chinese Army Headquarters at Hangchow. It was while traveling from Hangchow after receiving the money that John Birch encountered Colonel Doolittle and his crew. Prior to the meeting, Birch had already volunteered to enlist in the U.S. forces in China, preferably as a chaplain. Just days after he helped guide Doolittle and his men to safety, Birch was ordered to report immediately to Chu Chou airbase for duty, no doubt as a result of the glowing report Doolittle gave of him to headquarters.

After a scant four and a half weeks at Chu Chou, where John served as chaplain, he evacuated with several other preachers just ahead of the advancing Japanese, who quickly overran the base. Under orders to report to headquarters at Chungking, Birch made a harrowing overland journey by truck and train to Kweilin, where he had the astounding good luck to run into General Claire Chennault. The general, who was at the time in charge of the famed "Flying Tigers" of the American Volunteer Group (A.V.G.), gave John Birch a lift in an Army transport plane to Chungking. There, Birch was first assigned to serve as translator for Colonel Doolittle. The colonel, still in China, needed help discussing Chinese aviation with the locals, but Birch found the tech-

Doolittle strikes: Colonel Jimmy Doolittle led an unprecedented attack on Tokyo in April 1942 from the flight deck of the *USS Hornet*. For the crews of Doolittle's B-25 bombers, it was a one-way trip ending in China. Doolittle himself was met in China by John Birch and led to safety.

four crew members. Exhausted from their ordeal, but otherwise uninjured, Doolittle and his crew were nevertheless in need of a guide and translator to help them get to American headquarters in Chungking. Birch agreed to personally guide Doolittle and his "Tokyo Raiders" to safety, and accompanied them as far as Lanchi. From there, he saw that they had proper directions, told Colonel Doolittle where he could be reached, and left.

Partly as a result of this encounter — which brought to the attention of the American military Birch's unusual talents with the language and culture — the young missionary soon became a soldier, spy, saboteur, and liaison with Chinese rebel forces. In this capacity, Birch worked primarily behind enemy lines and lived off the land under conditions that most common soldiers would have found unendurable. Yet John Birch bore it with-

them to return to the milder climate of the United States. Young John Birch grew up a devout Southern Baptist, like his parents. By all accounts a sober, responsible youth, John was remembered by his younger siblings for his generosity and kindness. "In our family, we didn't have much money," his sister Betty recalled to a reporter many years later, "so John used to buy us younger children candy and gifts at the dime store with money he earned selling newspapers." Once, John even donated his entire savings to his parents to help defray Betty's medical bills.

A studious young man, Birch attended Mercer College in Macon, Georgia, where he graduated at the top of his class. While at Mercer, he decided to become a missionary, and enrolled in the Bible Baptist Seminary at Fort Worth, Texas. After completing a two-year curriculum in a single year, John Birch sailed for

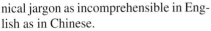
nical jargon as incomprehensible in English as in Chinese.

Soon, because of his unique language skills and adaptability, Birch became involved in intelligence work, both in Chungking proper and in the interior, working very closely with General Chennault himself. A natural leader, Birch drew up maps, organized intelligence networks, and, in general, seems to have nearly singlehandedly set up the Intelligence Headquarters for the A.V.G.'s replacement, the China Air Task Force (C.A.T.F.).

In 1943 Birch was sent to Changsha as a liaison and intelligence officer. He not only established an unending flow of intelligence on Japanese troop movements, but also developed a system to coordinate American air support for Chinese forces engaging the Japanese. Equipped with a field radio and a growing network of Chinese infiltrators and informants, Birch efficiently located enemy ammunition dumps, airfields, howitzers, and other objects of strategic importance, and, using a portable radio, directed American planes to these targets from the ground. On one occasion, when bombers were unable to locate a large, well-camouflaged ammunition dump concealed in the suburb of a small city, Birch slipped back across enemy lines and, flying in the nose of a bomber, personally guided the pilots to their target.

Birch's network of Chinese guerrillas and saboteurs set up posts along the Yangtse, to monitor the movements of Japanese naval forces and the shipping of supplies. General Chennault, in his autobiography, *Way of a Fighter*, lauded Birch as "the pioneer of our field intelligence net." But Birch's contribution to the war effort in China went beyond the collection of accurate and reliable intelligence. The brave young missionary also set up a network for rescuing American fliers shot down behind enemy lines. About 90 percent of Chennault's downed fliers were rescued by Birch's system. According to General Chennault, this incredible success rate was "the highest percentage of any war theater."

Birch spent much of his time in the field, usually disguised as a Chinese coolie. His command of the language had by then improved to the point where he was usually taken for a Chinese from another province. Often his missions involved grueling treks of hundreds of miles through the subtropical heat and humidity of China, living on little more than boiled water or tea with red rice, and enduring occasional bouts of malaria.

Birch the man apparently changed little during all these activities. He remained dedicated to spreading the Gospel, and looked

forward to the war's end when he could return to his proselytizing work full-time. To most of his comrades-at-arms, he was a bit of an oddity: He neither drank nor smoked; and he never used profanity. Yet he was never perceived as self-righteous, even by those who emphatically disagreed with his religious convictions.

More importantly, as far as his military work was concerned, Birch was, in the words of friend Captain Bill Drummond, "absolutely fearless, completely unselfish, never thinking of his personal discomfort or danger." Another friend, Captain James Hart, testified that "where brave men were common, John was the bravest man I knew." "Without reservation," recalled Lieutenant Arthur Hop-

Intelligence pioneer: General Claire Chennault **(above)** led the Flying Tigers **(left)** in defense of China. "John Birch," said Chennault, "was the pioneer" of the Tigers' and its successors' "field intelligence net."

kins, "I will say that he was the most brilliant, finest, most able, bravest officer I ever met." High praise indeed for a simple minister of the Gospel who had picked up most of his military training on the fly!

He was a man able to endure not only physical hardship but long stretches of isolation from his compatriots. Birch the ascetic was, except for the comforting

NARA

High praise: Birch was decorated by General Chennault with the Legion of Merit for "meritorious conduct in performance of outstanding service." Birch's "devotion to duty was beyond anything that was expected of him. I cannot praise his work sufficiently," said Chennault.

presence of his God, more often than not a man alone. Because of the secrecy of much of his work, he grew accustomed to keeping his own counsel, disappearing into the hinterland for weeks and months at a time on reconnaissance missions, and returning suddenly without giving any hint of where he had been. We can but imagine, for example, the solitude he endured during a mysterious journey to Tibet, presumably to gather or relay intelligence. Alone he bore the discomforts of another secret mission involving a 60-mile ride through a snowstorm on a hardy Mongolian pony.

This exemplary stoic and patriot, this fine Christian man, was also, as one might expect, a man of high ideals. Those ideals are evident in a touching piece of prose, entitled *The War Weary Farmer*, written by Birch in April 1945. In it, Birch outlined his personal aspirations and his hopes for a better world:

I should like to find the existence of what my father called "Plain living and high thinking."

I want some fields and hills, woodlands and streams I can call my own. I want to spend my strength in making fields green, and the cattle fat, so that I may give sustenance to my loved ones, and aid to those neighbors who suffer misfortune....

I do not want a hectic hurrying from place to place on whizzing machines or busy streets. I do not want an elbowing through crowds of impatient strangers who have time neither to think their own thoughts nor to know real friendship. I want to live slowly, to relax with my family before a glowing fireplace, to welcome the visits of my neighbors, to worship God, to enjoy a book, to lie on a shaded grassy bank and watch the clouds sail across the blue.

I want to love a wife who prefers rural peace to urban excitement, one who would rather climb a hilltop to watch a sunset with me than to take a taxi to any Broadway play. I want a woman who is not afraid of bearing children, and who is able to rear them with a love for home and the soil, and the fear of God.

I want of Government only protection against the violence and in-

justices of evil or selfish men.

I want to reach the sunset of life sound in body and mind, flanked by strong sons and grandsons, enjoying the friendship and respect of neighbors, surrounded by fertile fields and sleek cattle, and retaining my boyhood faith in Him who promised a life to come.

Where can I find this world? Would its anachronism doom it to ridicule or loneliness? Is there yet a place for such simple ways in my own America or must I seek a vale in Turkestan where peaceful flocks still graze the quiet hills?

Birch's qualities endeared him to General Chennault, who lavished praise and commendations on the young soldier-missionary. A case in point came on July 17, 1944, when Birch was awarded the Legion of Merit "for exceptionally meritorious conduct in performance of outstanding service." Modestly, he wrote to his mother that "they ought not to cheapen the decoration by giving it when a man merely does his duty. I shall feel guilty in accepting this one...." Birch shouldn't have felt guilty when General Chennault pinned the medal to his chest. History records Chennault as a great leader and an honest man. One therefore has great difficulty envisioning the general giving a decoration to a soldier undeserving of it. In fact, Chennault once wrote: "I always felt that he would do any job I gave him to do well and he could be depended upon to see things through. His loyalty to me personally and his devotion to duty was beyond anything that was expected of him. I cannot praise his work sufficiently."

Like most lovers of freedom and religion, Birch was acutely aware of the Communist menace. Before the war had ended, he already saw Communism as a potentially worse enemy than either the Japanese Imperialists or the German Nazis. In a 1942 letter to an aunt, he presciently remarked, "I believe this war and the ensuing federations will set the world stage, as never before, for the rise of the anti-Christ!"

August 1945 was a month of epochal events: The savage beginning of the nuclear age with the detonation of atomic bombs over Hiroshima and Nagasaki on August 6th and 9th; the entry into the war against Japan by an opportunistic Soviet Union on the 8th; and the broadcast in Japan on the 15th, V-J Day, of Emperor Hirohito's message of surrender. Ten days later, as the Allies rejoiced in the flush of victory, another critical event occurred. Unlike V-J Day, the event was concealed for years from the American public; had it been otherwise, this seemingly minor tragedy might have rerouted the whole course of history in the postwar 20th century.

On August 25, 1945, a small group of American and Chinese soldiers under the command of John Birch, who had been promoted to captain, left a surrendered Japanese garrison and proceeded by railroad handcar toward the city of Hsuchow. About noon, they reached a section of track that was being torn up by Communist guerrillas. After a tense confrontation, Birch persuaded the Communists to allow his party to pass.

After another hour's travel, though, Birch and his party encountered a second band of Communists. This group was more hostile, but a member of Birch's party, Lieutenant Tung of the Nationalist Chinese army, still attempted to negoti-ate an agreement with the Communists allowing Birch and his small team to pass. The negotiations failed, leading to the murder of Captain Birch, the attempted murder of Lt. Tung, and the capture of the remainder of Birch's party.

On what was thought to be his deathbed, an ailing Lt. Tung recounted to Lt. William T. Miller — a friend of Birch and a fellow intelligence agent in China — the tale of the Communist attack. After the Communists stated their intention to disarm the Americans, Birch refused, stating, "well so you want to disarm us. Presently the whole world has been liberated from the enemy and you people want to stop and disarm us." Birch then demanded to see the Communist leader responsible for the order to disarm the Americans and the Communist soldiers agreed, taking Tung and Birch with them. After repeatedly failing to be brought to the Communist commander, Birch, exasperated, grabbed a Communist soldier by the back of his collar and said: "you are worse than bandits." The Communist soldier did not respond and the group walked a little way further. Then someone called out: "Come over here, this is our responsible man."

Lt. Tung recalls:

This Communist then angrily commanded: "Load your guns and disarm him first," pointing to Capt.

Birch's contribution to the war effort in China went beyond the collection of accurate and reliable intelligence. The brave young missionary also set up a network for rescuing American fliers shot down behind enemy lines. About 90 percent of Chennault's downed fliers were rescued by Birch's system.

Birch. Realizing how seriously acute the situation was, I spoke up in desperation saying: "Wait a minute please, if you must disarm him I will get the gun for you lest a grave misunderstanding develop."

At this moment the Communist commander turned and pointed to me ordering, "shoot him first." In an instant I felt a terrible shock and fell to the ground, shot through the right thigh....

Though lying there on the street in a semi-faint, I heard another shot fired and a voice command, "bring him along."

To this I heard Capt. Birch's anguished reply, "I can't walk."

Tung passed out and never saw Captain Birch alive again. Later he was thrown into a ditch along with the dead body of John Birch and left to die. He was severely beaten, suffering from a broken nose and ruptured right eye, as well as from the severe bullet wound in his leg. Gruesome photos taken by Lt. William Miller show the mutilated body of John Birch, his hands bound behind his back as if he had been executed, his face destroyed by multiple bayonet thrusts. A second bullet may have passed through his skull from back to front.

Some have speculated that Birch, through a belligerent attitude, brought about his own death. A headline in the August 13, 1972 edition of the *Cleveland Plain Dealer* went so far as to state: "John

Elements of success: Birch (second from left) achieved success in China due to his fine Christian character, his language skills, and his affection for the Chinese people. "I will say that he was the most brilliant, finest, most able, bravest officer I ever met," said Lt. Arthur Hopkins.

Birch Aroused Chinese Reds Into Killing Him." Lt. General Charles B. Stone III, former commander of Birch's outfit — the 14th Air Force, which had replaced the C.A.T.F. on March 10, 1943 — dismissed such allegations as spurious years before. In a November 21, 1961 letter to *Newsweek*, Stone defended Birch's handling of the situation: "What else should an American officer do in these circumstances?" Stone asked. "Perhaps any argument with an organized Communist group is useless, but this should not inhibit an American officer from making the attempt in performance of his duty."

The death of John Birch, the first American casualty of the Cold War, sent ripples through an American Establishment swooning over Mao Tse-tung and his Communist band of "agrarian reformers." Mao's forces could never have defeated Chiang Kai-shek and his Nationalists, the greatest force for civilization and liberalization that China had ever seen, if the Nationalists had not already been slated for extinction by socialist elites in the West. With the collusion of State Department subversives, Communists in East Asia had been able to consolidate their gains at war's end. Communist Russia, which had opportunistically declared war on Japan scant days before the Japanese surrender, turned over huge caches of seized Japanese weapons to the Chinese and Korean Communists. American military aid intended for Chiang Kai-shek was blocked by treasonous Leftists in Washington bent on hastening the Communist apocalypse in the Far East. In the context of such cynical deceit and viciously duplicitous American foreign policy, the murder of an innocent American at the hands of Communist thugs would be disastrous for America's media- and State Department-sponsored Mao love-fest.

Accordingly, the Insiders embarked upon a cover-up of the circumstances of John Birch's death. A 1948 letter from Major General Edward Witsell to John Birch's mother claimed that John Birch was killed "as the result of stray bullets fired by Communist forces." Conse-

quently, the letter stated, he was not entitled to the Purple Heart "as he was not killed in action against an enemy of the United States or as a direct result of an act of such enemy." Mrs. Birch was not informed of the findings of a report compiled under the aegis of General Albert C. Wedemeyer that contained the testimony of Lt. Tung.

General Wedemeyer had also confronted Communist leaders Mao Tse-tung and Chou En-lai during a meeting

on August 30, 1945, expressing extreme displeasure at the murder of Birch and the capture of his party. Mao and Chou, feigning concern, promised to investigate the matter and punish the guilty parties. However, the U.S. pressed the matter no further. The incident was not mentioned again, the relevant documents were classified, and the official Washington campaign of deception on behalf of the Chinese Communists continued.

Not until the early 1950s did the details of John Birch's death become public. On September 5, 1950, California Senator William Knowland angrily announced on the Senate floor that the circumstances of John Birch's death had been deliberately covered up by pro-Communists in the United States government. Had the facts of the Birch incident been known at the time, he charged, Congress and the American people

would never have permitted the betrayal of Chiang Kai-shek and the Chinese people. But by then the Communist takeover in China was a *fait accompli*.

John Birch's life was tragically short. The war-weary farmer never lived to see the "fields and hills, woodlands and streams I can call my own," or the wife and family he dreamed about. His death, nasty and brutish, came precisely as millions of other servicemen were enjoying reunions with loved ones and laying plans for a brighter future. He was for a time consigned to oblivion in order to serve the twisted interests of diabolically cynical political manipulators. Only the freedom-loving organization that Robert Welch named in his honor brought John Birch to public attention, kept alive the memory of his extraordinary courage and quiet heroism.

In many respects, John Birch is a far more typical hero than others we have profiled in these pages. Unlike the statesmen, the generals, the scholars, the writers, and others who have left their mark on our tragic century, he led a modest, self-sacrificing existence and died a martyr's death without public acclaim. It never occurred to him to do other than what was right; he was unencumbered by the moral ambiguities associated with power politics. He defined all of his hopes and ambitions in terms of serving his God, his family, and his fellow men. John Birch, in a word, belonged to that most heroic of all classes of human beings — the so-called common men and women who, in order to preserve our civilization, have fought, suffered, and died by the countless millions. Their bones lie interred at Normandy, in Treblinka, in the Soviet gulags, in the Cambodian killing fields, in the waters of the Florida Strait. Like John Birch, they all died in the hope that generations unborn would benefit from their sufferings and sacrifices, even if their names were lost to posterity. Captains and kings depart this fallen world lavished with acclaim, but we must suppose that the millions of common heroes like John Birch will, in some future, better time, receive the higher honor. ■

Flight of the "Lone Eagle"

Charles Lindbergh's independent spirit led him to brave the skies over the Atlantic and to defend America's interests during WWII.

by Jane H. Ingraham

Corbis

Millions of words have been written about the life of Charles Augustus Lindbergh. Most loved and most despised, most admired and most ridiculed, most politically astute and most maligned, Charles Lindbergh was surely one of the most controversial as well as the most arresting of this century's American public figures.

This simple Minnesota farm boy of Swedish descent hardly seemed destined to become anyone of note. Yet he became an international aviation hero adored by the multitudes, a keen analyst of current affairs loathed by the Establishment, a pioneering genius of the aviation industry, and a dedicated scientist on the cutting edge of organ transplant research.

It has been said that outstanding people are often the children of parents who actively oppose the status quo. If this is true, then Charles Lindbergh was marked for fame from birth. His extraordinary mother, Evangeline Land of Detroit, graduated in 1900 with a bachelor's degree in chemistry from the University of Michigan at a time when it was considered unseemly for women to attend college and unheard of for them to major in science. His equally remarkable father, Charles August Lindbergh (called C.A.), rose from his practice as a country lawyer in the tiny town of Little Falls, Minnesota, to become a congressman in 1906 as a Progressive Republican opposed to the "conservative" wing led by Senator Nelson Aldrich (of Federal Reserve fame). C.A. devoted his congressional career to crusading against the J.P. Morgan Money Trust and the concept of a central bank. By 1913 he had come to believe, with startling perception, that inflation and economic panics were intentionally created by bankers as part of their "selfish plan to rule the world by the manipulation of finances."

It is hardly strange that Charles Lindbergh's main inherited attribute was an unshakable independence of mind and spirit. Whatever his endeavor, Lindbergh believed in himself and in his own thinking, a characteristic reinforced by his upbringing. Although his parents' marriage became troubled and they separated, both lived in Washington in winter and Little Falls in summer because of Charles, who remained close to both.

As often happens with extremely bright children, Charles was bored with his studies and not a good student. When a school complained of his inattentiveness and poor grades, his mother simply changed schools, 11 in all between the ages of 8 and 16. Neither parent took his schooling seriously, believing he could be better taught at home than with "censored textbooks." It certainly seemed so.

At the age of seven Charles designed a system for moving heavy blocks of ice from the icehouse to the kitchen. A few years later, after studying the theory of concrete construction, he built a pond for ducks which still exists. At the age of 11 he took over all driving for both his mother and father in a Model T Ford which he also maintained and often repaired, fascinated by the intricacies of the internal combustion engine. Loving to be with his father on his campaign trips, nevertheless Charles had no interest in politics. By the time he was a teenager, in his own words, he "worshiped science."

Meanwhile war had broken out in Europe and C.A., although no longer a congressman, was a passionate foe of becoming involved, believing that the Money Trust desired the conflict as an excuse to undermine civil liberties. After writing a book entitled *Why Is Your Country at War?*, C.A. agreed to run in the Republican primary for governor of Minnesota. But the sinking of the *Lusitania* (which carried a contraband cargo of munitions) was used to whip up public hysteria against Germany, so that anyone opposing intervention was viewed as

seditious or worse. As if in an uncanny preview of the media vilification his son faced many years later for the same reason, howling mobs tore up C.A.'s campaign banners, threw rotten eggs, shouted him down, and hanged him in effigy.

At this time Charles was a senior in high school with full responsibility of running the Little Falls farm and still getting poor grades. Just as it seemed as though he had no chance of graduating, senior boys who dropped out to work on the land in the Food for Victory program were allowed to graduate automatically. Charles never went back until graduation day in June. But he closely followed the exploits of the great air aces of the war — American, British, French, and German. He decided that if the war lasted another year, he would try to enlist as an army pilot and learn to fly. But in November 1918, when Charles was 16, the war ended.

Eager to be a scientific farmer, Charles invested his father's money heavily in machinery and stock, becoming the first in the area to apply advanced procedures. But Charles' mother strongly urged him to go to college. Turned down for MIT's aeronautical engineering program, in the fall of 1920 Charles entered the University of Wisconsin at Madison and was promptly disillusioned, claiming he was learning nothing. At the end of his freshman year his only success was as the crack shot of the ROTC's rifle team. Although Charles returned to Madison in 1921, he found it even more unbearable and in February the college dropped him on grounds of failing grades. Still just a lanky 6'2" 19-year-old, Charles immediately left for flying school in Lincoln, Nebraska.

In flying school Charles learned that he had an uncanny aptitude for planes, an instinctive touch with any of the instruction aircraft. He had "air sense." This unusual sense doubled the value of what he learned there. Turning next to stunt flying, he readily flew planes of any description and became known throughout the West for his daredevil barrels, loops, wing-walking, hanging by his teeth, and anything else that would

The great Atlantic air race had claimed the lives of six aviators when the unknown Lindbergh arrived at Roosevelt Field. "Lindy," with his boyish good looks, tousled hair and dazzling smile, immediately captured the hearts of the public.

thrill an audience. These were the days in which he perfected himself in his control of planes, unaware of how much this would mean in the future.

In 1924 Charles enrolled in the Army Air Service Cadet program. For the first time in his life he was motivated to study. Of 104 cadets who entered, only 18 graduated, with Charles at the top of the class, commissioned a second lieutenant in the Air Corps Reserve.

Two years later, Charles Lindbergh, still only 24 years old, became one of the first U.S. airmail pilots, flying between St. Louis and Chicago, narrowly escaping death in several crack-ups. Of the 40 pilots hired at this time, 31 were killed. This is not surprising, since airmail pilots flew at night without navigation lights or ground beacons, ditching in cow pastures when their engines konked out, which was frequently. Fog was a pilot's worst enemy. Charles, with an extraordinary ability to keep his wits about him in an emergency, developed a sense for blind flying. His quick thinking and calmness in a heavy fog and a dying plane saved his life more than once.

But Charles had no intention of flying mail for the rest of his life; he had already conceived a breathtaking plan. A $25,000 prize had been offered for a nonstop flight from New York to Paris, considered to be beyond the range of existing aircraft. Richard Byrd, the first to fly over the North Pole, was already preparing for

the attempt, waiting for a new Fokker tri-motor to be delivered. The French ace René Fonck was testing a giant new Sikorsky biplane equipped with a sofa bed, survival gear, and full-course meals. Attempting to take off at Roosevelt Field in 1926, the overloaded Sikorsky tumbled into a ditch and burst into flames.

In St. Louis, Charles Lindbergh, reading newspaper accounts, reacted with disbelief at the lack of knowledge shown. It was perfectly clear to him that the flight should be made by a single pilot in a single-engine plane with no other weight than fuel. However, none of the other contenders were both pilots *and* navigators, and few had experience flying at night or in bad weather. With his usual unbounded confidence in himself, Lindbergh fired off telegrams to every manufacturer in the country, asking if they would build a plane to his specifications. A bankrupt company in San Diego, Ryan Aircraft, was the only one that responded. In 60 days, Lindbergh had his plane, christened the *Spirit of St. Louis* in honor of his financial backers in that city.

Meanwhile, Byrd's Fokker flipped over in a test run, two other contenders suffocated when their plane sank in a swamp, and two French pilots disappeared en route from Paris to New York. The great Atlantic air race had claimed the lives of six celebrated aviators when the unknown Lindbergh arrived at New York's Roosevelt Field. By this time, a fever of excitement gripped the public. "Lindy," with his boyish good looks, tousled hair, and dazzling smile, immediately captured the hearts of the public. His photo was soon in all the popular magazines before he had done anything.

On the morning of May 20, 1927, when all his carefully thought-out details of engine, fuel, weight, weather, and route coalesced, Charles Lindbergh climbed into his plane. When someone asked if it was true he was taking along only a few sandwiches and water, Charles is said to have replied, "Yes, it's true. If I get to Paris I won't need any more, and if I don't get to Paris, I won't need any more either."

Spirit of adventure: When a $25,000 prize was offered for the first nonstop flight across the Atlantic from New York to Paris, Lindbergh accepted the challenge in 1927 even though many others had failed. Thirty-four hours after departing New York alone in his plane, the *Spirit of St. Louis*, "Lucky" Lindy made history by landing in Paris.

When Lindbergh set his plane down at Le Bourget airfield and ended the intense suspense in which two continents had been held for 34 hours, he became the idol of the Western world. The screaming crowds, celebrations, ticker-tape parades, honors, and medals that followed were the most extraordinary ever bestowed on a hero. So were the proposed million dollar contracts, endorsements, movie deals, and paid appearances, all of which gave rise to the next event of major importance in Lindbergh's life.

Bizarre as it might seem, Lindbergh was taken under the wing of the J.P. Morgan crowd at the suggestion of Dwight Morrow, a partner, in order to "save him from being exploited." Knowing a good thing when he saw it, Morrow arranged for Charles to be invited to the Long Island estate of the son of the late Harry Davison, the Morgan partner Charles' father (now deceased) had rightly accused

of using the Red Cross as a front for the Money Trust. Realizing he was unprepared to handle the flood of heady offers coming his way, and impressed with the expertise of these top bankers, Lindbergh agreed to hand over management of his financial affairs to them. These financiers, knowing that Charles' fame was a pot of gold for the development of the nascent airline industry, moved to monopolize the exploitation of his person and his name. Convincing Charles to reject all other offers (including a contract with Juan Trippe who was organizing Pan Am and $500,000 for a Hearst documentary), they added his name to their secret list of "preferred" J.P. Morgan clients. In this way, Charles missed the opportunity to become independently wealthy (although he cared very little for wealth).

At the height of the Lindbergh hero worship, Dwight Morrow was appointed ambassador to Mexico and suggested that

Charles make a goodwill tour there (which would increase Morrow's own visibility). The Mexicans went literally wild over Lindy, but none were more infatuated than Morrow's daughter Anne, on vacation from her classes at Smith College. A true romantic, Anne Morrow lost her heart to Charles' unpretentious ways, boyish smile, blue eyes, and elegant hands, so like an artist's. Now almost 26 years old, Charles had been too busy to ever date a girl. When he showed up later at Smith, the romance blossomed. They were married in a simple ceremony in 1929, vainly attempting to shun publicity. The famous couple could not go to a movie, a restaurant, or even take a stroll without attracting an adoring but raucous mob.

Meanwhile, Charles was trying to decide what to do with the rest of his life, while the Morgan partners were planning it for him. Using Lindbergh's "participation" as a "come-on" for investors, the Morgan bank raised ten million dollars to found the first airline across North America (later reorganized as TWA). But they were shocked when Lindbergh refused a corporate position. To this aeronautical genius, the thought of a corporate desk job was anathema, a feeling that stayed with him the rest of his life. He finally agreed to become an independent consultant at $10,000 a year and 25,000 shares of stock at a time when "aero stocks rocketed" at the mere mention of his name.

Although the year was only 1929, Lindbergh was intensely interested in promoting research in rocketry for the exploration of space. With habitual faith in his own thinking, he dismissed physicists' claims that heavier-than-air craft had reached their limits in size. Already absorbed in the vision of building a rocket that could reach the moon, he presented his ideas to the DuPont Corporation, but was turned down. Soon afterward, Robert Goddard in Massachusetts tested a liquid-propelled "moon rocket"; when Lindbergh arranged for Goddard to meet with DuPont engineers, they remained

No longer flying solo: During the height of Lindbergh's fame, Charles met Anne Morrow, the daughter of then-Ambassador to Mexico, Dwight Morrow. They were wed in 1929, and Anne became his copilot, an expert radio operator, and the first woman to secure a glider pilot's license.

unimpressed with what turned out to be the potential for jet propulsion.

Anne soon discovered that Charles, the son of a mother far ahead of her time, had advanced ideas about women. He persuaded her to take up flying with himself as a strict instructor. She became his copilot, an expert radio operator, and the first woman to secure a glider pilot's license. Together they blazed the Great Circle route across Alaska and the Bering Strait to Tokyo. Although their backgrounds couldn't have been more different (the

Morrows had four homes, 36 servants, and were surrounded by possessions), Anne and Charles agreed to live simply, gave away hundreds of wedding gifts to the Missouri Historical Society, tried to adjust to receiving a million letters a year, and sought ways to prevent their lives from becoming public property.

When Lindbergh met Dr. Alexis Carrel, head of Rockefeller University's experimental surgery laboratory and winner of a Nobel Prize in medicine, he seized the opportunity to become involved in biomedical engineering. Carrel's attempts at animal organ transplants and open-heart surgery were an inspiration to Lindbergh, who was offered the use of Princeton University's laboratory facilities. To be near Princeton, the Lindberghs, now parents of a son, built a home in Hopewell, New Jersey.

It was from this home that two-year-old Charles Jr. was abducted in 1932. What followed is beyond belief even with today's invasions of privacy. Bus tours of gawking strangers drove past the Lindbergh home snapping photos while aircraft flew overhead for an aerial view. In one month the Lindberghs received 12,000 letters from people who believed their dreams revealed the fate of their baby. The entire country, including the Salvation Army and the A.F. of L., took part in the hunt for the "Eaglet." Many radio stations canceled all programs and issued bulletins every hour.

In spite of the delivery of a ransom of $50,000 in marked bills, the baby's body was found, still clad in his little pajamas, several months later. Then the road to Hopewell became one long traffic jam; vendors were selling hot dogs, pretzels, and postcards of the Lindbergh home. From this time forward the Lindberghs viewed the media and the public with bitterness, never making their peace with either and finally fleeing to England.

In 1936, with rumors of German re-armament circulating in Europe, the American military attaché in Berlin, Major Truman Smith, asked Lindbergh to accept an invitation from General Goering to inspect Germany's military air installations and aircraft. Smith was confident that Goering, eager to impress the great Lindbergh, would allow him to see the most advanced planes, a matter of vital interest to the United States.

Smith was right. Lindbergh saw the aeronautical research institute at Adlershof, the Heinkel and Junkers airplane factories, the new designs for liquid-cooled engines, and the Stuka dive-bomber, already in mass production; his warnings to Washington were invaluable. Up to this time Lindbergh had tried to convince himself that the airplane was an instrument of peace, bringing people closer together in understanding. Now he realized that it could also be a terrible weapon of death and destruction; the only defense possible was retaliation, which meant a horrible war.

In the fall of 1937, Smith asked Lindbergh to return to Germany to obtain further intelligence. This time Lindbergh toured the top-secret Rechlin airfield and was allowed to sit in the cockpits of the new Messerschmitt fighter and Heinkel bomber. Contrary to later smears, Lindbergh was obviously dismayed by German re-armament. In his own words, his inspections "had given me disturbing insight into the magnitude of Hitler's intentions." At the same time he couldn't help being impressed by the industrious, efficient, and scientifically advanced Germans, quite apart from their objectives. Although this would have been the natural reaction of any engineer, it was later used by FDR and the pro-war media in malicious attacks against Lindbergh for his opposition to intervention.

As the situation in Europe deteriorated and Charles analyzed the developing scene, he was one of the first to propose that England and France do nothing but strengthen their military. He pointed out that Hitler's logical route of expansion was to the east, against Germany's natural enemy, Russia. Only in that direction could Hitler find the wheat, oil, and territory he sought. Lindbergh reasoned that the two totalitarian tyrants should be left alone to fight it out and exhaust each other, which would surely happen without English, French, and U.S. involvement. Then the West would be in a position to dictate terms of peace. This position was later espoused by many prominent American conservatives, including Senator Robert Taft.

But it was already too late. France and England were preparing to go to war over Czechoslovakia. Asked to return to active duty and help develop aircraft weaponry, Lindbergh, ideally suited for the job, accepted. But when offered a top job at the national Commission on Aeronautics, he bolted, once again panicked by the thought of losing his freedom in a desk job.

On September 1, 1939, the Wehrmacht swept into Poland, and England and France declared war against Germany. Although polls showed Americans opposed to U.S. intervention, the media were thoroughly saturated with pro-war propaganda, led by David Brinkley, Walter Lippman, and especially Henry Luce with his *Time*, *Life*, and *Fortune*. Lindbergh felt compelled to speak out. Before he could do so, he received an urgent message from the War Department: If he would desist, President Franklin D. Roosevelt would create a separate department of the Air Force (then under the Army) and make him Secretary. No request could have been more incongruous with Roosevelt's public anti-war posture. But FDR was trying to buy the wrong man. Lindbergh looked upon this despicable bribe as proof positive of Roosevelt's chicanery and secret plans for intervention.

Following his first speech, Lindbergh was approached by Republican leaders (as well as southern *Democrats* opposed to intervention) to run for President against Roosevelt, who was seeking a third term in 1940 based on his infamous pledge, "Your boys are not going to be

Glimpse of the future: Throughout 1936 and 1937, Major Truman Smith (left), the American military attaché in Berlin, asked Lindbergh to accept invitations from Germany to inspect Hitler's military aircraft and installations. These inspections convinced Lindbergh that aircraft had a terrible destructive potential in warfare and gave him "disturbing insight into the magnitude of Hitler's intentions."

sent into any foreign wars." But after listening to some of the compromises these politicians wanted him to make, Lindbergh bowed out, refusing to change his views for anyone.

In subsequent speeches, Lindbergh made it clear that he was also against military aid to Britain as leading inevitably to war and as being unnecessary, even though he had no way of knowing that at this very time Churchill had written a secret memo saying England was safe, the enemy had never contemplated invading Britain, and they could never have gotten across the English Channel anyway.

But Lindbergh's opposition to aid was the last straw for his old "friends" at the House of Morgan. In a weird replay of his father's crusade against the "Money Trust," Lindbergh denounced "powerful elements" that planned to profit from selling arms to the Allies and secretly driving the U.S. into the war. His break with the House of Morgan was complete. With a feeling of disgust, he severed ties with Harry Davison, Thomas Lamont, Henry Breckenridge, Harry Guggenheim, and Jack Morgan.

We now know that Lindbergh was severely handicapped in his struggle against Roosevelt because he had no way of knowing the actual facts about Roosevelt's machinations. Although he thoroughly distrusted the British and thought they would go to any lengths to trick America into war, he could scarcely have imagined that Churchill had arranged for Roosevelt and the appallingly ruthless chief of British intelligence to meet almost nightly in super secrecy to cook up abominable lies, plots, and counterplots to drag America unnecessarily into the war. Not until 1976, with the publication of *A Man Called Intrepid*,

by William Stevenson, would the world know the extent of the incredible deceptions of these three men. Relying on common sense and faith in his own reasoning, Lindbergh came closer than anyone else to blasting the cover off the Roosevelt intrigue. When Roosevelt attempted to terrify Americans into accepting war by declaring that Hitler was out to

America first: Before the start of World War II, Lindbergh realized that "powerful elements" planned to draw the U.S. into the conflict and to profit by selling arms to the Allies. Reasoning that the threat of a German invasion of the U.S. was unrealistic, he spoke up for nonintervention under the auspices of the Committee to Defend America First.

conquer the world, and that the U.S. was next and was in mortal danger of invasion, Lindbergh fearlessly went on the air and refuted these falsehoods with common sense: "Let us not be confused by this talk of invasion.... Great armies must still cross oceans by ship.... No foreign navy will dare approach within bombing range of our coasts. Let us stop this hysterical chatter of calamity and invasion.

If we desire peace we need only stop asking for war."

By 1941 Lindbergh was speaking under the auspices of the Committee to Defend America First, backed by many prominent Americans, including Henry Ford, Captain Edward Rickenbacker, and General Robert A. Wood. (America First, like Lindbergh, was smeared as being composed of fascists, racists, and pro-Nazis.) Tens of thousands flocked to hear Lindbergh speak in Madison Square Garden, the Hollywood Bowl, and other arenas across the nation. In every instance there were record crowds with every seat filled and thousands standing outside listening to loudspeakers.

After the Japanese attack on Pearl Harbor, Roosevelt ordered that Lindbergh not be allowed to serve in the military. When Curtis Wright, Pan Am, and United Aircraft tried to employ this brilliant specialist in aircraft, Roosevelt, like a true dictator, forbade it. It took Henry Ford to defy Roosevelt. Lindbergh worked at Ford's Willow Run facility for no salary and contributed enormously to the design and production of military aircraft. He also flew 50 combat missions in the Pacific, surreptitiously arranged by the Navy, the knowledge of which was kept from the public for many years.

In 1970, the publication of *The Wartime Journals of Charles A. Lindbergh* revealed that the hatred of Lindbergh by the pro-war party had not abated. The book and its author were maliciously condemned as a "shameless exhibition of the foul and discredited racist theories of the Nazis.... Lindbergh's anti-Semitism shouts to the heavens … the book will be a shot in the arm for the ultra-Right, pro-fascist, pro-Nazi forces...." (*Daily World*, September

8, 1970). Jewish organizations denounced him as anti-Semitic for having bluntly stated that Roosevelt, the British, and Jewish propaganda had pushed the U.S. into war. But far from being anti-Semitic, Lindbergh said something far different in 1941 (as quoted in the *San Francisco Chronicle* for August 31, 1970):

It is not difficult to understand why Jewish people desire the overthrow of Nazi Germany. The persecutions they suffered in Germany would be sufficient to make bitter enemies of any race. No person with a sense of the dignity of mankind can condone the persecution the Jewish race suffered in Germany. But no person of honesty and vision can look on their pro-war policy here today without seeing the dangers involved in such a policy both for us and for them.

Meditating upon the war, Lindbergh wrote in the introduction to *The Wartime Journals*:

We won the war in a military sense; but in a broader sense it seems to me we lost it.... In order to defeat Germany and Japan we supported the still greater menaces of Russia and China — which now confront us in a nuclear-weapon era.... Much of our Western culture was destroyed.... Meanwhile, the Soviets have dropped their iron curtain to screen off Eastern Europe.... More than a generation after the war's end, our occupying armies still must occupy, and the world has not been made safe for democracy and freedom.

It would be difficult to find a more prescient summary of what came out of the war. Surely Lindbergh should be celebrated for his intellect as well as his mechanical genius. As Holmes Alexander wrote of him at this time, "Lindbergh in his mature years has so much to offer … he should be considered a national resource."

In his 70th year, Charles was diagnosed with lymphoma. At first the doctors were hopeful of recovery, but by 1974, failing rapidly, Charles chose to die in his simple cottage on Maui in Hawaii, where he is buried. The following moving passage is from Joyce Milton's book *Loss of Eden*:

Several times that week he had been near death, and Anne had asked him to describe the experience so that she would know what to expect when her turn came. He found it impossible to put into words. But he did leave a note. Found on his nightstand after he breathed his last, it said: "I know there is infinity beyond ourselves. I wonder if there is infinity within."

If "infinity within" means honor, principle, nobility of mind and spirit, and the moral courage to speak the truth, then in his own case, the answer to Charles Lindbergh's wonderment is an unqualified yes. ■

A Man of Character

Farmer, scholar, statesman, and man of God, Ezra Taft Benson dedicated a lifetime of service to church, family, and country.

by Steve Bonta

Abraham Lincoln once asserted that "you will never get me to support a measure which I believe to be wrong, although by doing so I may accomplish that which I believe to be right." Such stirring words are seldom heard in Washington, D.C. today. Instead the capitol is increasingly known for political ambition, broken promises, backroom dealing, and compromised principles in the name of public welfare and other socialist bromides — with the result that a bloated, extra-constitutional federal monstrosity is masquerading as government by the people. Amidst the sordid, century-long sprawl of scandal and deceit, a scant handful of men have risen above the fray to ringingly endorse, through actions unsullied by lust for power and acclaim, the words of Lincoln. Ezra Taft Benson — farmer, patriot, statesman — was one of these.

Ezra Taft Benson, or "T," as he was affectionately known to friends and family, was born of noble pioneer stock in the tiny farming community of Whitney, Idaho, in 1899. He was the oldest of 11 children and a grandson of Ezra T. Benson, a Mormon Apostle under Brigham Young and a pioneer in Cache Valley in southern Idaho. Like most farm boys of the era, Ezra grew up quickly, developing early in life an excellent work ethic and unshakeable faith in God that were among his trademark lifelong virtues. When Ezra was in his early teens, his father George was unexpectedly called on a church mission in the eastern United States. During his father's absence, young Ezra was the man of the house; as with the many burdens he shouldered throughout his life, he bore his new responsibilities uncomplainingly.

At age 21, Ezra traveled to England as a missionary for his church. Intending eventually to pursue a quiet life of farming in Idaho, he enrolled in Brigham Young University after his mission to receive formal education in the field of agriculture. After graduating with distinction in

ganized the USDA to make it more efficient, stating that America had the right to expect her public servants to give "a full day's work for a full day's pay." For his team, he took great care to choose men who were not only professionally qualified, but also of good character. Of one candidate for a position, he simply asked: Are you happily married? Are you active in your church? Do you like your job? When the candidate, a noted economist, answered in the affirmative to all three questions, Benson hired him on the spot.

Benson also believed in calling on the aid of Almighty God for help in his duties. At his first staff meeting, he established the practice of opening meetings with a prayer, which he continued throughout his entire administration. Staff members took turns offering the prayer. Benson also encouraged President Eisenhower to have prayer at Cabinet meetings, a practice that the President soon adopted.

It didn't take long for such a pious and principled Americanist to become embroiled in controversy. In his very first major public speech as Secretary, delivered in St. Paul to the Central Livestock Association, Benson laid out in clear, unmistakable language his opposition to subsidies, price fixing, and other welfare-state policies. Upon his return to Washington, he was besieged by an angry liberal Establishment. Sniffed Congressman Eugene McCarthy (D-MN), "Benson is like a man standing on the bank of the river telling a drowning man that all he needs to do is take a deep breath of air." One prominent journalist predicted that Benson would be the first Cabinet official to resign. Despite the barrage of attacks in the press and in Congress, farmers themselves liked what they heard; letters received at the USDA ran about 15 to one in Benson's favor.

Throughout his administration, Secretary Benson fought for the reduction and elimination of subsidies, with mixed success. As a step in the right direction, he fought hard for the replacement of rigid price supports with a flexible-support system. The latter, he believed, while far from ideal, would at least be a more workable alternative to the system in place, and would alleviate some market distortions that government interference in agriculture had created. While still unconstitutional, flexible supports were at least a step in the right direction.

The House Agriculture Committee in particular resisted his vision. Nevertheless, with dogged persistence and the support of President Eisenhower, Benson logged several significant legislative victories. The Agricultural Act of 1954, which included provisions for flexible price supports, passed despite fierce opposition. Benson also persuaded a reluctant President Eisenhower to veto several popular bills that contained short-sighted socialist policies calculated to win the approval of farmers, but which, Benson was convinced, were in the farmers' long-term worst interests. Of the soil bank, another less than ideal measure he supported as a step in the right direction, he remarked ruefully "I could not get as enthusiastic about it as some of my staff. Maybe just the idea of paying farmers for not producing — even as a one-shot emergency measure — outraged my sensibilities. The only real justification was that the government itself had been so largely responsible for the mess farmers were in."

Benson continued to travel about the country trying to educate farmers on the evils of government interference in farming. "You can't run the farms of America from a desk in Washington," he emphasized. He earned respect, even among those who didn't agree with him, for sticking to his guns. Senator James Eastland (D-MS), one of his early critics, later accompanied Secretary Benson to a speech at the Delta Cotton Council in the senator's home state. Introducing Benson to a hostile crowd, the senator said, to Benson's delighted surprise: "My friends, today you're going to hear something you won't like, but it will be good for you because it's the truth." Eastland became one of Secretary Benson's strongest supporters in Washington.

In his long and fruitful life, as a scholar, farmer, patriot, and man of God, he had made American liberty one of his highest concerns, earning the admiration of America's patriotic remnant and the respect of even his most bitter enemies.

President Eisenhower, a political weathercock in many ways, was unswervingly committed to his controversial Agriculture Secretary. In 1953, with political pressures at the boiling point, Benson told Eisenhower he was willing to resign, if the President preferred. Replied Eisenhower, "That will never happen! I don't want to hear any more about it." A few years later, when a group of Republican congressmen pressured the administration to get rid of Benson, whom they believed to be an intolerable liability for their party, Eisenhower stood by his man: "When we find a man of this dedication, this kind of courage, this kind of intellectual and personal honesty, we should say to ourselves, 'We just don't believe that America has come to the point where it wants to dispense with the advice of that kind of person.'" Although some speculated that Eisenhower had chosen Benson to placate the Taft wing of the Republican Party, who were still angry at Eisenhower's unscrupulous campaigning tactics, Benson himself never found out for sure whether such claims were accurate. In any case, Eisenhower remained loyal to his Agriculture Secretary through his entire two terms in office, long after Senator Taft passed away in the summer of 1953.

While serving as Secretary of Agriculture, Benson also met with many world leaders, some of whom left lasting impressions on him. He appreciated the courage of Israel's David Ben-Gurion and the principled anti-Communist statesmanship of Free China's Chiang Kai-shek. He was less enthusiastic about meeting Soviet

Premier Nikita Khrushchev in 1959, during the Communist dictator's visit to Washington. Asked by Eisenhower to accompany Khrushchev and his entourage on a tour of a USDA station, Benson agreed with extreme reluctance. He was opposed to bringing the boasting tyrant to the United States at all. "My enthusiasm for the project," he later recorded, "could have been put in a small thimble.... [Khrushchev] has about as much conception of right and wrong as a jungle animal." Nevertheless, he made the most of the occasion, unambiguously spelling out the advantages of freedom in a speech at the Plant Industry building to the Communist dictator and his minions. He recalled: "I told about the way research is conducted and how it is carried to the people through our *free press*; and how new ideas … are *freely available* to everyone interested.... Our farmers have transformed American agriculture under our *capitalistic free enterprise system*.... As I finished I thought, And I hope you get the message."

At one point during Khrushchev's visit, the Soviet Premier boasted to the Agriculture Secretary that Benson's own grandchildren would live under Communism. Benson replied tartly that he expected to do all in his power to assure that Khrushchev's and all other grandchildren would live under freedom. The Communist leader then responded in essence, according to Benson's personal account: "You Americans are so gullible. No, you won't accept communism outright, but we'll keep feeding you small doses of socialism until you'll finally wake up and find you already have communism."

In the late 1950s, many Americans were beginning to swallow this and other Soviet propaganda touting her economic, military, and technological prowess. Cooked statistics proclaiming robust economic growth in the Soviet Union, backed by a nuclear arms buildup and Russian "firsts" in the space race, suggested to some that the American free enterprise system was being bested. Ezra Taft Benson had no doubt that Americans

were being hoodwinked by a crafty foe adept at concealing massive inefficiency and poverty. A few weeks after Khrushchev's visit to the United States, Secretary Benson paid a visit to the Soviet Union, where he intended to take full advantage of his close-up view of life in the Communist slave state.

Secretary of Agriculture Benson found Soviet Russia to be a land of contrasts. He stayed at luxurious

Anti-Communists meet: While serving as Secretary of Agriculture, Ezra Taft Benson met with Chiang Kai-shek, China's great soldier and statesman.

hotels with glittering, ornate lobbies — as well as ancient, cage-like elevators and creaking floors. He saw the broad, impressive boulevards of Moscow — with scarcely a car on them. At an agricultural exposition, Benson and his entourage were shown a modern-looking piece of farm machinery, a three-row beet-topper. Later, while touring the beet farms near Kiev, Benson indicated a wish to see one of the toppers in operation. His guide pointed out one in a distant field. Benson insisted they stop the car and walk over for a closer look, which his guide was reluctant to do. Finally, Benson strode off across the field to inspect the machine himself. He found that,

The machine was operating on three rows of beets, but the results were calamitous. It was dropping the beets in piles, and women with butcher knives were following be-

hind picking up each beet; about one-third of the beets were not topped at all, another third were poorly-topped and the rest were pretty well topped.... In charge of the sugar beet operation was a robust, chubby woman with a continuing smile and apple-red cheeks.... Later we saw her picture in the halls of the Ukrainian Exhibition of Economic Achievement. She had been decorated with the Order of Lenin and was known as "The Sugar Beet Hero."

Secretary Benson had seen laid bare the inefficiencies of the Soviet system.

Being an ecclesiastical leader, Ezra Taft Benson was acutely sensitive to the problem of religious persecution under the Soviet Communists. From the moment of his arrival, Benson importuned his hosts to show him one of Moscow's Protestant Church services, but was repeatedly rebuffed. Finally, on the last night of his visit, he made one final attempt. As his car ploughed through the rain on the way to the airport, he told his guide he had been disappointed not to have been shown a Christian worship service. His guide snapped an order to the chauffeur, and the car abruptly swung onto a side street and pulled up at the Central Baptist Church, not far from Red Square.

The church was packed with worshippers of all ages, contrary to what Benson had been led to expect. One newsman described the scene as Benson and his entourage were led to the front of the church and seated beside the pulpit: "Every face in the old sanctuary gaped incredulously as our obviously American group was led down the aisle.... They reached out to touch us almost as one would reach out for the final last caress of one's most-beloved just before the casket is lowered. They were in misery and yet a light shone through the misery. They gripped our hands like frightened children."

To Benson's surprise, the minister asked him to address the congregation. Greeting them on behalf of "millions and

millions of church people in America and around the world," Benson testified that "Our Heavenly Father is not far away.... God lives, I know that he lives.... Jesus Christ, the Redeemer of the World, watches over this earth.... Be unafraid, keep His commandments, love one another, pray for peace and all will be well." Benson spoke of the power of prayer and of the reality of eternity and the resurrection. Finally, he concluded with a witness that "the truth will endure. Time is on the side of truth."

As they left the warmth of the little church and returned into the chilly, rain-soaked night, the congregation broke into a familiar hymn, "God Be With You Till We Meet Again." The members of the American press in Benson's entourage, who had witnessed the scene, were especially moved. The most cynical among them wept openly. Wrote Grant Salisbury in *U.S. News & World Report*, "It turned out to be one of the most moving experiences in the lifetime of many of us. One newsman ... ranked it with the sight of the American flag rising over the old American compound in Tientsin, China, at the end of World War II." Another recorded: "Imagine getting your greatest spiritual experience in atheistic Russia.... What the atheists don't know is that God can't be stamped out by legislated atheism.... This Methodist backslider who occasionally grumbles about having to go to church, stood crying unashamedly, throat lumped, and chills running from spine to toes. It was the most heart-rending and most inspiring scene I've ever witnessed." As Secretary Benson and his entourage quietly boarded their waiting cars, one of the reporters summed up the entire episode: "I believe they were the only really happy people we saw in Russia."

During his years in Washington, Secretary Benson was increasingly dismayed at the expansion of Communism worldwide. He had already seen — and understood — the betrayal of China and Eastern Europe to Communism. While Benson was in Poland after the war, U.S. Ambassador Arthur Bliss Lane, who was later to write the devas-

tating exposé *I Saw Poland Betrayed*, had explained to him the duplicity of American policy there. Benson also watched in frustration as his own government encouraged Hungarians, with promises of support, to revolt against Communist rule, only to sit passively by during the ensuing bloody Soviet crackdown.

He also saw firsthand the success of Communist disinformation during the 1950s. Acting on intelligence from his agricultural attaché in Havana, Benson warned the State Department that Cas-

Khrushchev: The Soviet tyrant met with Secretary Benson in 1959. Khrushchev had, said Benson, "about as much conception of right and wrong as a jungle animal."

tro was a thinly disguised Communist and a Moscow stooge. His warnings went unheeded, impressing on Benson yet again both the deviousness of Communists and the complicity of American leaders.

With the conclusion of Eisenhower's second term in early 1961, Ezra Taft Benson returned gratefully to full-time ecclesiastical work in the Mormon Church. Yet his experience had so strengthened his patriotic convictions that his religion and his political convictions had become inseparable. He spoke often and forthrightly for civic gatherings on the principles of free-

dom, on the threat of Communism and socialism, on the threat to our freedom and sovereignty posed by the United Nations, and on the citizens' duty to acquaint themselves with the U.S. Constitution, which, in accordance with the teachings of his church, he believed to be divinely inspired. His personal political creed he expressed as follows:

I am for freedom and against slavery.

I am for social progress and against socialism.

I am for a dynamic economy and against waste.

I am for the private competitive market and against unnecessary government intervention.

I am for national security and against appeasement and capitulation to an obvious enemy.

He wrote voluminously on freedom; his lucid, straightforward writing style bore witness to his extraordinary depth of understanding in fields such as free-market economics, constitutional law, and American history. In such books as *An Enemy Hath Done This* and *The Red Carpet*, Benson bore eloquent witness of the growing threat of Communism/socialism in all of its guises.

Among his other writings, Benson's unusual book *Cross Fire* stands out as a candid account of his years in the Eisenhower administration, while splendid pamphlets like *The Constitution: A Heavenly Banner* laid out in elegantly simple language the principles enshrined in the Constitution.

Some of his writings, such as the last-mentioned pamphlet above, were specifically directed to members of his church; among the rising generation of Americans were many who were ignorant of the U.S. Constitution and the principles of freedom, and many members of his own church were among them. At one address to the students of Brigham Young University, for example, he spoke plainly about the evils of welfare handouts: "When you accept food stamps, you accept an unearned handout that other people are paying for.... If you do not have the finances to complete your education, drop out a semester and go to work and save."

Addressing a church audience in 1968, Benson noted that "no people can maintain freedom unless their political institutions are founded upon faith in God and belief in the existence of moral law. God has endowed men with certain unalienable rights and no legislature and no majority, however great, may morally limit or destroy these. The function of government is to protect life, liberty and property and anything more or less than this is usurpation and oppression." In this same talk he observed that "we can never survive unless our young people understand and appreciate our American system which has given more of the good things of life than any other system in the world — unless they have a dedication that exceeds the dedication of the enemy."

Concerning his love of the U.S. Constitution, he told a church audience in 1964: "the power of Heaven rested on [America's] founders as they drafted that greatest document for governing men, the Constitution of the United States.... From them we were endowed with a legacy of liberty — a Constitutional Republic."

Predictably, his boldness in declaring the eternal truths of liberty aroused controversy among a few members of his church, who felt that his political teachings were an infringement on their religious freedoms. But Benson persevered with the encouragement and support of church President David O. McKay.

He also continued to participate in patriotic activities outside his church, though he wisely refrained from endorsing political candidates. In the early 1960s, he became acquainted with the young John Birch Society and its dynamic leader, Robert Welch. While he himself did not join the Society, his wife Flora and son Reed did. Reed even accepted employment with the JBS and helped to bring about much of the Society's early growth in Utah. Regarding this organization, Benson said:

When my son, Reed, was invited to be a state coordinator for the John Birch Society, he asked me if he should accept it. I had read the *Blue Book*.... I had met Mr. Welch and other leaders and members.... I knew Reed would be enrolling in an unpopular cause.... Nevertheless, I told him to go ahead if he thought this was the most effective way to defend the Constitution and fight the Socialist-Communist menace.... When he joined I expressed my opinion that I was con-

Champion of freedom: Despite harsh criticism, Benson campaigned assiduously for the cause of liberty, believing that one should "stand up for the right ... especially when it is unpopular."

vinced that the John Birch Society was the most effective non-church organization in our fight against creeping Socialism and godless Communism.... I feel it is always good strategy to stand up for the right, even when it is unpopular. Perhaps I should say, especially when it is unpopular.

In November 1985, Ezra Taft Benson became the President of the Mormon Church. To mark the occasion,

the liberal media unleashed a salvo of name-calling and character assassination, portraying him as a "rabid anti-communist" and a political and religious extremist. True to character, though, Benson continued to teach, whenever appropriate, the sweet doctrines of freedom.

At an address to a church General Conference, which, because of declining health turned out to be one of his last, he re-emphasized the basic beliefs he had embraced and taught for so many years: "America is a choice land. God raised up the Founding Fathers of the United States of America and established an inspired Constitution.... Secret combinations lusting for power, gain and glory are flourishing. A secret combination [conspiracy] that seeks to overthrow the freedom of all lands, nations, and countries, is increasing in its evil influence and control over America and the world."

At his 90th birthday celebration, near the end of his distinguished life, Ezra Taft Benson received the Presidential Citizens Medal from President George Bush. A copy is on display in the Benson Building on the Brigham Young University campus. The inscription reads, in part: "A lifetime of dedicated service to country, community, church and family, make Ezra Taft Benson one of the most distinguished Americans of his time.... His devotion to family and commitment to the principles of freedom are an example for all Americans."

On May 30, 1994, Ezra Taft Benson passed away. In his long and fruitful life, as a scholar, farmer, patriot, and man of God, he had made American liberty one of his highest concerns, earning the admiration of America's patriotic remnant and the respect of even his most bitter enemies. Were he alive today, he would no doubt be disappointed that the long slide toward tyranny, which he worked so hard to reverse during his life, is still underway. Yet he would doubtless remind all of us, as he did a congregation of Russian faithful on a cold, rainy night many years ago, that "time is on the side of truth." ∎

Emancipation by Example

Born in obscurity, poverty, and slavery, Booker T. Washington became the first widely recognized leader of black Americans.

by William Norman Grigg

Although his most significant accomplishments took place in the late 19th century, Booker Taliaferro Washington (who died in 1915) committed his public life to an issue that has been particularly nettlesome in the 20th century — the question of race relations. Born into slavery on April 5, 1856 on the plantation of James Burroughs near Hale's Ford, Virginia, Washington's origins were so obscure that he knew neither his specific date of birth, nor the identity of his father. On one occasion, alluding to the skimpy knowledge of his origins, Washington wryly noted that he "felt assured that his birth was a certainty," but could attest with reasonable certainty of little else in his background.

Well into adulthood, Washington was unsure even of the name with which he was born. "From the time when I could remember anything, I had simply been called 'Booker,'" recalled Washington in his 1901 memoir *Up From Slavery*. "Before going to school it had never occurred to me that it was needful or appropriate to have an additional name. When I heard the school-roll called, I noticed that all of the children had at least two names, and some of them indulged in what seemed to me the extravagance of having three." Knowing that a surname would be demanded of him, the youngster quickly improvised: When the teacher "asked me what my full name was, I calmly told him, 'Booker Washington' as if I had been called by that name all my life; and by that name I have since been known."

After learning later in life that his mother had named him Booker Taliaferro, Washington adapted the long-lost surname as a middle name. With his characteristic gentle wit, Washington described what for many would be an unpleasant reflection upon illegitimacy and uncertain identity as an ironic blessing: "I think there are not many men in our country who have had the privilege of naming themselves in the way that I have." Despite the fact that he was born onto a pile of rags

on the dirt floor of a slave's shack, Washington never expressed anything but gratitude for being born in America. While he acknowledged the "cruelty and moral wrong of slavery," he reflected that "Providence so often uses men and institutions to accomplish his purpose."

"I have never seen [a former slave] who did not want to be free, or one who would return to slavery," observed Washington. He maintained that "the ten million Negroes inhabiting this country, who themselves or whose ancestors went through the school of American slavery, are in a stronger and more hopeful condition, materially, intellectually, morally, and religiously, than is true of an equal number of black people in any other portion of the globe.... When persons ask me in these days how, in the midst of what sometimes seem hopelessly discouraging

Emancipated slaves: "In a few hours the great question with which the Anglo-Saxon race had been grappling for centuries had been thrown upon these people to be solved," Washington recalled. "These were questions of a home, a living, the rearing of children, education, citizenship, and the establishment and support of churches."

conditions, I can have such faith in the future of my race in this country, I remind them of the wilderness through which and out of which, a good Providence has already led us."

Propelled by an insatiable appetite for learning, blessed with personal discipline and a love of honest work, and guided by Christian principles, Washington ascended from the abysm of poverty, slavery, and ignorance to become the first widely recognized leader of black Americans. In that role, Washington championed racial reconciliation, equality of all Americans before the law, and ordered social progress for black Americans through thrift, industry, and education. "The great human love that in the end recognizes and rewards merit is elevating and universal," opined Washington. "In the long run, the world is going to have the best, and any difference in race, religion, or previous history will not long keep the world from what it wants."

For the first nine years of his life, Washington lived as "a slave among slaves," in the words of biographer Louis R. Harlan. He was constantly barefoot until the age of eight, at which time he was given a pair of uncomfortable wooden shoes. Aside from a single pair of breeches, his only clothing was a flax shirt that scourged his skin like "a dozen or more chestnut burrs." During his time as a slave, Washington recalled, he never once ate a regular sit-down meal. Harlan points out that the young Booker and his older brother John "ate what they could snatch from the kitchen fire, the Burroughs' leftovers, or the livestock."

While Washington did not minimize the "cruel wrongs" inflicted upon the slave population, he maintained that the harmful influence of the peculiar institution was "not by any means confined to the Negro.... The whole machinery of slavery was so constructed as to cause labor, as a rule, to be looked upon as a badge of degradation, of inferiority. Hence labor was something that both races on the slave plantation sought to es-cape. The slave system on our place, in a large measure, took the spirit of self-reliance and self-help out of the white people. My old master had many boys and girls, but not one, so far as I know, ever mastered a single trade or special line of productive industry."

Washington wrote of his mother "kneeling over her children and fervently praying … that one day she and her children might be free." With the collapse of the South, the nine-year-old Booker was gathered along with the rest of Burroughs' servants to the master's house, where a military officer read the Emancipation Proclamation. Despite the fact that when the Proclamation was issued it was a cynical act of war propaganda, the Union's victory did bring liberty to Washington and his fellow slaves, and the moment was a poignant one for the youngster and his family. "My mother, who was standing by my side, leaned over and kissed her children, while tears of joy ran down her cheeks," recalled Washington. "She explained to us what it all meant, that this was the day for which she had been so long praying, but fearing she would never live to see."

The ecstasy of the newly liberated slaves was short-lived, Washington recalled, as a sobering sense of the responsibilities of freedom descended upon them. "The great responsibility of being free, of having charge of themselves, of having to think and plan for themselves and their children, seemed to take possession of them," wrote Washington. "It was very much like suddenly turning a youth of ten or twelve years out into the world to provide for himself. In a few hours the great question with which the Anglo-Saxon race had been grappling for centuries had been thrown upon these people to be solved. These were questions of a home, a living, the rearing of children, education, citizenship, and the establishment and support of churches. Was it any wonder that within a few hours the wild rejoicing ceased and a feeling of deep gloom seemed to pervade the slave quarters?" As Washington wisely concluded, to many of the newly liberated slaves, "it seemed that, now that they were in actual possession of it, freedom was a more serious thing than they had expected to find it."

Shortly after receiving his freedom, Booker, along with his mother and older brother, traveled to Malden, West Virginia, where Booker's stepfather was working in the local salt furnaces. The ten-year-old was unceremoniously rousted from bed one morning and brought to work as a salt packer, shoveling crystallized salt into barrels and pounding it vigorously until the container held the required weight. From four in the morning until well after dark the youngster toiled at this task, and as he did so his curiosity was piqued by the figure used to mark his barrel — the number 18. Untutored as yet in either letters or numbers, Washington was nonetheless intrigued by the figure. "I soon learned to recognize that figure wherever I saw it, and after a while got to the point where I could make that figure, though I knew nothing about any other figures or letters," he recalled in his memoir.

Washington had always longed to learn how to read, and determined as a small child that, "if I accomplished nothing else in life, I would in some way get enough education to enable me to read common books and newspapers." Immediately upon settling in West Virginia, Booker prevailed upon his mother to get him a book — "an old copy of Webster's 'blueback' spelling book, which contained the alphabet.... I began at once to devour this book, and I think that it was the first one I ever had in my hands." Since none of his black friends or co-workers could read, and because he was afraid of approaching any of the white population for help, Booker was required to teach himself. Within a few weeks, the young autodidact had "mastered the greater portion of the alphabet." In this effort he had the constant support of his mother, who despite her illiteracy "had high ambitions for her children, and a large fund of good, hard, common sense...."

Booker also came to an early understanding of his spiritual needs and responsibilities. Given to playing marbles

in the streets of Malden with his friends on Sundays, which offered the youngster his only respite from hard labor, Booker found himself one Sabbath morning being rebuked by an elderly man for failing to attend church. The account of the spiritual benefits of worship "so impressed Booker that he gave up his game and followed the old man," recalls Louis Harlan. In short order, Booker was baptized by Elder Lewis Rice, pastor of the Tinkersville African Zion Baptist Church, where he was soon regarded as a pillar of the congregation.

As an adult, Washington reflected upon the spiritual benefits that flowed from the old man's gentle rebuke. As a noted educator whose oratorical skills commanded audiences throughout the United States and Europe, Washington readily acknowledged that his eloquence was a divine gift: "I make it a rule never to go before an audience, on any occasion, without asking the blessing of God upon what I want to say." He also wrote of his great love for the Bible, stating that "when I am at home, no matter how busy I am, I always make it a rule to read a chapter or a portion in the morning, before beginning the work of the day."

The old man's rebuke led to terrestrial benefits as well: Had Booker not been invited to church in Tinkersville that Sunday morning, he may not have had the opportunity to attend the Tinkersville school, which was established in Elder Rice's home. "Father Rice," as he was fondly known in West Virginia's Kanawha Valley, was besieged with requests from black residents to start a school. In September 1865, a teacher materialized in the person of an 18-year-old Union veteran named William Davis, who had obtained a basic education shortly before enlisting in 1863. The Tinkersville school was a self-help project funded entirely by the poor black people of the village, without so much as a penny from the federal Freedmen's Bureau or either county or local governments.

Unfortunately for Booker, his stepfather initially refused to allow him to attend school, insisting that the family was too poor to allow the youngster to live at

Despite the fact that he was born onto a pile of rags on the dirt floor of a slave's shack, Washington never expressed anything but gratitude for being born in America. While he acknowledged the "cruelty and moral wrong of slavery," he reflected that "Providence so often uses men and institutions to accomplish his purpose."

home without working. "Booker's disappointment at missing school became keener when he looked out from the salt-packing shed and saw other children passing happily to and from the school," notes Louis Harlan. However, "I determined that I would learn something, anyway," wrote Washington. "I applied myself with greater earnestness than ever to the mastering of what was in the 'blue-back' speller." He also enrolled in a night-school class that Davis had primarily organized for adults. Through determination and discipline, and because he genuinely coveted any opportunity to learn, Booker learned much more at night — despite the rigors of his schedule — than more fortunate children were learning during the day.

"Finally I won," recalled Washington, "and was permitted to go to the school in the day for a few months, with the understanding that I was to rise early in the morning and work in the furnace till nine o'clock, and return immediately after school closed in the afternoon for at least two more hours of work." This posed a predicament, since school began at nine o'clock as well, and Booker resented the fact that his forced tardiness was cheating him of precious learning time. In order to solve this problem, the ingenuous youngster would move up the hands of the clock used by workers and supervi-

sors to regulate their shifts. "I got the idea that the way for me to reach school on time was to move the clock hands from half-past eight up to the nine o'clock mark," Washington ruefully confessed. Once his subterfuge was discovered by the furnace boss, the clock was safely locked away in a glass case. "I did not mean to inconvenience anybody," wrote Washington. "I simply meant to reach that schoolhouse on time."

Washington's innocent ruse was born not out of an aversion to work, or an intent to defraud his employer, but out of a desire to learn. When, in his justly famous 1895 Atlanta Exposition address, he would admonish black Americans that "it is at the bottom of life we must begin, not at the top," and urge them to find "as much dignity in tilling a field as in writing a poem," he was speaking with the earned moral authority of one whose life exemplified the self-help ethic.

In 1867, after spending a stint working in a West Virginia coal mine, Booker learned of an employment opening for a houseboy (at a wage of five dollars a month) in the household of General Lewis Ruffner and his wife, Viola. Mrs. Ruffner, a formidable matron of Vermont Yankee extraction, was noted for her granite disposition and exacting nature, and she had put to flight several houseboys who couldn't measure up to her expectations. Shortly after being hired by the Ruffners, young Booker fled as well — only to return, chastened and willing to resume his labors. The young ex-slave and the Yankee aristocrat soon became close friends.

"From fearing Mrs. Ruffner I soon learned to look upon her as one of my best friends," wrote Washington. "When she found that she could trust me she did so implicitly." She also encouraged his efforts to educate himself, granting him daily leave during the winter months to attend a few hours of school and helping him acquire a private tutor to study at night. While living in the Ruffner household, Booker also began to assemble his first private library: He obtained a large, empty dry-goods box, placed some shelves in it, "and began putting into it every kind of book that I could get my hands upon, and called it my 'library.'"

Mrs. Ruffner's demanding personality also helped refine Booker's work habits, and taught him the value of tidiness and order — traits that would serve him well as an educator and administrator. "I soon began to learn that, first of all, she wanted everything kept clean about her, that she wanted things done promptly and systematically, and that at [the] bottom of everything she wanted absolute honesty and frankness," recalled Washington. "Nothing must be sloven or slipshod; every door, every fence, must be kept in repair." From his perspective, "the lessons that I learned in the home of Mrs. Ruffner were as valuable to me as any education I have ever gotten anywhere since."

Just as important was the genuine friendship that grew between Booker and his employer. Viola Ruffner, a shy and melancholy woman married to a man 20 years her senior, had few close friends, and according to one close relative knew "nothing of domestic happiness." At the time that Booker was hired as a houseboy, Viola Ruffner's son was a cadet at West Point and her daughter was away at boarding school. Louis Harlan comments that Booker was "a godsend" to Mrs. Ruffner. "The black youth became the chief beneficiary of the energy, intellectual vigor, and sense of purpose of a frustrated New England schoolmarm." It is likely that Mrs. Ruffner took an almost maternal interest in the bright, eager, hardworking boy.

"A remarkable bond of affection and trust grew up between the gentle-spoken black boy and the sharp-tongued white woman," continues Harlan. "The lonely woman even may have made a confidant of the boy and poured out to him all of her loneliness and bitterness...." After Booker obtained renown for his work as an educator and social activist, Mrs. Ruffner fondly recalled that Booker was "quiet, determined to make good, and never wasteful of time": "His conduct has always been without fault, and what more can you wish? He seemed peculiarly determined to emerge from his obscurity.

> *"When persons ask me in these days how, in the midst of what sometimes seem hopelessly discouraging conditions, I can have such faith in the future of my race in this country, I remind them of the wilderness through which and out of which, a good Providence has already led us."*
>
> *— Booker T. Washington*

He was ever restless, uneasy, as if knowing that contentment would mean inaction. 'Am I getting on?' — that was his principal question."

While living with the Ruffners, recalled Washington, "I saw one open battle take place at Malden between some of the colored and white people." A payday altercation erupted between a white man named John Fewell and a black man named Tom Preston in which the latter "came out first best." Fewell swore vengeance upon Preston, prompting Preston to file assault charges. By seeking legal redress at court, Preston provoked a local Ku Klux Klan contingent called "Gideon's Band," who swore to prevent Preston from appearing in court.

On the day of the trial, narrates Harlan, "ten Negroes armed with revolvers surrounded Tom Preston as he walked from Tinkersville to Malden. Six white men, friends of the defendant John Fewell, ordered the black men to leave town." After a brief gun battle, Preston and his bodyguards ended up near the Ruffner home. General Ruffner, with the young Booker behind him, intervened to restore the peace. According to one account, the General told Preston and his defenders to accompany him to town, where "he would see that they should have a fair trial." As General Ruffner tried to act as a mediator between the contending factions, he was struck from behind with a "brick-bat," suffering an injury from which he never fully recovered, and the riot resumed.

"As a young man," wrote Washington later, "the acts of these lawless bands made a great impression upon me." Among the lessons he took away from this experience was the futility of violent agitation as a means of bringing about social progress for black Americans. Although as a young man he witnessed firsthand the hateful depredations of the Klan, he understood that reciprocal hatred was not only self-defeating but sinful; he resolved that he "would permit no man, no matter what his color might be, to narrow and degrade my soul by making me hate him."

In 1872, Booker enrolled as a student at the Hampton, Virginia Normal and Agricultural Institute, where he worked as a janitor to earn his room and board. Upon arriving at Hampton, he recalled, he had "a surplus of exactly fifty cents with which to begin my education." Hungry, poorly dressed, and long unbathed when he presented himself before the head teacher, "I did not, of course, make a very favorable impression upon her, and I could see at once that there were doubts in her mind about the wisdom of admitting me as a student." After keeping Booker on tenterhooks while several other students were processed, the head teacher informed him that "the adjoining recitation-room needs sweeping. Take the broom and sweep it."

"It occurred to me that here was my chance," recalled Washington. He eagerly grabbed the broom and, with the fastidiousness he had learned from Viola Ruffner, "swept the recitation-room three times. Then I got a dusting-cloth and I dusted it four times." Having banished every speck of dust from the room, he invited an inspection by the head teacher. After surveying Booker's handiwork, the teacher calmly informed the anxious young man, "I guess you'll do to enter the institution." "I was one of the happiest souls on earth," recalled Washington. "The sweeping of that room was my college examination, and never did any youth pass an examination for entrance into Harvard or Yale that gave him more

genuine satisfaction. I have passed several examinations since then, but I have always felt that this was the best one I ever passed."

During his three years at the Hampton Institute, Booker came to admire the school's superintendent, General Samuel C. Armstrong, whom he came to regard as "the noblest, rarest human being that it has ever been my privilege to meet." "The older I grow, the more I am convinced that there is no education which one can get from books and costly apparatus that is equal to that which can be gotten from contact with great men and women," wrote Washington, and in his view General Armstrong was such a

Student days: Young Booker did not allow lack of opportunity to impede his insatiable appetite for learning. He is shown here during his enrollment at the Hampton Normal and Agricultural Institute, where he worked as a janitor to earn his room and board.

man. The General was "Christlike" in his capacity for selfless service, Washington recalled: "I do not believe he ever had a selfish thought.... Although he fought the Southern white man in the Civil War, I never heard him utter a bitter word against him afterward. On the other hand, he was constantly seeking to find ways by which he could be of service to the Southern whites."

After his graduation from the Hampton Institute, Washington was offered an

opportunity by General Armstrong to serve as a "house father" to 75 American Indians who were part of a special educational program. Although there were a few black students at Hampton who resented the presence of the Indians, recalled Washington, most of the Negro students "gladly took the Indians as roommates, in order that they might teach them to speak English and to acquire civilized habits."

It was while he worked with Indian students that Washington "had one or two experiences which illustrate the curious workings of caste in America." When one of the Indian students took ill, Booker was required to take him to Washington, D.C., where he would be taken under the care of the Interior Department. During the steamboat trip, Washington and his ailing Indian charge presented themselves at the dining saloon for dinner, only to be politely informed "that the Indian could be served, but I could not." Without rancor, but with a discernible note of cultured sarcasm, Washington commented: "I could never understand how he knew just where to draw the color line, since the Indian and I were about the same complexion. The steward, however, seemed to be an expert in this matter." The same useless expertise was displayed by the clerk at the Washington hotel to which the weary travelers repaired upon their arrival in the Capitol city.

Reflecting upon such incidents, Washington wrote that "the time to test a true gentleman is to observe him when he is in contact with individuals of a race that is less fortunate than his own. This is illustrated in no better way than by observing the conduct of the old-school type of Southern gentleman" in social settings involving black people. To illustrate, Booker referred to the familiar incident in which George Washington, meeting a black man who lifted his hat in greeting, reciprocated the polite tribute. When he was criticized by some of his friends for his gesture, Washington — artfully using against them their prejudices, which he did not share — replied: "Do you suppose that I am go-

Organizer and educator: Washington built the fledgling Tuskegee Institute into a thriving, expanding center of learning. At the time of his death in 1915, Tuskegee had an enrollment of 1,500 black students studying 38 trades and professions.

ing to permit a poor, ignorant, colored man to be more polite than I am?"

Despite occasional incidents of the kind he experienced during his first trip to Washington, Booker reported that "in all my contact with the white people of the South I have never received a single personal insult." After becoming head of Alabama's Tuskegee Institute, Washington found that white Southerners treated him with respect and appreciation. Thus it is not surprising that Washington was a critic of the policy of military occupation and social engineering known to history as the "Reconstruction" of the South.

"I think ... that the opportunity to freely exercise [the franchise and other] political rights will not come in any large degree through outside or artificial forcing, but will be accorded to the Negro by Southern white people themselves, and that they will protect him in the exercise of those rights," observed Washington at the dawn of the 20th century. "Just as soon as the South gets over the old feeling that it is being forced by 'foreigners,' or 'aliens,' to do something which it does not want to do, I believe that the change in the direction that I have indicated is going to begin. In fact, there are indications that it is already beginning...."

Washington was also critical of the

way in which "Reconstruction" cultivated dependence on the part of black Southerners. "I felt that the Reconstruction policy, so far as it related to my race, was in a large measure on a false foundation, which was artificial and forced. In many cases it seemed to me that the ignorance of my race was being used as a tool with which to help white men into office, and that there was an element in the North which wanted to punish the Southern white men by forcing the Negro into positions over the heads of the Southern whites. I felt that the Negro would be the one to suffer for this in the end."

Indeed, by becoming wards of the central government, contended Washington, blacks were as much victims of Reconstruction as were the whites who were being punished: "During the whole of the Reconstruction period our people throughout the South looked to the Federal Government for everything, very much as a child looks to its mother." This was intolerable to someone such as Washington, who fervently believed in the value and virtue of work and individual effort. From his perspective, the way to mitigate the South's racial predicament was for blacks and whites to engage in honorable and productive commerce, and thus create a society based upon merit. With regard to the franchise, Washington supported non-

racial literacy requirements and insisted that "each state that finds it necessary to change the law bearing upon the franchise [must] make the law apply with absolute honesty, and without opportunity for double dealing or evasion, to both races alike."

Despite the fact that his labors consumed nearly all of his time, Washington made time for his family. Since he had never known his father or even known the pleasure of a sit-down meal, Washington strictly regulated his time in order to fulfill his duties as a husband and father to his four children. His home life was not without tragedy, however, as death claimed his first two wives at a very young age.

In 1881, after several years of teaching and a brief stint as a student at Wayland seminary in Washington, D.C., Booker was selected to head the newly established Tuskegee Institute, which at the time boasted assets totaling two converted buildings (one of them an old hen-house) and almost no money. With the help of generous donors in both the North and South, and through the application of the industry for which he became properly famous, Booker built Tuskegee into a thriving, expanding center of learning. At the time of his death in 1915, Tuskegee encompassed over 100 well-equipped buildings, a teaching staff of 200, an enrollment of 1,500 black students studying 38 trades and professions, and an endowment of $2 million. Washington also pointed out that although Tuskegee was strictly non-denominational, the education it provided was "thoroughly Christian and the spiritual training of students is not neglected."

As he traveled the country raising funds for Tuskegee, Washington found himself in demand as an orator. In September 1895, Washington was invited to attend the Atlanta Cotton States and Industrial Exposition, one of the most significant gatherings of political, religious, and industrial leaders in the post-war South. Although Washington was never deeply involved in partisan politics, he was acutely aware of the Exposition's potential political fallout, and that the prospects for the Tuskegee Institute could depend upon the reception that his speech received. He was also sensible of the potential impact his speech could have on race relations in a South that was still deeply injured from the War and Reconstruction.

As he strode to the dais at the Exposition on September 18, 1895, Washington bore a burden he had not sought, and he dispatched it by speaking candidly about the need for black and white Southerners to join in the mutually enriching work of economic development. He urged Southern blacks to "cast down your bucket where you are": "Cast it down in agriculture, mechanics, in commerce, in domestic service, and in the professions. And in this connection it is well to bear in mind that whatever other sins the South may be called to bear, when it comes to business, pure and simple, it is in the South that the Negro is given a man's chance in the commercial world.... Our greatest danger is that in the great leap from slavery to freedom we may overlook the fact that the masses of us are to live by the productions of our hands, and fail to keep in mind that we shall prosper in proportion as we learn to dignify and glorify common labor and put our brains and skill into the common occupations of life...."

He also admonished white Southerners to "cast down [their] bucket where [they] are" by encouraging blacks to seek education and productive employment, remembering that blacks have "tilled your fields, cleared your forests, builded your railroads and cities, and brought forth treasures from the bowels of the earth, and helped make possible this magnificent representation of the progress of the South." Given the opportunity, black Southerners would be willing to "stand by [white Southerners] … interlacing our industrial, commercial, civil, and religious life with yours in a way that shall make the interests of both races one." Washington's speech was greeted with a prolonged ovation, and earned laudatory notices from news-

papers across the country. Clark Howell, editor of the *Atlanta Constitution*, expressed the view of millions of Americans in a telegram to Washington in which he referred to the address as "a platform upon which blacks and whites can stand with full justice to each other."

Within a few years, a far different approach to "social progress" would be championed by one of Washington's chief antagonists, William Edward Burghardt DuBois. Born in Great Barrington, Mas-

Contrasting contemporary: W.E.B. DuBois rejected Washington's vision of progress through industry, literacy, and racial conciliation in favor of political confrontation and social agitation.

sachusetts, and raised in modest, if comfortable, middle-class surroundings, W.E.B. DuBois was one of the founders of the National Association for the Advancement of Colored People (NAACP), which rejected Washington's vision of progress through industry, literacy, and racial conciliation. The NAACP's preferred strategy was political confrontation and social agitation, and its program reflected the Marxist worldview of DuBois and his comrades.

Where Washington resolved never to succumb to racial resentment, DuBois — who had never known the privations and brutality of slave life, and whose career benefited from the patronage of wealthy white philanthropists — re-

solved at Harvard to "disdain and forget as far as possible that outer, whiter world." In a 1909 editorial for the NAACP organ *Crisis,* DuBois wrote that "the most ordinary Negro is a distinct gentleman, but it takes extraordinary training and opportunity to make the average white man anything but a hog." In 1911, DuBois joined the Socialist Party; a few years later — as DuBois recalled in a 1961 letter applying for membership in the Communist Party of the United States of America (CPUSA) — he "hailed the Russian Revolution of 1917." In that same letter, which was sent to Gus Hall, the Soviet quisling who headed the CPUSA, DuBois proclaimed that Communism "is the only way of human life.... In the end Communism will triumph. I want to help bring that day."

W.E.B. DuBois despised Washington and execrated him as a tool of white capitalists. It is also not surprising that the modern "civil rights" movement drew from DuBois' vision — kept alive by the campus network of "W.E.B. DuBois Clubs," which were organized by the CPUSA as front groups in 1959 — rather than that of Booker T. Washington. In his introduction to the 1967 edition of *Up From Slavery,* Professor Clarence A. Andrews of the University of Iowa paid fealty to the prevailing prejudices of our unfortunate age: "I know where I stand — my heart is with Booker T. Washington but my brain is with DuBois." In 1991, the U.S. Postal Service issued a commemorative stamp featuring the likeness of DuBois, who died in 1963 in Ghana as an honored guest of Marxist dictator Kwame Nkrumah.

It is almost certain that black Americans, and the country as a whole, would have fared much better had the vision of Booker T. Washington prevailed. To the extent that the values he championed and personified are followed, those who do so find that America remains a land of opportunity for everyone, irrespective of race or color. Washington himself remained industrious until literally the last day that God gave him — November 14, 1915, when he expired at Tuskegee, a casualty, at age 59, of overwork. ∎

Archive Photos

Sch

The human
in the fre
many wo
Armed with a
es illuminated th
lationship to hu
publication of M
is still catching

Blessed with
sight, G.K. Che
faith, family, ar
joyed material st
ings continues t
seek out the wis
C.S. Lewis d

Free Market Champion

The most brilliant economist of his time, Ludwig von Mises fought for freedom in the marketplace.

by Jane H. Ingraham

Preeminent economic theorist of the century; heroic and lifelong opponent of statism; most devastating demolition of socialism; brilliant refutation of economic fallacies of Marx and Keynes; great searchlight of a mind.

Who was the man about whom such accolades were written? Born in 1881 in Galicia in the Austro-Hungarian Empire, Ludwig von Mises was perhaps the most innovative and creative economist of all time. His long and eventful career in both Europe and America, his marriage at age 58 to a beautiful Viennese actress, his escape from Hitler's fanatical anti-Semitism, his preservation of the best of European culture and erudition, his intellectual triumph over collectivist fallacies — all read like an extraordinary drama of courage and uncompromising principle.

From the beginning, Mises' unusual perception brought him into conflict with the prevailing orthodoxy. As a student at the University of Vienna he rejected the statism inherent in his studies; this early insight determined the course of his life's work. He began to realize that all improvements in the condition of workers came about through capitalism, not government. In 1903 he discovered the Austrian school of economics (newly founded by Carl Menger with his *Principles of Economics*), which opened the way to a new world of economic theory and free market liberalism compatible with his own inspiration.

Mises first major work, *The Theory of Money and Credit*, published in 1912, pinpointed the cause of business cycles with irrefutable clarity. Booms and busts, he wrote, are caused by monetary expansion by central banks, not by rising prices or low unemployment. When government inflates, it artificially lowers the interest

Mises Institute

rate, which misleads businesses into unwise expansions and investments, creating an inflationary boom. When the credit expansion stops, as it must, these bad investments cannot survive and unemployment results. Mises, far ahead of his time, argued that money should be taken out of the hands of government and returned to the market, where it originated as a commodity. Banking should be treated as any other industry in a market economy, subject to competition and tied to gold through free convertibility.

In his *Ludwig von Mises: Scholar, Creator, Hero*, Murray Rothbard, a renowned economist in his own right, relates that *The Theory of Money and Credit* would have been far more influential had it not been for a belittling and totally uncomprehending review by the young British economist John Maynard Keynes, who said it was not "constructive" or "original," exactly the opposite of its true merits. Later Keynes confessed, "In German, I can only clearly understand what I already know — so that new ideas are apt to be veiled from me...." This revelation properly enraged Rothbard, who calls Keynes' denunciation of a book written in a language he didn't understand "sheer gall" and "breathtaking arrogance," "characteristic of Keynes."

The development of Mises' free market thought was put on hold by World War I, during which he served for five years as a captain in the Austrian army. But Mises had already run into another kind of roadblock that was to plague him for most of his life: the refusal of academia to grant him a full-time, paid position. This brilliant scholar with a major seminal work already to his credit was forced to earn his living as an economist at the Vienna Chamber of Commerce into his mid-50s, writing his profoundly original articles and books in his spare time.

The war over, the Austrian Empire torn to pieces, the gold standard discarded, a runaway inflation raging, and socialism sold as the wave of the future, Mises turned his penetrating mind to the problem of centralized government. In 1920, his groundbreaking *Economic Calculation in the Socialist Commonwealth* devastated the socialist position by proving the impossibility of economic calculation under central control. Prior criticism of socialism had been strictly moral or political; for the first time Mises demolished socialism on its own terms. For socialism to "work," central planners must have the ability to allocate resources to fulfill their own plans.

Loving partners: Mises' wife Margit was the stable center of his life. She provided him the security, encouragement, and privacy that was integral to his work as a leading economist.

But as Rothbard writes, Mises demonstrated that since a socialist planning board would lack a genuine price system for the means of production, "the planners would be unable to rationally calculate the costs, the profitability, or the productivity of these resources, and hence would be unable to allocate resources rationally ... to achieve their own goals."

This profound insight, says Rothbard,

"In all matters Mises was the soul of rigor and consistency.... Never would he compromise his principles.... Mises was a joy and an inspiration, an exemplar for us all."

— *Murray Rothbard*

had a blockbuster impact on European socialists, who for 20 years afterward tried in vain to refute Mises' reasoning.

But Mises remained unshakable, expanding his arguments in articles and in his comprehensive critique, *Socialism*, in 1922. One of the first to predict the dissolution of Communism, Mises also demonstrated that mixed economies cannot function efficiently either. Through taxes, regulation, and spending, government distorts the price system and prevents the allocation of resources to their most highly valued uses.

In 1925 a chance meeting at a dinner party changed Mises' life forever. Although he was now 44 years old, it was love at first sight when he met Margit Sereny, famous actress of the Vienna stage, now at 27 a widow with two small children. This remarkable woman was to become the stable center of Mises' life, protecting him, nurturing him, arranging privacy and time for his writing, sustaining him no matter what the discouragement or danger.

But all this was still in the future, for this romance and engagement lasted for 13 years. In love but afraid that marriage, change, responsibility, and children might disrupt his passionate dedication to his work, Mises tirelessly lectured (unsalaried) at the University of Vienna, held his famous seminar that produced leading Austrian economists such as

Friend and admirer: Henry Hazlitt, at the time financial editor of the *New York Times*, befriended Mises when the Austrian economist arrived in the United States. Hazlitt introduced Mises to his colleagues and helped spread the word about his reputation.

Friedrich von Hayek and Fritz Matchlup, attended conferences with leading authorities, and yet kept up his research and writing.

Following the election of Hitler in 1933, Mises saw where Austria was headed and decided to leave, accepting a part-time position at the Graduate Institute of International Studies in Geneva, Switzerland. Much as it distressed him to leave his beloved Vienna, this wise move probably saved his life. In 1938 German SS troops and the Gestapo broke into the apartment where he had lived and seized all his papers, books, and writings and carted them away. Mises' writings were hated by socialists of all stripes: Nazis, Communists, Fascists, and (later) the British and American collectivists. Only recently has this treasure trove of papers been recovered from KGB files in Moscow (where they ended up) and made available to scholars.

Galvanized into action by the chaos in Vienna and fearful for Margit's safety, Mises sent for her to come to Geneva, where they were married in 1938. At that time Mises was working on a French translation of his superb *Socialism*, as well as the German language predeces-

sor of his crowning accomplishment, *Human Action*. In her wonderfully personal memoir, *My Years with Ludwig von Mises*, Margit von Mises tells of how, during this period, Mises would fall into terrible outbursts of rage, flaring up unexpectedly about small, unimportant things. Slowly Margit came to realize that these outbursts were based on Mises' deep feeling of a coming catastrophe for Europe against which he was powerless to fight and about which he couldn't even bring himself to talk. Mises was not alone; this losing battle against the foes of liberty broke the spirit of many leading conservative European intellectuals, including Carl Menger, Max Weber, and Wilhelm Rosenberg.

In September 1939 Hitler invaded Poland, followed by Norway, Denmark, and the Netherlands. The tension in Geneva became unbearable. Many professors left for the U.S., but Mises refused to go. Almost 60, he feared the strangeness of America and a new language, his crucial tool. But when Hitler took Paris, Mises gave in. Through a friend at Chase Bank in Geneva, a non-

quota visa to enter the U.S. immediately was obtained. But by that time Switzerland was surrounded by German troops, making it extremely hazardous to leave. Finally the agonizing decision was made. Gaining passage on a special bus, Mises and Margit were driven through France dodging German troops at every crossroad until they crossed the border into Spain. From there they flew to Lisbon; a ship of the American Export Line carried them to New York.

Then followed dark days with no money and no recognition, although every socialist professor who fled Europe was quickly given a faculty position at a leading university. The first to befriend Mises was Henry Hazlitt, at that time financial editor of the *New York Times*, who knew of Mises through his books. Hazlitt did much to get Mises established by introducing him to the "right" people and spreading word of his reputation. Invitations as guest speaker or lecturer began to come in from Columbia University, the Political Economy Club, the New School for Social Research, and even Harvard and Princeton. These helped, but a bigger financial break came when the Rocke-

Nazi troops raise flag in Poland, 1939: Many professors fled to U.S., but Mises refused to leave Europe until Hitler took France.

Murray Rothbard: A renowned economist in his own right, Rothbard was an admiring student of Mises at the latter's famous two-hour evening seminars at New York University.

feller Foundation (of all places!) awarded Mises a grant of $5,000 for two years of research at the National Bureau of Economic Research.

A very private man, Mises never talked about himself or his feelings. Although he wrote millions of words about economics and money, the only semi-autobiography he ever wrote was not much more than notes about his schooling, his intellectual development, his work, and his ideas for future books. Nothing about his personal life or his family. When Margit suggested he write a real autobiography, his answer was: "You have my notes; that's all people need to know about me."

Although Mises was right about everything else, he couldn't have been more wrong about this. As it has turned out, people seem to want to know more and more about Mises as his fame continues to spread and increase. Astonishing things, such as that from March 1942 to July 1943 Mises wrote nine articles for the *New York Times*, for each of which he was paid $10!

But people especially want to know about Mises' famous two-hour evening seminars at New York University from 1948 to 1969. According to Margit von Mises, a tiny piece of paper with notes was all Mises needed for the evening. "The composition of his lectures was always the same: he began with a statement and returned with a closing word to exactly the point from whence he had started. His thoughts completed a perfect circle."

Margit quotes a prominent New York corporation lawyer who regularly attended the seminar:

> The seminar was the most enriching experience of my life.... In the first seminar Dr. Mises had finished his lecture on welfare legislation, attacking the economics of various social policies. The entire class was astonished at his critical attitude. They arranged a special meeting afterward … to teach Mises the social facts of life. And what happened? Wonder of wonders! After all the arguments had been submitted and Mises had explained everything anew, the class came away in complete agreement with him and shared a new conception of economic realities and economic freedom.

Most of the students who flocked to these seminars admired Mises' quick and brilliant answers, but there were also plenty of hostile questioners and derisive professors, steeped in the New Deal and Keynesianism. Yet Mises' influence was incalculable. Many of the best students went on to become famous professors of Austrian economics in their own right, including Murray Rothbard, Hans Sennholz, Israel Kirzner, Lawrence Moss, Edward Facey, George Reisman, and Ralph Raico (the latter two still in high school at the time).

Even later, when these scholars were offered posts at leading universities, Mises continued to be denied a university chair. In fact, his seminars were underwritten by the staunchly supportive Volker Fund, not New York University.

However, Mises' ideas spread well beyond academia through two splendid organizations in which he played a prominent role. In 1947 the Mont Pelerin Society was founded by a group of European and American economists, historians, philosophers, and journalists alarmed over the erosion of the free society. As one of the "founding fathers," Mises was the star of the show, although members included such luminaries as Friedrich von Hayek, Milton Friedman, Wilhelm Roepke, George Stigler, and Arthur Shenfield. Papers presented by Mises at these international meetings converted numerous important intellectuals throughout Europe and the U.S.

Perhaps even more widely influential was Mises' association with the Foundation for Economic Education, established in 1946 by Leonard Read, who was already an admirer and disciple of Mises. For many years Mises served as a director and conducted seminars at this fine institution, helping to assure its success. The Foundation's publication, *The Freeman*, was the first magazine devoted exclusively to the beautiful logic of the freedom philosophy and carried the ideas of Mises and his disciples far and wide, inspiring readers from housewives to college presidents.

By 1944 Mises' first book written in English, *Omnipotent Government: The Rise of the Total State and Total War*, was published by the prestigious Yale University Press, with which Mises had developed a good relationship through Henry Hazlitt. Amazingly, the Press brought out this book in the teeth of an avalanche of socialism and statism flowing from the major book publishers of the time.

As explained by Murray Rothbard, the dominant interpretation of Nazism in that era was the Marxist view; supposedly Nazism was the last desperate gasp of German big business (capitalists) anxious to crush the rising power of the lower classes. Mises thoroughly discredited that analysis by pointing out that interventionism and national planning were the underlying conditions leading to war; that "what is needed to make peace durable is neither international treaties and covenants nor international tribunals and organizations [such as the United Nations].... If the principle of the market economy is universally accepted, such makeshifts are unnecessary; if it is not accepted, they are futile. Durable peace can only be the outgrowth of a change in ideologies."

In the same year of 1944, inspired by his observation of the extraordinary growth of the federal government in the U.S., Mises wrote an expanded warning against the mixed economy in his powerful book *Bureaucracy*. The first systematic economic analysis of government intervention, in this work Mises demonstrated that "government regulatory agencies, lacking a test of profit and loss, grow larger and more intrusive even while they confer no social or economic benefit."

It was to the Yale University Press that Mises once again turned in 1948 for publication of his English edition of *Human Action*: *A Treatise on Economics*, the most important work on general economic theory of this century. This book created a tremendous impression, going into a third printing after only one month and soon translated into Italian, French, Spanish, and Japanese. This masterwork is about "everything," defending sound Austrian economics against all its opponents. Murray Rothbard, perhaps Mises' best known student from the NYU seminars, describes how this remarkable accomplishment kindled the flames of liberty:

The book was a revelation to those of us drenched in modern economics.... It provided eager libertarians with a policy of uncompromising laissez faire ... there were no escape hatches, no giving the case away with "of course, the government must break up monopolies," or "of course, the government must provide and regulate the money supply." In all matters, Mises was the soul of rigor and consistency.... Never would he compromise his principles.... Mises was a joy and an inspiration, an exemplar for us all.

Mises' intellectual triumph was so hated by entrenched academic collectivists that in 1963 a revised edition of *Human Action* was horribly botched by a new and vindictive team at Yale University Press, which was willing to blacken its own reputation in order to "punish" the author. Some paragraphs or even whole pages were printed in dark ink as though the author wished to emphasize them. Other pages were so lightly printed as to be scarcely legible. Whole paragraphs were left out. Mises, traumatized by this shocking experience, had nothing but

scorn for this contemptible act, especially because the Press continued to reap a high profit from the six printings of this painfully defective product sold to unsuspecting buyers.

Although New York University never bestowed a professorship upon Mises, in 1963 it awarded him an honorary doctorate of law. The citation eloquently summed up Mises' life and influence:

Author of literally hundreds of books and articles, his major works are recognized as classics of economic thought. He has brought one of the most powerful minds of his age to bear on his subject and has clarified it with philosophic con-

science and a scientific integrity of a rare order....

He is an eloquent scholar, a scholar's scholar, and the force of his ideas has been multiplied manyfold by the able economists he has trained and influenced. For his great scholarship, his exposition of the philosophy of the free market, and his advocacy of a free society, he is here presented with our Doctorate of Law.

Recipient of countless numbers of distinguished honors and academic honorary degrees, admired, loved, and respected, Ludwig von Mises was the oldest active professor in the U.S. when he retired in 1969 at age 88. He continued his labors for liberty — which included 25 books and more than 250 scholarly articles — right up until the end. He died quietly in 1973 at the age of 92.

It is impossible to calculate the breadth and depth of this great economist's influence. What we do know is that events have proven that centralized government is an unmitigated disaster, and that the concepts of limited government and faith in freedom are now more broadly accepted than at any time since FDR's collectivist New Deal. Understanding is increasing worldwide that collectivism of any stripe is a con game played by power-seeking politicians promoting economic fallacies exposed by Mises as tyrannical and pernicious. This kind of knowledge is the hope of the future.

With the founding of the Ludwig von Mises Institute at Auburn University in 1982 by the outstanding organizer, writer, and speaker Llewellyn Rockwell, the compelling insights taught by Mises are assured of continuity into the next century. Young professors from Auburn with doctorates in Austrian economics are teaching in universities across the land. Their essential message is that Mises was right, the collectivists were wrong.

This is the great lesson of the 20th century. ■

Faith, Family, Freedom

Lecturer, poet, writer — of all the hats G.K. Chesterton wore, none fit better than that of heroic Christian apologist.

by Fr. James Thornton

Gilbert Keith Chesterton was neither statesman nor warrior, neither law-giver nor political leader. In any conventional history of the 20th century, he would not loom very large. In fact he would not appear at all, for he never commanded armies or determined the fate of nations. Yet, Chesterton — poet, novelist, essayist, social commentator, editor, and lecturer — was one of the heroes of our time. Standing at a crossroads early in his life and contemplating two divergent paths ahead of him — a wide, glittering boulevard to fame and fortune, and the steep, narrow, rocky trail reserved for those who challenge the Spirit of the Time — Chesterton chose the more arduous; he chose the heroic. In doing so, he left us with a treasure trove of wisdom in defense of the Christian tradition.

Chesterton was born May 29, 1874 in Kensington, a suburb of London, to Edward and Mary Louise Chesterton, members of Britain's well-to-do middle class. That background allowed him access to an excellent education, capped by several years at the Slade School of Art, a prestigious institution then part of the University of London. Chesterton's parents were convinced that their son was gifted in the field of fine art and imagined him one day making a comfortable living as an artist. But that was not to be. He insisted, in a characteristic bit of self-effacement, that despite his years at the Slade he "entirely failed to learn how to draw and paint." Chesterton, in actual fact, possessed considerable artistic ability and his illustrations have appeared in many books. Nevertheless, shortly after graduation, Chesterton decided on a career as a writer.

It was at about this same period that he met a young lady whom he was to marry in 1901. Frances Chesterton quickly came to grasp the fact that while her husband was a genius with the pen, he was absent-minded, even incompetent,

"It is idle to talk always of the alternative of reason and faith. Reason is itself a matter of faith. It is an act of faith to assert that our thoughts have any relation to reality at all."
— *G.K. Chesterton*

insofar as the commonplace, practical things of life were concerned. Hopeless in money matters, notoriously forgetful, habitually late to appointments, and neglectful of his personal appearance, Chesterton came to rely on Frances in all these things. It was she who suggested what came to be his trademark attire, a flowing cloak (to shield his carelessness in dress), a soft wide-brimmed hat (no damage done should he mistakenly sit on it), and pince-nez spectacles (with black ribbon around the neck, impossible to lose). Frances devoted herself completely to removing all concern about the mundane matters of life so that her husband could concentrate his entire attention on his work.

Chesterton began his writing career as a critic and journalist. His weekly columns became an institution at the *London Illustrated News*, where they appeared from 1905 until shortly before his death in 1936. Chesterton was a prolific writer, producing almost 80 books in which he set forth his views on subjects as diverse as literature, philosophy, theology, history, sociology, science, and economics. Chesterton was renowned for his inimitable style, with its paradoxes, parallelisms, and epigrams. His friend, Hilaire Belloc, writes that the "heart of [Chesterton's] style is lucidity, produced by a complete rejection of ambiguity" and a "complete exactitude of definition." Style is so closely wedded to ideas in Chesterton's works that more than one of his biographers have noted that Chesterton is best quoted, not paraphrased. To characterize Chesterton's style is one thing, but to characterize his

outlook, given the countless subjects he wrote about, is a much more daunting task. Suffice it to say that he was a traditionalist and a conservative in matters touching on the foundations of human life and society, such as religion, family, morality, and freedom, and something of a revolutionary in his battle against concepts or institutions that threatened those fundamentals. Expressing himself bluntly and fearlessly, Chesterton was a man of decidedly strong opinions.

In considering Chesterton's outlook as expressed in his works, the first attribute that stands out is the importance he ascribes to the Christian religion. Taking religion very seriously, living it, and boldly professing it, Chesterton became one of the great Christian apologists of our century, similar in many ways to C.S. Lewis. He was not always a Christian, and in fact he dabbled in his youth in various shades of agnosticism, as many bright young people are wont to do. Upon reaching maturity, however, he "put away childish things," moving on to the firm ground of faith, first as an Anglican and later as a Roman Catholic. He defended the traditional Christian worldview against the scoffers and skeptics of his day, against the liberal theologians who would reduce Christianity to an impoverished shadow of itself, and against those who would make false gods out of ideologies, like socialism, or out of vapid nebulosities, like progress or science. To Chesterton, Christianity was a matter of simple logic, common sense, and orderly thought processes. Without belief in God the world was a howling hurricane of lunacy. Faith, in contrast, offered a serenity and sanity that existed nowhere else.

Chesterton understood that, in their unholy war against religious belief, Christianity's enemies seek to dismantle religion as a force in modern life and to abolish any awareness of its spiritual truths. To accomplish this, it must undermine and demolish the very structure of two thousand years of Christian civilization, right down to its foundations. Thus, the anti-Christianity of our time is an assault on the souls of men, and an assault on high culture, an unholy, sickly exalta-

tion of the primitive, a reversion to savagery and despotism. These were arresting notions at the beginning of the 20th century, when to superficial observers all seemed right with the world and the prospects for so-called progress and material abundance appeared limitless. Looking back over the bloodiest century in history, we now see how right Chesterton was and we can appreciate the depth of his amazing insights.

In one of his early masterpieces, *Orthodoxy*, Chesterton writes about how modern arguments against traditional religious authority serve to cripple religion, all legitimate authority, and even our ability to reason critically:

The sages, it is often said, can see no answer to the riddle of religion. But the trouble with our sages is not that they cannot see the answer; it is that they cannot even see the riddle. They are like children so stupid as to notice nothing paradoxical in the playful assertion that a door is not a door. The modern latitudinarians speak, for instance, about authority in religion not only as if there were no reason in it, but as if there had never been any reason for it. Apart from seeing its philosophical basis, they cannot even see its historical cause. Religious authority has often, doubtless, been oppressive or unreasonable; just as every legal system (and especially our present one) has been callous and full of a cruel apathy.... But the modern critics of religious authority are like men who should attack the police without ever having heard of burglars. For there is a great and possible peril to the human mind: a peril as practical as burglary. Against it religious authority was reared, rightly or wrongly, as a barrier. And against it something certainly must be reared as a barrier, if our race is to avoid ruin.

That peril is that the human intellect is free to destroy itself. Just as one generation could prevent the very existence of the next generation, by all entering a monastery or

Chesterton's trademark attire, suggested by his wife to shield his carelessness in dress, lent itself to caricature.

jumping into the sea, so one set of thinkers can in some degree prevent further thinking by teaching the next generation that there is no validity in any human thought. It is idle to talk always of the alternative of reason and faith. Reason is itself a matter of faith. It is an act of faith to assert that our thoughts have any relation to reality at all.

The entire edifice of human knowledge rests upon layer after layer of the strivings and struggling of our ancestors to acquire and refine knowledge, so that each successive generation stands, as it were, upon the shoulders of its forebears. We may use another metaphor and say that knowledge is a delicate silver chain that runs back through more than 25 centuries. Break the silver chain of knowledge, and leave it broken for a generation or two, and we lose our connection with the entire body; we become brutes once again; we become jabbering, witless barbarians. We lose even our ability to formulate our thoughts in logical sequence, and so concepts like freedom are meaningless. We can only think and speak gibberish. We exchange the silver chain of knowledge for the iron chain of slavery. The demolition of Christianity as a living force in our society *is* the destruction of those silver links, because our religion embodies

all that was, is, and can be the focus of the possibilities of our civilization. Chesterton continues:

> There is a thought that stops thought. That is the only thought that ought to be stopped. That is the ultimate evil against which all religious authority was aimed. It appears at the end of decadent ages like our own: and already Mr. H.G. Wells has raised its ruinous banner; he has raised a delicate piece of skepticism called "Doubts of the Instrument." In this he questions the brain itself, and endeavors to remove all reality from all his own assertions, past, present, and to come. But it was against this remote ruin that all the military systems in religion were originally ranked and ruled. The creeds and the crusades, the hierarchies and the horrible persecutions were not organized, as is ignorantly said, for the suppression of reason. They were organized for the defence of reason. Man, by blind instinct, knew that if once things were wildly questioned, reason could be questioned first.... [T]hese were all only dark defences erected

round one central authority, more undemonstrable, more supernatural than all — the authority of a man to think. We know now that this is so; we have no excuse for not knowing it. For we can hear skepticism crashing through the old ring of authorities, and at the same moment we can see reason swaying upon her throne. In so far as religion is gone, reason is going. For they are both of the same primary and authoritative kind. They are both methods of proof which cannot themselves be proved.

Modernist atheistic and antitheistic philosophies that seek to supplant Christianity, Chesterton argues, proffer formlessness in place of ordered perception, a wallowing in empty perplexity in place of substance and stability.

Evolution is a good example of that modern intelligence which, if it destroys anything, destroys itself. Evolution is either an innocent scientific description of how certain earthly things came about; or, if it is anything more than this, it is an attack on thought itself. If evolution destroys anything, it does not destroy religion but rationalism. If evolution simply means that a positive thing called an ape turned very slowly into a positive thing called a man, then it is stingless for the most orthodox; for a personal God might just as well do things slowly as quickly, especially if, like the Christian God, he were outside time. But if it means anything more, it means that there is no such thing as an ape to change, and no such thing as a man for him to change into. It means that there is no such thing as a thing. At best, there is only one thing, and that is a flux of everything and anything. This is an attack not upon the faith, but upon the mind; you cannot think if there are no things to think about. You cannot think if you are not separate from the subject of thought. Descartes

True devotion: Frances attended to the everyday cares of life so that her husband could focus entirely on his work.

said, "I think; therefore I am." The philosophic evolutionist reverses and negatives the epigram. He says, "I am not; therefore I cannot think."

The philosophies of our time are nothing more than a "suicidal mania," writes Chesterton, a mania of nihilism that destroys us and and then destroys itself.

[T]he most characteristic current philosophies have not only a touch of mania, but a touch of suicidal mania. The mere questioner has knocked his head against the limits of human thought; and cracked it. This is what makes so futile the warnings of the orthodox and the boasts of the advanced about the dangerous boyhood of free thought; it is the old age and ultimate dissolution of free thought. It is vain for bishops and pious bigwigs to discuss what dreadful things will happen if wild skepticism runs its course. It has run its course. It is vain for eloquent atheists to talk of the great truths that will be revealed if once we see free thought begin.

We have seen it end. It has no more questions to ask; it has questioned itself. You cannot call up any wilder vision than a city in which men ask themselves if they have any selves. You cannot fancy a more skeptical world than that in which men doubt if there is a world.

Some years later, in his book *The Well and the Shallows*, Chesterton commented on the appalling superficiality of the imagined wisdom of our age.

We need not deny that modern doubt, like ancient doubt, does ask deep questions; we only deny that, as compared with our own philosophy, it gives any deeper answers. And it is a general rule, touching what is called modern thought, that while the questions are often really deep, the answers are often decidedly shallow. And it is even more important to remark that, while the questions are in a sense eternal, the answers are in every sense ephemeral.... Those who leave the tradition of truth do not escape into something we call Freedom. They only escape into something else, which we call Fashion.

Read any of the books by or about G.K. Chesterton and one of two things will stand out. The first is Chesterton's reputation as a explicator of Christian teaching and defender of Christian truths and the Christian ethos, samples of which we have just read. The second is his fierce advocacy of property, family, and tradition, which he believed were the chief bulwarks of human liberty.

In Chesterton's view, modern men are beset all around by giant institutions, especially big government and giant corporations. These organizations tend, as time goes on, to grow ever larger, dwarfing the ordinary citizen, gradually robbing him of his independence, and rendering him ever more reliant on the good will of the nabobs of government and industry who actually run things. These men, the "elite," the "ruling class," the

"Establishment," the "Insiders," or whatever you want to call them, have learned to influence the thinking of most citizens through their control of communications and education. By such means they have shaped national and international policy — which the everyday citizen must pay for in confiscatory taxes, and, not infrequently, with his blood when it is in the interests of the reigning big shots to launch a war in some far-away place.

In countries like Chesterton's England, or in our own United States, the elite accomplishes its political ends through a party system. Two ostensibly antagonistic political parties, both rigorously controlled by the Establishment, maintain an illusion of choice, of opposition, and of self-government. As a bonus, the pretense of political campaigns entertains the people, keeping them preoccupied. That, we remember, is one of the components in the old "bread and circuses" formula of Imperial Rome. "It is a mark of our whole modern history," writes Chesterton, "that the masses are kept quiet with a fight. They are kept quiet by the fight because it is a sham-fight; thus most of us know by this time that the Party System has been popular only in the sense that a football match is popular."

Most politicians, in Chesterton's judgment, are self-serving mediocrities: "The whole modern world has divided itself into Conservatives and Progressives. The business of Progressives is to go on making mistakes. The business of Conservatives is to prevent mistakes from being corrected." His reference here is to what informed Americans would call liberals and neo-conservatives. Substitute "Democrats" for "Progressives" and "Republicans" for "Conservatives," and one can see how well his aphorism applies to modern American political life. "The Party System," he wrote, "was founded on one national notion of fair play. It was the notion that folly and futility should be fairly divided between both sides."

Politics, of course, is inextricably intertwined with economics. Like his associate Hilaire Belloc, and like many other men throughout the 20th century, Chesterton understood that the false dichoto-

my of "capitalism versus socialism" did not address the real questions of our time. Chesterton did not oppose the idea of free enterprise; on the contrary he demanded that it be truly free. Free enterprise to him meant small and medium-sized companies, shops, and farms owned by individual persons and families. These businesses, he believed, are the backbone of a healthy nation. What he opposed was the practice of giant, impersonal, bureaucratic corporations, monopolies, and cartels, benefiting from government interventionism because they are controlled by the same men who control government, using unlimited power to undercut and squeeze the small property owner, drive him under, deprive him finally of his property and liberty, and turn him into a rootless, urbanized worker — a process known as "proletarianization." In the Britain of Chesterton's time, this meant widespread and truly horrifying poverty. This theft of the dignity, pride, and honor of ordinary Englishmen exasperated and infuriated Chesterton, for this was not what his countrymen had fought for centuries to achieve.

"Big Business and State Socialism are very much alike...," Chesterton remarked. His response to this false dichotomy was to propose a *true* private enterprise sys-

Contemporary, colleague, and comrade: Hilaire Belloc valued not only Chesterton's lucid writing style but his virtuous character.

tem called "distributism," a word signifying simply that property should be distributed widely in a society. What is suggested, in Chesterton's terse language, is that "too much capitalism does not mean too many capitalists, but too few capitalists." Property — and by this he meant genuinely productive property like farms and small businesses — should be in the hands of many, not just a few, making the citizens of a country responsible, productive, independent, and self-reliant and creating conditions that enhance liberty. Writes Chesterton, "For the mass of men the idea of artistic creation can only be expressed by an idea unpopular in present discussions — the idea of property. The average man cannot cut clay into the shape of a man; but he can cut earth into the shape of a garden; and though he arranges it with red geraniums and blue potatoes in alternate straight lines, he is still an artist; because he has chosen. The average man cannot paint the sunset whose colours he admires; but he can paint his own house with what colour he chooses; and though he paints it pea green with pink spots, he is still an artist; because that is his choice. Property … means that every man should have something that he can shape in his own image as he is shaped in the image of heaven."

Chesterton reasoned that if ownership of property is widespread, citizens are much less likely to look to giant institutions to solve their problems. Such citizens solve their own problems, and government becomes truly a servant, not a master. Socialism is stopped dead in its tracks, for a nation of independent entrepreneurs would never look kindly on high taxes, intrusive bureaucracies, or welfarism. Is this concept compatible with American ideals? Without doubt it is. Thomas Jefferson's dream for America was a free nation made up, for the most part, of tough, independent farmers, supporting themselves and their families with minimal interference from government. Jefferson, in the words of Professor Robert A. Nisbet, "feared, in the name of individual liberty, the great cities, industries, and bureaucracies which he saw forming in Europe."

> *"Those who leave the tradition of truth do not escape into something we call Freedom. They only escape into something else, which we call Fashion."*
>
> *— G.K. Chesterton*

Discussing Chesterton's distributism, renowned author and poet E. Merrill Root said this:

It is hardly necessary to say that Chesterton was the enemy of Communism and of socialism. He was such because he believed in the freedom and worth of *individual men*. The collectivity, the arrogant "experts," the commissars, the State usurping the choices of man and the sovereignty of God, seemed to him an evil to be fought to the death. He saw Communism or socialism as a bulldozer driven by stiff-minded and groove-minded madmen.... He regarded both as a sort of arteriosclerosis of the soul, stiffening man towards an existential death. He abhorred both.

It is interesting and heartening, also, to know that Chesterton distrusted and opposed the *Insiders* of finance-capitalism. He saw the wealthy of the world assuming the *mask* of socialism to destroy both socialism and the freedom of individual enterprise. Like his great friend, Hilaire Belloc, he foresaw the *Servile State* — i.e., the Welfare State — where the *Insiders* use the superficial easy panaceas of socialism (applied to most men but escaped by themselves) to seduce men into servitude at the price of freedom. He and Belloc both saw, as the alternative, what they called "distributism" — *not* a distribution of wealth such as the Establishment pretends and upholds today, but a capitalism in which many, indeed more and more *individuals*, own capital property — land, businesses, resources — so that free enterprise may indeed be both enterprise and free.

This may not be the way, this may not be possible in our day, but Chesterton saw no other way.... And neither do I.

Chesterton also decried the decline of the traditional family, for the family is another of those bulwarks of freedom, as we have noted, since, he writes, it "is the only check on the state that is bound to renew itself as eternally as the state." He was well aware that those who would rob us of our freedom would, in the words of Ian Crowther in his book *G.K. Chesterton*, "much rather deal with mobile, isolated individuals, whether it's for the purpose of employing them, exploiting them, entertaining them, organizing them, reforming them, regimenting them, or simply ruling them." The family, with its overriding inward loyalties and its need for continuity and stability, is by its very nature an enemy of tyranny, and that is precisely why the family has been under attack throughout most of the last century. Chesterton argued that easy divorce laws and radical feminism were the chief weapons employed in this attack.

Near the end of his life Chesterton observed that "freedom has remained exactly in so far as the faith has remained," and he warned that "where it is true that all our Faith has gone, all our freedom is going." Faith and freedom are bound together; they are inseparable. In opposition to faith, modern ideologies offer only materialism. If we do not believe in God, then the only thing remaining is belief in material things — the Marxists go so far as to glorify what they call "scientific materialism." But, Chesterton said, a "servile fatalism dogs the creed of materialism; because nothing, as Dante said, less than the generosity of God could give Man, after all ordinary orderly gifts, the noblest of all things, which is liberty." In other words, freedom is a gift from God, but if there is no God, or at least no meaningful recognition of Him, where does that leave freedom?

Let us conclude by saying a few words

about Chesterton the man. Chesterton was, as we have seen, a courageous fighter for light, freedom, and human dignity and against darkness, oppression, injustice, and ignorance. And while the lessons we can learn from his books are nearly endless, the lessons we learn from his character are likewise invaluable — like perseverance, fortitude, and hope. One of the most remarkable of his qualities was that he never allowed his struggle to corrode his own soul with personal hatreds or bitterness, even to the smallest degree.

Chesterton was a happy man, loving life, loving his family and friends, and loving laughter. Moreover, his biographers note that he was gracious and generous to everyone he encountered, even those whom he opposed philosophically or politically. Shortly after Chesterton's death in 1936, Hilaire Belloc wrote a small book entitled *The Place of Gilbert Chesterton in English Letters*, a tribute to his friend of many years in which he praises this wonderful Chesterton trait:

> [Chesterton] was blessed in knowing nothing of the acerbities which bite into the life of writing men. The life of writing men has always been, since our remote fathers engaged upon it in the high Greek world, a bitter business. It is notoriously accompanied, for those who write well, by poverty and contempt; or by fatuity and wealth for those who

write ill. It is unrewarded in this world and probably in the next — (seeing, that those who write well do so with their backs put up like spitting cats — witness the immortal Swift). The writing man, I say, is a most unhappy beast of burden (and I know something about it); he bears upon his back for conveyance to others the joys and consolations, the visions that make life in this bad world tolerable. But he may not enjoy them himself any more than the donkey may enjoy the vegetables that he bears to market. Now Gilbert Chesterton enjoyed this singular, this very happy fate, that, though he was a writing man the bitterness of the trade never approached him. He was spared its ignominies and its trials, which are a sort of martyrdom whereby the writer earns fame — which is worth nothing. He himself had something much more worth while, called Virtue.

G.K. Chesterton was blessed with great gifts. He refused, however, to sell those gifts to a corrupt and corrupting establishment, renouncing the immense material rewards he could have enjoyed had he done so and rejecting anything he saw as a compromise of truth. As a result his success in a *worldly* sense was of a very modest kind, his popularity limited to a relatively small following, his books never "best sellers," and his personal wealth always quite humble, so humble that there was some concern among Chesterton's friends for Frances' financial well-being when he died. Nevertheless, his thoughts remain as alive and as fresh as when he put them down on paper. And in a hundred or in two hundred years his books, essays, and poetry will still be read and they will still be alive and fresh, remaining so long after the ideological monstrosities concocted by his opponents are buried and forgotten forever. As long as men fight God, and as long as tyrants and their minions fight the liberty that comes from God, Chesterton's heroic words will enlighten, uplift, and embolden truth's defenders. ■

Pillar of Western Culture

A reluctant yet reasonable convert to Christianity, C.S. Lewis became a master apologist and champion of the Western tradition.

by Thomas R. Eddlem

O ne of C.S. Lewis' most popular and enduring works is *The Screwtape Letters*. This witty and insightful satire explores the problems of the world from the perspective of devils in Hell and outlines the means by which they go about tempting souls and pulling "patients" (people) away from God. The serialized newspaper columns (later published as a book) centered around a senior fiend, Screwtape, who advised his nephew Wormwood, an apprentice tempter, on how to tempt his human "patient" away from Christianity. But not all readers of this literary work recognized the satire, which was intended to warn of the many subtle techniques Satan employs in leading people to damnation. *The Guardian* informed C.S. Lewis that one not-too-observant clergyman had canceled his newspaper subscription because "much of the advice given in these letters seemed to him not only erroneous but positively diabolical." That clergyman would not have said the same about any of C.S. Lewis' many other works of Christian apologetics, which — together with his vast literary works and social commentary — make him a pillar of the Western cultural tradition.

Yet if one looks at his early life, the Belfast-born Lewis can only be considered an unlikely Christian, let alone a hero of Western Civilization. Clive Staples Lewis was born in 1898. He disliked his birth name so much that from childhood he insisted upon being called "Jack" by his family and friends. Though he was baptized into the Anglican Church of Ireland as an infant, his resentment over the death of his mother when he was nine caused Lewis to become a staunch atheist at a young age. Still, an important element in Lewis' early life was an emphasis on learning. This originated in part with his relatively erudite parents but also from within the young scholar himself, as the many books that cluttered the family home continually piqued his curiosity. He

recalled in his 1955 autobiographical book, *Surprised by Joy*, that "My father bought all the books he read and never got rid of any of them. There were books in the study, books in the drawing room, books in the cloakroom, books (two deep) in the great bookcase on the landing, books in a bedroom, books piled as high as my shoulder in the cistern attic, books of all kinds reflecting every transient stage of my parents' interest, books readable and unreadable, books suitable for a child and books most emphatically not. Nothing was forbidden me. In the seemingly endless rainy afternoons I took volume after volume from the shelves. I had always the same certainty of finding a book that was new to me as a man who walks into a field has of finding a new blade of grass."

Lewis' father soon sent the brilliant young man to England, where he was tutored in the classics by W.T. Kirkpatrick, a fervent atheist. Lewis went on to teach for most of his adult life at the two most establishmentarian of British universities: Oxford and Cambridge. "Looking back on my life now," Lewis recounted, "I am astonished that I did not progress into the opposite orthodoxy … a Leftist, Atheist, satiric Intellectual of the type we all know so well. All the conditions seem

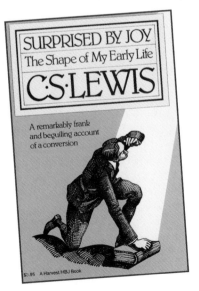

"Reluctant convert": The remarkable story of C.S. Lewis' conversion to Christianity is told in his autobiography.

Prodigal son returns: Oxford's Magdalen College, where C.S. Lewis admitted that "God was God."

to be present. I hated my public school. I hated whatever I knew or imagined of the British Empire. And though I took very little notice of Morris' socialism (there were too many things in him that interested me far more), continual reading of Shaw had brought it about that such embryonic political opinions as I had were vaguely socialistic."

"He never attacked religion in my presence," Lewis later observed of Kirkpatrick, although from Kirkpatrick he regularly received atheism "indirectly from the tone of his mind or independently from reading his books." Kirkpatrick — or as Lewis and his family came to call him, "the Great Knock" — nevertheless implanted the seed that led to his eventual religious conversion to Christianity. "[T]here was one really wholesome element" in Kirkpatrick's teaching, Lewis recalled. "The Absolute was 'there.'" Kirkpatrick did instill a desire for an absolute and transcendent truth, even if he never concluded that truth involves God.

The "Great Knock" had set Lewis' reason to work, and his academic studies compelled him to reconsider the logic of his atheism. Soon Lewis found that "All the books were beginning to turn against me.... George McDonald had done more to me than any other writer; of course it was a pity he had that bee in his bonnet about Christianity. He was good *in spite of it*. Chesterton had more sense than all the other moderns put together; bating, of course, his Christianity. Johnson was one of the few authors I felt I could trust utterly; curiously enough, he had the same kink. Spenser

and Milton by a strange coincidence had it too." Finally, Lewis "read Chesterton's *Everlasting Man* and for the first time saw the whole Christian outline of history set out in a form that seemed to me to make sense." But despite the overwhelming logic of the God of the Scriptures, Lewis was still determined to retain his atheism — or at the least not adopt the Christianity he had rejected in his youth. "Really, a young Atheist cannot guard his faith too carefully," Lewis later admitted. "Dangers lie in wait for him on every side." But the unrelenting logic of McDonald and Chesterton left Lewis with a painful choice: abandon logic and truth altogether; or conclude that what he had been told — and rejected — in the nursery was right all along. "The Prodigal Son at least walked home on his own feet," Lewis wrote, in contrast to his own conversion whereby he "was brought in kicking, struggling, resentful, and darting [my] eyes in every direction for a chance to escape." The Professor of English Language and Literature at Magdalen College (at Oxford University) wrote: "You must picture me alone in that room in Magdalen, night after night, feeling, whenever my mind lifted even for a second from my work, the steady, unrelenting approach of Him whom I so earnestly desired not to meet. That which I had greatly feared had at last come upon me. In the Trinity Term of 1929 I gave in, and admitted that God was God, and knelt and prayed: perhaps, that night, the most dejected and reluctant convert in all England."

Lewis' theistic view of an omnipotent and semi-personal God was still a long way from the God of the Christian Bible. But his reading and discussions with friends on the subject continued. After a long talk in September 1931 with his friends and fellow Oxford instructors, Hugo Dyson and J.R.R. Tolkien (author of *The Lord of the Rings* series and a devout Christian), Lewis wrote, "I have just passed on from believing in God to definitely believing in Christ." Lewis soon became a regular communicant in the Church of England. Two years later Tolkien, Dyson, and Lewis began meeting regularly with a group of friends from Oxford, and attendees at these meetings called themselves the "Inklings." Other Inkling members included Lewis' only brother Warren ("Warnie"), Robert Havard, Charles Williams, Neville Coghill, and Lewis' close friend Owen Barfield. The Inklings met in Lewis' rooms at Oxford's Magdalen College or at a local pub called The Eagle and Child, where they discussed religion, philosophy, literature, mythology, and other subjects. The meetings continued regularly until 1949, and one can only guess the influence of the meetings on Lewis' writings.

Those who did guess at what influenced his writing during Lewis' lifetime did so at their own peril, however. Lewis was often stung by absurd reviews of his works which devoted little space to his actual work and multitudinous space to "imaginary histories of the process by which you wrote it." He went on to conclude that "My impression is that in the whole of my experience not one of these guesses has on any one point been right; that the method shows a record of 100 per cent failure. You would expect that by mere chance they would hit as often as they miss. But it is my impression that they do no such thing. I can't remember a single hit."

Nevertheless, it is worth a try for a first hit. Lewis had to be at least indirectly influenced to write his seven-volume *Chronicles of Narnia* by Tolkien's immensely popular 1936 book *The Hobbit* and its sequels. Tolkien was working on them throughout the time of the Inkling meetings, and soon after the

meetings ended Lewis came out with his first Narnia book, *The Lion, the Witch, and the Wardrobe* (1950). It may be Lewis' best known and most read book. An instant international success, it has enthralled millions of readers, young and old, since its introduction. *The Lion, the Witch, and the Wardrobe* is an allegorical story of the life, death, sacrifice, and resurrection of Christ in the mythical land of Narnia. Like Lewis' science fiction "space trilogy" before it and the six other Narnia books after it, Lewis employed fiction in *The Lion, the Witch, and the Wardrobe* as a means of teaching various tenets of Christian and Western principles.

Though highly respected as a literary critic, Lewis' theological works were sometimes dismissed by other Oxford academicians. It is true that in the area of theology, his educational background made him — technically speaking — an amateur. He hadn't studied theology; he had studied literature. But Lewis made no pretense to being a professional theologian. Nevertheless, Lewis was England's most capable amateur. He wielded his literary cudgel with devastating efficiency against the forces of liberalism within his own church. Among his prime targets was the modern tendency to view the miracles of the Bible as allegories — mere stories for teaching lessons — rather than historical record. He warned his church that advocating and teaching such a theology — one that "denies the historicity of nearly everything in the Gospels to which Christian life and affections and thought have been fastened for nearly two millennia," will likely drive the uneducated believer to atheism or drive him to a church (he specifically cited the Roman Catholic) that still maintains that historicity.

In criticizing allegorical Christianity, Lewis could speak as a true literary expert. "[W]hatever these men may be as Biblical critics, I distrust them as critics. They seem to me to lack literary judgement, to be imperceptive about the very quality of the texts they are reading." Lewis explained that the Bible doesn't

"The Prodigal Son at least walked home on his own feet," Lewis wrote, in contrast to his own conversion whereby he *"was brought in kicking, struggling, resentful, and darting [my] eyes in every direction for a chance to escape."*

read like a fairy tale or legendary story. "Either this is reportage ... [o]r else, some unknown writer in the second century, without known predecessors or successors, suddenly anticipated the whole technique of modern, novelistic, realistic narrative. If it is untrue, it must be narrative of that kind. The reader who doesn't see this has simply not learned to read." He concluded, in what was a rather prophetic remark regarding church attendance in England: "Once a layman was anxious to hide the fact that he believed so much less than the Vicar: now he tends to hide the fact that he believes so much more. Missionary to the priests of one's own church is an embarrassing role; though I have a horrid feeling that if such mission work is not soon undertaken the future history of the Church of England is likely to be short." Lewis was also generally skeptical of the grand discoveries claimed by many modern liberal "scholars," exclaiming that "all theology of the liberal type involves at some point — and often involves throughout — the claim that the real behaviour and purpose of the teaching of Christ came very rapidly to be misunderstood and misrepresented by His followers, and has been recovered or exhumed only by modern scholars."

Not unexpectedly, considering the rational nature of his conversion, Lewis fervently defended the complete congruity of faith and reason. Most of his works at least touch on that subject. In *The Screwtape Letters*, the arch-fiend Screwtape advises the apprentice tempter to employ propaganda and to avoid reason whenever possible. "Jargon, not argument, is your best ally in keeping [the patient] from the Church.... The trouble with argument is that it moves the whole struggle onto the Enemy's own ground.... By the very act of arguing, you awake the patient's reason; and once it is awake, who can foresee the result? Even if a particular train of thought can be twisted so as to end in our favour, you will find that you have been strengthening in your patient the fatal habit of attending to universal issues and withdrawing his attention from the stream of immediate sense experiences. Your business is to fix his attention on the stream." Clearly one cannot foresee the result of a reason awakened, to which the life of C.S. Lewis himself — once a young atheist — serves as evidence.

Attention to the "stream of immediate sense experiences" mentioned by Screwtape is being heartily advocated by the mass media and the educational systems in America today. In *Screwtape Proposes a Toast*, a follow-up to his original *Screwtape Letters*, Lewis goes even so far as to have Screwtape suggest: "Every dictator or even demagogue — almost every film star or crooner — can now draw tens of thousands of the human sheep with him.... There may come a time when we shall have no need to bother about individual temptation at all, except a few. Catch the bellwether, and his whole flock comes after him." Lewis arrayed his brilliant pen against the modern bellwethers leading Western culture in the direction of nihilism and totalitarian government, and the replacement of the education of youth with the conditioning of youth in the schools.

Among the features of Lewis' hellish bureaucracy in *Screwtape* are a rigorously enforced official party line (a.k.a., "political correctness"), backbiting, and fear of exposure. The Christian worldview contends that God does not cast anyone into Hell, but that the damned cast themselves into Hell because of their own actions. Lewis brilliantly portrays this politically correct, hellish bureaucracy reflecting this reality through a pathetic inability to understand the concept of love, the prime plank in the platform of Hell. Screwtape advises Wormwood: "The whole philosophy of Hell rests on recognition of the axiom that one thing is not another

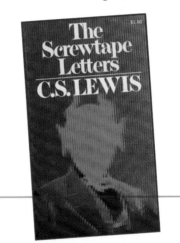

Mere masterpiece: Lewis' *Screwtape Letters* cleverly describes a demonic bureaucracy in an attempt to warn of Satan's cunning.

thing.... My good is my good, and your good is yours. What one gains another loses." And in a zero sum reality, the party line of Hell becomes one in which love — where we give ourselves back to God and yet remain distinct and individual beings — is mathematically impossible: "We know that He [God] cannot really love: nobody can; it doesn't make sense. If only we could find out what He is *really* up to! Hypothesis after hypothesis has been tried, and still we can't find out. Yet we must never lose hope; more and more complicated theories, fuller and fuller collections of data, richer rewards for researchers who make progress, more and more terrible punishments for those who fail — all this, pursued and acceler-

ated to the very end of time, cannot, surely, fail to succeed." The depiction of diabolical bureaucrats insanely obsessed with their rebellion against God, and laboring to the end of time to solve the nonexistent riddle of love, is but one example of Lewis' brilliant ability to express the Christian worldview with simple, credible pictures.

Nowhere does Lewis paint these simple pictures of complex issues better than in *Mere Christianity*, a book which began as a series of wartime BBC radio broadcasts on the basic philosophical tenets of Christianity. Lewis also chases the quacks of pseudo-psychoanalysis and the flakes of pseudo-science back to their legitimate domains in *Mere Christianity*. While respecting both psychology and science as worthwhile and valuable pursuits, Lewis tried to put matters about the origin of man and the earth outside the realm of science (whether it be evolutionism or creationism). "You can not find out which view is the right one by science in the ordinary sense. Science works by experiments. It watches how things behave. Every scientific statement in the long run, however complicated it looks, really means something like, 'I pointed the telescope to such and such a part of the sky at 2:20 AM on January 15th and saw so-and-so,' or 'I put some of this stuff in a pot and heated it to such-and-such a temperature and it did so-and-so.'" But "None of us has seen the Norman Conquest or the defeat of the Armada. None of us could prove them by pure logic as you prove a thing in mathematics." Lewis concludes that science is an inadequate foundation upon which to build beliefs about the past.

Lewis also takes up his cudgel against Freud's attempt to explain the whole world in terms of psychological phenomena, while acknowledging the need to distinguish "between the actual medical theories and technique of the psychoanalysts, and the general philosophical view of the world which Freud and some others have gone on to add to this. The second thing — the philosophy of Freud — is in direct contradiction to Christianity." Lewis essentially argued that once a subject — for instance, sexual morality — is discussed or thought about openly and freely, the decision or conclusion can hardly be dismissed as the result of subconscious or repressed feelings. Once a person is cured of irrational fears and feelings, "it is just then that the psychoanalytical problem is over and the moral problem begins." Lewis explained: "what psychoanalysis undertakes to do is to remove the abnormal feelings, that is, to give the man better raw material for his acts of choice; morality is concerned with the acts of choice themselves." Lewis observed that "when Freud is talking about how to cure neurotics he is speaking as a specialist in his own subject, but when he goes on to talk general philosophy he is speaking as an amateur. It is therefore quite sensible to attend to him with respect in the one case and not in the other — and that is what I do. I am all the readier to do it because I have found that when he is talking off his own subject and on a subject I do know something about (namely, languages) he is very ignorant."

Lewis also did his best to destroy the evil of collectivism. As weapons against collectivism, Lewis used the classroom lectionary as well as the pen. One of Lewis' leftist students in the late 1930s, John Lawlor, wrote of Lewis' effectiveness in dispelling Lawlor's collectivism after Lawlor entered Oxford's Magdalen College. "It was the time of the Spanish Civil War, and those on the political Left (though few in Magdalen) were busy organising lunches for refugee funds, collecting money by point-blank asking, and getting up meetings and demonstrations in support of the [Soviet-allied] Spanish Government. I must have been the last man Lewis wanted to see." Yet Lewis displayed "increasing goodwill" toward Lawlor in their weekly tutorial. "I was allowed the initiative on every occasion; Lewis gave me the choice of ground and of weapons and of course beat me every time." By his third year of Lewis' tutoring at Magdalen College, Lawlor had found that for him the "attractions of

Marxism had faded."

Despite his undermining of Marxism in the classroom and general warnings about totalitarian societies in his books, C.S. Lewis never got involved in political issues directly. Most of his effort went into constantly girding the Western moral infrastructure for political battle. Lewis viewed politics as only one element of a broader cultural war. For example, he exploded a popular fetish among many Americans who fancy themselves well

Used by permission of The Marion E. Wade Center, Wheaton College, Wheaton, IL.

Teaching against tyranny: An excellent teacher, Lewis' lectures dispelled the fallacies of collectivism and totalitarianism.

educated — that there should be a divorce of religious values from politics — in his classic philosophical essay, *The Abolition of Man*. "A dogmatic belief in objective value is necessary to the very idea of a rule which is not tyranny or an obedience which is not slavery," Lewis wrote. "When all that says 'it is good' has been debunked, what says 'I want' remains.... Either we are rational spirits obliged for ever to obey the absolute values of the [will of God], or else we are mere nature to be kneaded and cut into new shapes for the pleasures of masters who must, by hypothesis, have no motive but their own 'natural' impulses." Lewis concludes that "I am doubtful whether history shows us one example of a man who, having stepped outside traditional

morality and attained power, has used that power benevolently. I am inclined to think that the Conditioners will hate the conditioned." Lewis warned that this conditioning process, which, "if not checked, will abolish Man, goes on apace among Communists and Democrats no less than among Fascists. The methods may (at first) differ in brutality."

In social society, Lewis warned of the social conditioners who invoke the word "democracy" to bring traditional values down to the lowest common denominator. "You are to use it purely as an incantation; if you like, purely for its selling power. It is a name they venerate," says Lewis' Screwtape. "*Democracy* is the word with which you must lead them by the nose." Under the democratic and more tolerant values of the social conditioners, a girl who wishes to be "normal" will increasingly find that what she is really wishing is: "Make me a minx, a moron, and a parasite." Lewis felt that the "greatest evil is not now done in those sordid 'dens of crime' that Dickens loved to paint. It is not done even in concentration camps and labor camps. In those we see its final result. But it is conceived and ordered (moved, seconded, carried, and minuted) in clean, carpeted, warmed and well-lighted offices, by quiet men with white collars and cut fingernails and smooth shaven cheeks who do not need to raise their voice." Thus it is not surprising that in *The Screwtape Letters* the "symbol for Hell is something like the bureaucracy of a police state." Lewis quipped that he did not depict a hell with all of the time-worn images of devils with horns and bat wings, because he likes "bats much better than bureaucrats." In fact, Lewis' depiction of the bureaucracy of Hell is starkly reminiscent of the American political scene today. Specifically, it is "a state where everyone is perpetually concerned about his own dignity and advancement, where everyone has a grievance, and where everyone lives the deadly serious passions of envy, self-importance, and resentment."

Clearly, Western culture needs C.S. Lewis now more than ever. ∎

Novel Novelist

The most widely read living author of her day, Taylor Caldwell skillfully used "fiction" as a weapon in the freedom fight.

by Mark Samuel Anderson

When a young, precocious Taylor Caldwell foreshadowed her future greatness by winning a gold medal for an essay on Charles Dickens at the age of six, and brashly announced her plan to craft a career through the written word, her parents, relatives, and friends were doubtful. "A writer? That's lovely dear," was their usual reply.

Irrepressibly resolute despite her lack of years, Caldwell persisted in her efforts and at the tender age of 12 completed work on her first novel. That effort served as prelude to a 42-year career as a published writer that saw her produce some 34 historical and romantic novels in the course of becoming the most widely read living author in the world. Oftentimes her novels were not mere works of "fiction" but were intended to acquaint her readers with important historical insights, and to warn them against a real-life contemporary conspiracy that intends to, as she put it, "drive freedom off the face of the earth." She also sounded the alarm by writing an array of nonfiction essays. And she wrote a collection of autobiographical essays appropriately entitled *On Growing Up Tough*, which she accurately called "an irreverent memoir."

A number of Caldwell's novels were set in the latter 19th or early 20th century, a point in history when "old republic" America began to succumb to the depredations of socialists, Communists, anarchists, amoral financial barons, and others bent on ruthlessly remolding the republic into a Godless socialist state. In *Captains and the Kings* and *Ceremony of the Innocent*, in particular, her protagonists become aware of the existence of a secret cabal of powerful elitists working to destroy the American republic from within. Ultimately, Caldwell's central characters such as Congressman Jeremy Porter struggle, frequently in vain, against this high-level cabal and its coterie of street-level radical allies.

The conspiratorially orchestrated transition from a free, republican form of government to a despotic empire is a recurring theme in many of Caldwell's novels. It is also a theme not limited to the contemporary conspiratorial onslaught seeking to subvert the United States. In *A Pillar of Iron*, Caldwell brought to life Cicero's heroic fight to prevent the Roman republic's slide into Empire, and in *Glory and the Lightning* she recounted Pericles' struggle to preserve Athenian freedom centuries earlier. In other novels she recreated the lives of St. Paul (*Great Lion of God*) and St. Luke (*Dear and Glorious Physician*).

Her historical novels are rich in detail and in many ways more historically accurate than most of what now passes for "history." This is particularly the case with regard to the lessons of history — lessons we ignore at our own peril.

In general, whether creating an historical, contemporary, or futuristic setting, Caldwell used the novel as her chosen weapon in the age-old fight between freedom and slavery. She wrote so skillfully that she won millions of devoted fans. But because of the side she had chosen, and her willingness to expose the conspiratorial machinations behind our present retreat from greatness, she also earned the wrath of America's Establishment — which was very willing to trash her powerful prose as worthless fiction.

Janet Miriam Taylor Holland Caldwell was born on September 7, 1900, in Prestwich, a suburb of Manchester, England. Her parents were both natives of Scotland. The budding author, who had one younger brother, attended a nearby private school while spending most of her spare time tending to household duties. "Saturday and Sunday were tough days" she recalled in *On Growing Up Tough*. Those days were spent "ironing, mending, darning, snowshoveling, glass polishing, and sundry other arduous tasks...."

Although her parents did not have strong political opinions, they raised their daughter with a healthy dose of discipline and a fear of God, administering corporal punishment when necessary and faithfully attending church. The Caldwells' strict approach to running a household gave their daughter a strong sense of responsibility. "I was earning my spending money when I was seven after I finished my school work and chores at home," she recalled.

Just before her family moved to America, the seeds of Caldwell's conservatism were unwittingly planted by a "bleeding-heart" relative. In *On Growing Up Tough*, Caldwell wrote of her liberal aunt in England, whose "passion for the poor" manifested itself in two curious ways. First, her aunt would keep as much distance as possible between herself and the poor; second, "Auntie would frequently gather together outworn garments which her family had discarded and prepare them for the Women's Guild of our local Anglican Church. Singing some sad Scots or Irish ballad in a very moving soprano, she would carefully snip every single button off the clothing."

When the young Caldwell asked her aunt how the poor are supposed to wear clothes without buttons, the aunt is said to have shrieked, "A wicked, wicked girl. She has no heart for the poor!" Her button-snipping aunt was matched by Caldwell's uncle, who also loved the poor he had never met. He bellowed something about "impudence" and proceeded to thrash his niece for asking questions about the button-snipping. Of this experience, Caldwell wrote: "Thrift is an estimable virtue, but somehow when I encounter thrifty liberals — and they are inevitably tight with their own money — I always seem to see those damned buttons being snipped off the clothing for the poor. To this day I often find myself referring to male and female liberals as 'Mr. Buttons' and 'Mrs. Buttons.'"

Factual fiction: Caldwell's novels about the age-old battle between freedom and slavery are in many respects more accurate than what now passes for history. In *A Pillar of Iron*, she recreated the life and times of Cicero, who fought to prevent the transformation of the Roman republic into a despotic empire. In *Captains and the Kings* and *Ceremony of the Innocent*, she warned against a modern-day conspiracy to, as she put it, "drive freedom off the face of the earth."

A similar incident a few years later added nourishment to the seed of conservatism that had been planted by her experience with her aunt and uncle. Shortly after her family moved from England to Buffalo, New York, Caldwell began attending school and, at age 11, was "just about as happy as a child that age can be." But her contentment was soon shattered when one of those "new" teachers marinated in "new" ideas began to play the race card. One day, Caldwell recalled in her vivid essay "Irma Jones

Never Came Back," the teacher, whom Caldwell had taken to calling "Miss Blank," abruptly pointed out that Caldwell's bright, talented friend, Irma Jones, was black. "Miss Blank's suffused eye slowly settled on Irma Jones," said Caldwell, at which point the teacher began her sermon. "You must not despise Irma because she is a … Negress," pontificated the teacher. "She cannot help it. You must not look at her color. She is just as human as the rest of you." Caldwell and her fellow students sat in stunned and amazed silence, as they had never thought Irma any different from themselves, except that she had "nicer clothes" and "a more indulgent mother" and "somewhat better manners" than most other children.

Not yet satisfied with the dissension she had sown, Miss Blank directed her diatribe at other students. "Nor," sang Miss Blank, "must you hate Fanny and Anna because they are Jews. You must love them dearly … in spite of what you are taught in your Sunday schools." Finally, the teacher's gaze settled on Taylor Caldwell. "And there's Janet Caldwell. In spite of the American Revolution, you must not hate Janet because she was born in England!"

Caldwell's response is best described by the author herself: "I am usually a peaceful person, slow to wrath. But what I had witnessed … filled me with the blackest rage. I stood up and hurled a book at Miss Blank. It caught her smartly on the cheek and she howled and fell sideways. Then I went to the door, followed by whistles and jeers and exclamations of dismay."

Irma transferred to another school, as did Fanny and Anna. But Caldwell's action of throwing a book at a mushy-minded teacher ended up being an apt metaphor for the author's life. As an intensely patriotic author, Caldwell would continue "throwing the book" at liberals and subversives, one novel — or essay — at a time.

But Caldwell first had to deal with the vicissitudes of growing up. By all accounts, she grew up quickly, taking a job at a local grocery store at the age of 10 due to the family's financial problems and a personal desire to succeed. She also took a full-time job in a factory at age 15, and pursued secretarial training and earned a high school degree by taking night classes. In 1919, she married a handsome West Virginian, William Fairfax Combs, and homesteaded with him in Appalachia. They had one child, Mary Margaret.

When financial problems encroached on the young family's tough but idyllic life, Caldwell and her daughter moved back to Buffalo, where, in 1923, Caldwell became a court reporter for the New York State Department of Labor. Combs joined them for a time, and Caldwell began attending night classes at the University of Buffalo, receiving her B.A. in 1931. That same year saw the end of her marriage with Combs. Prior to earning her degree, she started working for the U.S. Department of Immigration and Naturalization in Buffalo. There she met Marcus Reback, whom she married in 1931. Caldwell would spend the happiest and most productive years of her life with Reback, who became her adviser, research assistant, and business manager during her many successful, yet trying, years behind her typewriter.

Reback had seen his new wife's unpublished manuscripts and realized that she had a genuine talent. With his help, Caldwell scored her first breakthrough by finishing *Dynasty of Death* and striking a deal with Scribner's Sons to have it published. Released in 1938, the novel centered around the intrigues and machinations of a munitions dynasty. It portrayed the munitions industry as a key, perhaps dominant, clique in sowing the seeds of war and revolution. *Dynasty of Death* was an immediate bestseller, and in literary circles Caldwell was lauded as "a female American Balzac." Her first three novels sold well in excess of two million hardbound copies.

Millions of readers in America and abroad were intrigued with the way Caldwell mingled compelling facts with fiction and wove her stirring views on world affairs into the fabric of her writings.

The conspiratorially orchestrated transition from a free, republican form of government to a despotic empire is a recurring theme in many of Caldwell's novels.

Caldwell successfully used this general formula for the rest of her career.

From 1938 through 1951, Caldwell's typewriter must have literally smoked as she cranked out one novel per year, except for 1939. This pace barely abated, even as recently as the 1970s. "Steamroller" was how she was described by one early critic, who was intrigued by the content of her writings as well as taken aback by the sheer volume. Another critic, writing in the *New York Times* in 1945, called her "one of the most industrious of our contemporary novelists." The *Times* critic, who had reviewed her novel *The Wide House* that year, said that while its style was "creaking and antiquated," the book was "still surprisingly effective." Her characters, he opined, may be "caricatures" but they "never lack vitality and force. Her story may be fantastic, but there is plenty of it. Things keep happening in these tumultuous pages."

The factual elements of her fictional works continued to zero in on freedom's real enemies, and the inclusion of Communists on her list of real-world subversives would arouse the ire of the dupes and operatives in the conspiratorial network; consequently, softball reviews that mainly took exception with matters of style did not remain the norm. A "shot over the bow" from the left was fired on May 19, 1947, when *Time* magazine published a scathing review of *There Was a Time*, Caldwell's novel of that year. Complete with perhaps the most unflattering photograph of the novelist that one could imagine, the diatribe, written by former Communist Whittaker Chambers, was chock full of verbal shards.

Chambers scribbled that the novel "has the color-blind prose and inability to distinguish real emotions from salable affectations...." He also fumed that the book's main character, "flaccid Frank Clair," is a frustrated artist who becomes a "literary prostitute" and pens some "poisoned pap" that focuses on "international bankers who cunningly and sedulously plotted wars for their own profit...." Chambers also levied personal remarks, referring to the author as "sickly Author Caldwell" while throwing in sarcastic observations about her childhood and her life with Marcus Reback. Taylor Caldwell, who considered it a sport to fire back at leftists in general and literary southpaws in particular, quickly sent a letter to *Time's* editor and then wrote several articles over the years about her experiences with Chambers and other hostile reviewers.

In her letter to *Time*, published June 23, 1947, she wrote that she had read Chambers' review while at her ill husband's bedside in Geneva. She stated that the "alleged critic" should have stuck to his sophomoric criticism of the book itself and should not have resorted to personal attacks. After pointing out that she gives large portions of her royalties to charities (Chambers had portrayed her as a wealthy skinflint), she showed her caustic sense of humor when she inquired, "Where did you get that dreadful photograph? It shows me to be snaggletooth, whereas my teeth are white and even small." Many years later, in the January-February 1964 issue of *Fact* magazine, Caldwell, who didn't mind using an occasional expletive to make a point, recalled, "I wrote Chambers five times asking why he had attacked me so maliciously but the b*****d never replied. The horror of it is that excerpts from Chambers' ridiculing article keep reappearing in the press after nearly 20 years."

Unfortunately, by the early 1950s, scathing reviews gave way to actual harassment of Caldwell, especially after her novels *The Balance Wheel* (1951) and *The Devil's Advocate* (1952) were published. The latter — a futuristic look at a Communist America in

the tradition of George Orwell's *1984* — was so controversial, Caldwell recalled, that Scribner's Sons decided not to publish the book, forcing her to find another publisher. Even worse, "the U.S. government came down on me furiously for daring to write anti-communist books," Caldwell wrote. "The government warned us repeatedly to stop our anti-communist activities.... We didn't stop."

Over the years she repeatedly proved that she wouldn't back down, specifical-

Caustic critic: Whittaker Chambers wrote a scathing review of Caldwell's 1947 novel *There Was a Time* for *Time* magazine. That review constituted the American Establishment's "shot over the bow" against the embattled author and was still quoted decades later.

ly describing in several of her novels the plot to establish a world government. She also included references to one "Colonel" Edward Mandell House, the shadowy right-hand man of President Woodrow Wilson. House's grubby fingerprints were all over America's involvement in World War I, the post-war effort to create the League of Nations, the establishment of the Federal Reserve System, and the creation of the Council on Foreign Relations. Caldwell, who had an uncanny

habit of naming real names and telling it like it is, was indeed a force to reckon with.

Many of her characters, as has already been noted, struggled against great odds to preserve the American republic. Likewise, Caldwell's real-life struggle to do the same ran into a variety of serious roadblocks — not the least of which was the IRS. To defend themselves, Caldwell and her husband even enlisted the help of the FBI, arranging to have their house bugged and their phone tapped so that their conversations with intrusive IRS agents could be recorded.

This gathering of information and the "grace of God," said Caldwell, were the only things that prevented hostile elements within the U.S. government from destroying her writing career. But her career already had been hobbled by newspaper accounts that portrayed her as a "tax evader" and by extremely unfair and arbitrary rules under which the IRS didn't allow the author and her husband the normal expense deductions routinely afforded to other authors. "I have met writers beloved of the Communist Party USA in New York, and they tell me they never have to pay Fed tax," Caldwell noted, perhaps with a bit of exaggeration. "Treason, it seems, pays off...."

Nevertheless, she continued her career with dogged determination. Her many insightful essays in *American Opinion* (a precursor to THE NEW AMERICAN), and her membership in the John Birch Society, indicated that while hostile forces had instilled in her a sometimes deep cynicism bordering on defeatism, she could still summon the strength and courage to fight back as an essayist and citizen-activist, as well as a novelist. She proved herself able to withstand virtually anything, even a March 20, 1967 home invasion and attempted murder the day after she and her husband had returned to their Buffalo residence from a vacation.

Caldwell, whose essay in the *Buffalo Evening News* that year described this life-changing event, recalled that two strange men who pretended to be delivering a telegram forced their way into her home. Marcus Reback was brutally subdued by one of the armed men; the other went after Caldwell and pistol-whipped her while trying to strangle and smother her. Caldwell, true to her nature, valiantly resisted, much to the frustration of her masked attacker, who muttered "I'm going to kill you" and then demanded, "Where's your jewelry, Mrs. Reback?" Caldwell later reflected that only two people besides her husband knew that her jewelry was still in the house and hadn't yet been returned to a safe-deposit box after the vacation. The assailants also seemed to know the unusual layout of the large house exceedingly well. But Caldwell's housekeeper, Mrs. Graham, had managed to call the police from a private room and the intruders fled, narrowly escaping capture.

This 10 minutes of terror, which convinced the Rebacks to purchase a gun, may have been perpetrated by garden-variety criminals in search of easy loot, but Caldwell suspected that the attack had been ordered by higher-ups who had resorted to force when smears and other tactics to erase or subdue her influence had failed. The attack itself was bad enough, but the truly tragic result was that her beloved husband, who was 78 at the time, never fully recovered from it. The brave defender and promoter of her literary works died less than three years later.

Thanks in no small measure to Marcus Reback's assistance, the 1960s had been a banner decade for the author's career. During those years she cranked out eight novels, including the *tour de force*, *A Pillar of Iron* (1965). The story of Marcus Tullius Cicero (106-43 B.C.), *A Pillar of Iron* portrayed in vivid detail the drama of the great Roman scholar, orator, lawyer, and statesman striving to preserve the Roman republic from threats external and internal. Tying the past to the present, she observed in the foreword of this book:

The histories of the Roman Republic and the United States of America are oddly parallel, such as Cincinnatus, "the father of his country," strangely like George Washington. Present politicians may find many of their private images in Catilina, and many of their secret desires. Were Cicero alive in the America of today he would be aghast and appalled. He would find it so familiar.

Dogged determination: Caldwell could have backed down when the opinion cartel trashed her works and refused to give her the literary recognition she deserved. But Caldwell continued to write what was right and true.

Varden Studio, Buffalo, NY

In her own way, Caldwell warned against the decline of the American republic, just as Cicero had warned against the decline of the Roman republic two millennia earlier. Cicero's speeches on treason in Rome boomed through the Forum before throngs of onlookers; Caldwell's writings reverberated around the world, warning free people everywhere that liberty was not a natural condition of human societies, but must be constitutionally established and vigilantly protected by an in-

"Amid the almost universal treason of the intellectuals, Taylor Caldwell stands proud and firm for sanity and freedom — a brilliant artist, a wise philosopher, a great woman."

— E. Merrill Root
Poet, Essayist, Author

formed and moral populace.

To that end she completed in 1972 the monumental *Captains and the Kings*, her boldest attempt to point out the existence of a real conspiracy operating behind the scenes to destroy America. Caldwell even included in the novel a lengthy bibliography of nonfiction books so the reader could do more research on the Conspiracy and (hopefully) get involved. In the novel's foreword she warned:

There is not, to my knowledge, any family like the "Armagh Family" in America … and all characters, except those obviously historical, are my own invention. However, the historical background and the political background of this novel are authentic. The "Committee for Foreign Studies" does indeed exist, today as of yesterday, and so does the "Scardo Society," but not by these names.

There is indeed a "plot against the people," and probably always will be, for government has always been hostile towards the governed. It is not a new story, and the conspirators and conspiracies have varied from era to era, depending on the political or economic situation in their various countries.

But it was not until the era of the League of Just Men and Karl Marx that conspirators and conspiracies became one, with one aim, one objective, and one determination. This has nothing to do with "ideology" or form of government, or ideals or "materialism" or any other catch-phrases generously fed to the unthinking masses. It has absolutely nothing to do with races or religions, for the conspirators are beyond what they call "such trivialities." They are also beyond good and evil. The Caesars they put into power are their creatures, whether they know it or not, and the peoples of all nations are helpless.... They will always be helpless until they are aware of their real enemy....

This is probably the last hour for mankind as a rational species, before it becomes the slave of a "planned society." A bibliography ends this book, and I hope many of my readers will avail themselves of the facts. That is all the hope I have.

Captains and the Kings, considered by some to be loosely based on the life of the Kennedy family, hit the bestseller list of the *New York Times* immediately upon its release. Later it became the basis for a mid-1970s television miniseries starring popular actress Jane Seymour.

Infinitely more could be said about the life and works of such a prolific writer. While in many respects she was a very private person and few people knew her intimately, she revealed herself to be of a bittersweet disposition. Although a sense of defeat sometimes engulfed her, she was imbued with an unstoppable determination to succeed, a cutting sense of humor, and an eye for the truth that delighted fans but made critics gnash their teeth.

Caldwell once summarized how the critics had turned on her when her books began to cut too close to the truth. "From being a female Balzac, I became a 'worthless, housewife scribbler.' From 'writing lyrically and with wonderful descriptive power,' my writing became 'copy-book rococo,' and worse." She also noted that the titles of her novels would sometimes prematurely disappear off the

New York Times bestseller list without explanation. But her talent and popularity could not be fully ignored or erased. Even *Life* magazine, not exactly a shimmering beacon of conservatism, conceded: "The lofty peaks of best sellerdom are traditionally difficult to scale ... but there are three American novelists who've climbed to the top not once or twice, but over and over again. In so doing, they

March of time: Caldwell tirelessly fought the enemies of freedom over many decades. Although her favorite weapon was the novel, she also sounded the alarm as an essayist and as a citizen-activist.

Varden Studio, Buffalo, NY

have established themselves as an elite among fiction writers. All three are women: Edna Ferber, Frances Parkinson Keyes and Taylor Caldwell."

Besides being lauded by her loyal readership, Caldwell was admired by fellow patriots who, like her, steadfastly refused to back down in the face of freedom's enemies. She became a life member of the John Birch Society and received a special Society award inscribed with the words "great American patriot and scholar." She was in close correspondence for several years with JBS founder Robert Welch, with whom

she shared insights on the state of the world and the machinations of the powers that be.

Captains and the Kings and a follow-up book, *Ceremony of the Innocent* (1976), were among Caldwell's last works, but they were also among her best. In their breadth, depth, characterization, and intense focus on a conspiratorial design that threatened the free world, they formed a double-barreled shot over the bow of tyranny. In the latter, the fictitious Congressman Jeremy Porter, speaking to unsympathetic fellow legislators who were about to censure him for daring to expose the conspiratorial plans for global control, courageously declared:

I tell you gentlemen that the Apocalypse is upon us, and from this time henceforth there will be no peace in this tormented world, only a programmed and systematic series of wars and calamities — until the plotters have gained their objective: an exhausted world willing to submit to a planned Marxist economy and total and meek enslavement, in the name of peace.... They want to destroy the middle class, which stands between them and the exercise of the tyranny they want.

Taylor Caldwell worked tirelessly to forestall in America the onset of the tyranny that so often formed the backdrop of her novels. But the bestselling novelist who had "grown up tough" could not forestall the inexorable march of time. She passed away in 1985 at the home in Connecticut she shared with her last husband, Robert Prestie. Of her, the great poet, essayist, and author E. Merrill Root wrote: "Amid the almost universal treason of the intellectuals, Taylor Caldwell stands proud and firm for sanity and freedom — a brilliant artist, a wise philosopher, a great woman." ■

Freedom Activism

The fight to preserve freedom requires that its enemies be exposed, confronted, and — God willing — defeated. Each of the heroes profiled in this section recognized and acted upon this responsibility.

Economist John T. Flynn was such an effective critic of the Roosevelt administration's collectivist policies and foreign adventurism that FDR personally undertook to ruin him. As a leader of the America First Committee, Flynn warned that entanglement in foreign wars would eventually mean the end of our free republic.

As chairman of the House Committee on Un-American Activities in the 1930s, Martin Dies, a Democrat congressman from Texas, fought to expose the extent to which the federal government had been infiltrated with Communists and fellow subversives. At every step his efforts were hindered by FDR and his subordinates.

With the possible — and well-deserved — exception of the murderous Adolf Hitler, no human being who lived in the 20th century has been more heartily despised than Senator Joseph McCarthy. The much-maligned Senate investigator understood that Communism was not an ideology in which people believe, but a criminal conspiracy in which people participate — and that service in a position of government trust was incompatible with membership in such a criminal cabal. Time — and access to previously inaccessible archival material — has vindicated McCarthy's investigations.

Dan Smoot pulled himself up by his bootstraps. The one-time hobo worked his way to a Harvard degree and a position as an investigator for J. Edgar Hoover's FBI. Smoot was among the first to understand the educational potential of mass media such as radio and television, which he used to educate the public in Americanist principles and to expose the machinations of freedom's enemies. Smoot was also among the first to expose and document the malign influence of America's "invisible government," the Council on Foreign Relations.

Organized evil must be countered with organized defense of truth. Robert Welch, a former child prodigy and brilliant businessman, acted upon this principle in 1958 by organizing the John Birch Society to give institutional continuity to the fight to preserve freedom.

Principles First

Old-school "liberal" John T. Flynn fought for limited government and noninterventionism against the rising tides of socialism and militarism.

by John F. McManus

It's hardly a bombshell to report that labels can be misleading. But trying to pin one on John T. Flynn must have been a daunting exercise. Flynn considered himself a "liberal" throughout his entire life. Yet, when his fellow liberals cast aside the principles of limited government and a noninterventionist foreign policy in favor of President Franklin D. Roosevelt's socialistic New Deal and America's entry into World War II, Flynn refused to go along with the pack. He used his influential pen as a "liberal" journalist to warn against the totalitarian implications of both the Welfare State and the Warfare State, and for this he became anathema to America's power elite. FDR so feared Flynn's powerful pen that he personally tried to blacklist him and drive him into obscurity.

As he began his journalistic career, Flynn focused on economic topics and regularly targeted big business, particularly monopolies. But by the time he retired in 1960, he had become the ultimate "Old Right" conservative — the ardent foe of the total state represented by Rooseveltian liberalism, Fabian socialism, Italian and German fascism, and Soviet Communism.

In her 1976 study, *An American First: John T. Flynn and the America First Committee*, Flynn's daughter, Michele Flynn Stenehjem, offered a definition of what her father's brand of liberalism entailed:

John Flynn and other America Firsters believed that government should regulate business by preventing monopolies and cartels from controlling large sectors of the economy. However, Flynn and his colleagues did not think that government itself should become a large economic power. This condition would restrict individual freedom, which was the essence of their definition of liberalism.... Flynn and his colleagues rejected

Franklin D. Roosevelt's brand of liberalism, in which government entered the economic community as a large employer and customer.

John T. Flynn was born on October 25, 1882 in Bladensburg, Maryland, near the nation's capital. He never attended college but graduated from Georgetown Law School a few years after the turn of the century. Even though he was the son of an attorney, he never practiced law but worked as a clerk in his father's office. He passionately wanted to be a writer, and in 1916 he began his journalism career by accepting a post at Connecticut's *New Haven Register*. By 1920, he went to New York where he was hired as financial editor and soon became managing editor of the *New York Globe*. When that newspaper went under in 1923, he turned to freelance writing.

While never ceasing his criticism of unrestrained big business, Flynn soon began criticizing big government as well. In 1932, he eagerly supported the candidacy of Franklin Delano Roosevelt. Like many others, he was lured to do so by a belief that the candidate would adhere to the promises in the Democratic Party's platform, which called for: an end to the extravagant spending of the Republicans under Herbert Hoover; a balanced budget; and the elimination of an array of federal bureaus, agencies, and commissions. He was also impressed by Roosevelt's campaign oratory against welfare and his demands for across-the-board cuts in federal spending.

After he took office in March 1933, FDR quickly abandoned his campaign promises in favor of greater spending, a huge boost in the federal deficit, and far more bureaus, agencies and commissions than before. More courageous than others, Flynn spoke out against this betrayal.

Flynn began achieving national attention in 1933 with a column entitled "Other People's Money" in the very liberal *New Republic*. He also wrote for *Harper's* and *Collier's*, supplied a syndicated column for the Scripps-Howard chain, and provided a series of articles he la-

"A born militarist": According to Flynn, FDR (shown aboard *USS Indianapolis*) led U.S. into war.

beled "Plain Economics" for newspapers in New York and Washington.

In the mid-1930s, America was mired in the Great Depression. The major element of Roosevelt's New Deal, the National Recovery Administration (NRA), created a maze of regulation over practically every aspect of business and industry. Flynn wasted little time in calling the NRA, enacted in 1933, a grave attack on fundamental American principles. Writing in the September 1934 issue of *Harper's*, he thundered: "Regimentation of American life means forming society into regiments, subjecting it to orders, drills, commanders."

At the time, Flynn expected some of his liberal colleagues to assist in slaying the NRA monster. At the close of his *Harper's* article, he forecast grave consequences for the nation "unless liberals maintain a more effective vigilance than they have in the past." But he soon found that most of his liberal friends succumbed to the power wielded by the White House and supported FDR's every wish. Nevertheless, he must have enjoyed some consolation when the Supreme Court declared the NRA unconstitutional.

By the mid-1930s, Flynn realized that his defense of true liberalism had become a lonely endeavor. Yet, he fought on with characteristic courage and integrity. His column in *The New Republic* lashed out at FDR's escalating deficits, faulted the newly created Securities and Exchange Commission as a toothless compromise with Wall Street, and described the Social Security Act as laudable in principle

but potentially dangerous because of the way it would be financed.

By 1936, his illusions about FDR long gone, he stated in a speech broadcast by radio that the President was "a born militarist." With great foresight, he worried that FDR would "do his best to entangle us" in an eventual European war and that he was "engaged in a desperate attempt to break down the democratic system in America."

In a September 1937 *Collier's* article, Flynn targeted the government's fraudulent practice of lending money it had created out of thin air. In a bow to the Constitution's separation of powers, he pointed out that various government bureaus were "supplying one another with money as part of this new system of eliminating Congress from its historic role of controlling the purse strings."

After several years of watching government programs shovel freshly created money at farmers and home owners, Flynn noted that "the government today holds twice as many home mortgages as all the commercial banks in the country put together, more than all life insurance companies or more than all the savings banks, and more, even, than the 8,000 building and loan associations combined." He targeted the Reconstruction Finance Corporation (RFC) as "the biggest and most sensational of all the government lending plants." But he also made the point that the RFC had been created during the Hoover administration, adding the telling point that it was "roundly criticized by Candidate Roo-

Flynn wanted Americans to realize that our nation was being undermined from within to accept a despotic ideology, writing in 1941: "Fascism is not the result of dictatorship. Fascism is the consequence of economic jam and dictatorship is the product of Fascism, for Fascism cannot be managed save by a dictator."

sevelt, and then adopted and enlarged by him" after taking office.

In 1939, Flynn was stunned when FDR tapped Harry Hopkins, his Works Progress Administration head, for Secretary of Commerce. Flynn's attitude about Hopkins was that he was "an able welfare worker wandering in a couple of strange jungles — a babe lost in two woods — business and politics." His "Mr. Hopkins and Mr. Roosevelt" column in the *Yale Review*, however, was much more an attack on the President than on Hopkins.

FDR, who was aware of Flynn's attacks on his policies, was enraged by this column. He fired off a letter to the *Yale Review's* editor claiming that Flynn was "a destructive rather than a constructive force" whose work "should be barred from … any presentable daily paper, monthly magazine or national quarterly." Before too long, that is precisely what happened. Historian Harry Elmer Barnes would write years later: "Probably the most extreme job of smearing ever turned in on a liberal who attacked the foreign policy of Roosevelt was done on John T. Flynn." Barnes also made the point that Flynn's "erstwhile liberal admirers, who had taken to warmongering, turned on him savagely."

As signs multiplied that Roosevelt was preparing to take the nation into war, Flynn and several other "noninterventionists," a term they always preferred to "isolationists," gath-

ered in mid-1938 to form the Keep America Out of War Committee (KAOWC) with Flynn as its national chairman. Unlike the soon-to-be-formed America First Committee (AFC), KAOWC wasn't a membership organization but a small circle of prestigious individuals who would coordinate the activities of several smaller groups. In 1940, when Roosevelt proposed sending 50 destroyers to England for her use in the ongoing war with Germany, Flynn not only objected but labeled the move a grave usurpation of power and called for impeachment of the President.

Allies for America: Retired General Robert Wood joined with Flynn and others to form the noninterventionist America First Committee.

Hammering away at what he contended were the inevitably destructive fruits of war, Flynn wrote in 1940: "The real peril of war lies not in military defeat. It lies in war itself, whether we win or lose." And he repeatedly identified its chief fruits as a controlled society and enormous national debt. He also accused the President of turning to war and the preparations for war as one way of

pulling the nation out of the still-existing depression.

Perhaps the greatest example of his foresight during this period was his concern that the American people were being led to believe that, no matter what problem they faced, the answer was government intervention. He wrote: "Thus the young and the old, the manufacturer, the farmer, the laborer, the little merchant and the big merchant, all swell the chorus of demand for order, law, regulation, rule — control." He warned against subjecting the capitalist system to "extensive controls," and he pointed out that those controls could be made to succeed "only when backed up by a grim and ruthless authoritarian government which enforces compliance with an iron hand."

America, he contended, was headed in the direction of fascism. Nations don't succumb to fascism "at one fell dive," he wrote in 1940, but through a series of steps that few recognize for the harm they do. Combining his intense abhorrence of war with a growing fear that America would adopt the fascism of Italy or Germany, he summarized: "We seem to be a long way off from the kind of Fascism which we behold in Italy today, but we are not so far from the kind of Fascism which Mussolini preached in Italy *before* he assumed power, and we are slowly approaching the conditions which made Fascism there possible. All that is needed to set us definitely on the road to a Fascist society is war. It will of course be a modified form of Fascism at first. But Fascism cannot continue in a modified form…. Thus, though Hitler will never come here to impose his Fascist abom-

Rally 'round the flag: The America First Committee's rally at Madison Square Garden drew 50,000 attendees.

ination upon us, we may go to him to impose it upon ourselves."

Continuing his warnings about growing fascism in America, he wrote in 1941 that it should not be associated with "such grotesque and futile excrescences as the Bunds, Christian fronts, and the like." He wanted the docile American people to realize that our nation was being undermined from within to accept a despotic ideology. Taking aim at the "self-appointed" intellectuals on whom he blamed the transformation, he wrote: "They think that to be a Fascist you must have some sort of shirt uniform, must drill and goose-step, must have a demonstrative salute, must hate the Jews, and believe in dictatorship. Fascism is not the result of dictatorship. Fascism is the consequence of economic jam and dictator-

ship is the product of Fascism, for Fascism cannot be managed save by a dictator."

In August 1940, Flynn and retired Army General Robert A. Wood, the head of Sears, Roebuck and Company, gathered with several others to form the noninterventionist America First Committee (AFC). Differing markedly from KAOWC's intellectual approach and its distance from the people, AFC was to be a mass movement formed to unite large numbers of citizens around the issue of keeping the nation out of war. Almost immediately, chapters were established all over America. In time, AFC grew to include 800,000 members.

During late 1940 as Roosevelt campaigned for a third term, Flynn became convinced of the need for a vigorous AFC chapter in New York, the "interventionist capital city." Flynn initially declined the chairmanship of this chapter because of his writing commitments and his desire to serve the effort mostly as a journalist, but he accepted the post in January 1941 and devoted great energy to the task. In time, Flynn's jurisdiction extended to 84 separate chapters in greater New York, and he maintained an advisory role over chapters in several surrounding states.

Ever the journalist, Flynn took a major role in the organization's publicity campaigns. Beyond writing or editing all of the chapter's literature, he delivered a public speech or a radio address every five days. The pamphlets he produced were adopted and used by the national AFC. He also created several advertisements to focus attention on the many

horrible consequences of war. Stenehjem reported that one ad, reprinted by the AFC nationwide, posed the frightening thought: "The Last War Brought: Communism to Russia, Fascism to Italy, Nazism to Germany. What Will Another War Bring To America?"

When members badgered NYC-AFC's executive board for more dramatic programs, Flynn agreed to hold huge rallies, six of which the group eventually sponsored. The largest of these, held at Madison Square Garden, attracted approximately 50,000 people. But he vetoed several proposals, including the call for a march on Washington, out of fear that participants might become disorderly and harm the group's reputation.

Flynn contended that a conspiracy involving the mass media and the motion picture industry was assisting the forces of intervention and dishonestly smearing AFC as pro-fascist and anti-Semitic. Stenehjem related Flynn's statements at a December 1940 Chicago AFC rally: "The plain and terrifying fact is that this great and peaceful nation is in the grip of one of the most subtle and successful conspiracies … to embroil us in a foreign war."

Ever the researcher, Flynn examined the most prominent pro-intervention organization, the Committee to Defend America by Aiding the Allies, and found that this group had been cooperating with several prominent interventionist journalists and motion picture producers. He then discovered links between these various pro-war elements and both the Roosevelt administration and the British government. He pointed to "great sums of money … being spent on [interventionist] literature and advertisements, frequently by persons or organizations which could hardly be supposed to have such funds at their disposal."

Flynn's research efforts also uncovered plots to infiltrate NYC-AFC for the purpose of disrupting its proceedings and discrediting the organization with outrageous outbursts. When an unknown individual shouted "Hang Roosevelt" at an AFC Madison Square Garden rally, there was little doubt that the intent was

to invite condemnation of the entire movement.

NYC-AFC commissioned polls to counter the Gallup and Roper surveys that its own research had determined were biased in favor of war. One AFC poll, questioning every voter in a New York-area congressional district, found 90 percent of respondents opposed to entry into a war. A *New York Daily News* poll, paid for by Flynn out of his own pocket, contacted ten percent of New York State's voters and found 70 percent opposed.

But Pearl Harbor changed everything. The America First Committee disbanded immediately, and many of its young members volunteered for military duty. Flynn himself completely supported the war effort. Stenehjem noted, however, that her father's opponents in the great debate over entry into the war didn't cease their campaign against him. She reported: "However, when attacks against America First continued for years after the committee dissolved, Flynn became angry and renewed his investigations. His discoveries were to shock him deeply and to have a seminal effect on his later view of life in the United States."

Fighting against militarism and exposing the plans of FDR proved costly to John Flynn. At *The New Republic*, editors had begun appending comments to his "Other People's Money" column claiming that his anti-militarism attitude was "nonsense" and that he was guilty of "blindness" and "prejudice." So it came as no surprise in the fall of 1940 when the magazine dropped him as a contributor. In late 1941, Flynn confided to General Wood that one consequence of his efforts "has been that I have sacrificed all of my own personal income and even the connection out of which I made that income."

Even though he was denied access to many of his former readers and increasingly isolated in the journalistic world, Flynn still lashed out at FDR's treachery whenever he could get a hearing. Even prior to the end of the war, his uneasiness about FDR's every move

National Park Service

Infamous betrayal: *USS Arizona* at Pearl Harbor; Flynn worked heroically to uncover the Roosevelt administration's complicity in provoking and facilitating the "surprise" attack.

led him to investigate the events that led to Japan's December 7, 1941 attack at Pearl Harbor. Flynn published his findings in a 32-page October 1944 pamphlet entitled *The Truth About Pearl Harbor.* There was no shortage of criticism aimed at Flynn for questioning the nation's President while men were still fighting and dying. Opponents charged him with disloyalty; Flynn obviously felt otherwise.

Flynn reported that, by mid-1941, our nation was supplying arms, ammunition, planes, and naval vessels to the British and had sent troops to Iceland to join in the British occupation of the island. In addition, FDR had ordered our naval vessels to patrol the Atlantic for the purpose of locating German submarines and reporting those findings to the British, and directed other vessels to convoy British shipping. These were warlike acts, intended to provoke Germany to attack the U.S. In September 1941, the President announced that the *USS Greer* had been attacked while hunting a German sub.

As Flynn stated, "To say that we were not at war with Germany ... is to close our eyes to the truth." He pointed to a

speech given in 1943 by *New York Times* publisher Arthur Sulzberger wherein that pro-FDR partisan concluded: "I am not one of those who believed we entered the war because we were attacked at Pearl Harbor, but that we were attacked at Pearl Harbor because we were already at war."

By early 1941, claimed Flynn, the President had decided that war with Japan (an ally of Nazi Germany) would accomplish his goal. Hoping to provoke the Japanese to fire the first shot, he froze Japanese assets in the U.S., sent American pilots and planes to aid China in her war with Japan, ignored Japan's plans to leave China and terminate that war, and rejected an offer by Japanese Premier Konoye to meet with him in Hawaii to defuse escalating tensions between the two nations. As Flynn reported, Konoye's lack of success with FDR resulted in the downfall of Konoye's government and the rise to power of the far more militant Tojo. Finally, on November 26th, Secretary of State Cordell Hull presented the Japanese with an ultimatum they could not accept. War was now a certainty, and FDR and his top advisors knew it was.

ists, educators and high-ranking government officials — almost all Americans — to force the American State Department to betray China and Korea into the hands of the Communists." Chief among those he indicted, obviously, was Owen Lattimore, the man Senator Joseph McCarthy had earlier branded as a top Communist and the man the Senate Subcommittee on Internal Security had labeled "a conscious, articulate instrument of the Soviet conspiracy."

Flynn sprang to the defense of McCarthy with an article entitled "What is Senator McCarthy Really Trying to Do?" Answering his own question, Flynn wrote that McCarthy "is opposed to admitting Americans who are enemies of our American system of government — Communists or Socialists — into the Government of the United States." And he added, "I should like to inquire, what is wrong about it?"

In a separate article that same year, Flynn committed the unforgivable sin of exposing President Dwight Eisenhower's "Phoney War on Communism." Noting that the President had exhibited great concern about the threat of Communism in Europe, Asia, and Africa, he found it revealing that there wasn't any such concern about the threat in the United States. Not only was Eisenhower uninterested in domestic Communist subversion, Flynn wrote, he "actually takes assaults on American Communists as a personal affront. In the war on world Communism, he is a roaring lion. In the war on Communism at home, he is a critical and muttering lamb."

Calling the United Nations a "racket" in a 1955 piece, Flynn insisted that it was "not an instrument for preserving peace in the world." His recommendation was unequivocal: "We must rid this nation of the United Nations, which provides the communist conspiracy with a headquarters here on our own shores, and which actually makes it impossible for the United States to form its own decisions about its conduct and policies in Europe and Asia."

In 1956, when William F. Buckley, Jr. solicited an article for publication in his brand new *National Review*, Flynn jumped at the opportunity and sent one likening the Eisenhower administration to its New Deal predecessors. He argued that Eisenhower was continuing the militarism that formed the basis for "one of the oldest rackets in history … the use of government money, acquired through taxation and created by debt, to buy the votes of numerous minorities and thus remain in power." Buckley rejected the article, sent the author a check for $100 dollars (which Flynn returned), and in a letter chided Flynn for failing to appreciate the Buckley view of the Cold War. Previously spurned by liberals, then embraced by the Old Right, Flynn would henceforth be rejected by the New Right led by Buckley.

Flynn's health began to decline in 1958 and he retired from writing in 1960. He died peacefully in 1964.

John T. Flynn paid repeatedly for his commitment to freedom. His efforts surely bought time for those who came later and continued his fight for America. No greater honor could be paid him than achieving victory in the monumental struggle to which he devoted his life. ■

Americanist Chairman

Martin Dies, as chairman of the House Committee on Un-American Activities, fought a desperate battle to expose Red subversives.

by Jane H. Ingraham

W ho was Martin Dies? Why is he worthy of honorable recognition as one of our 20th century heroes? Unfortunately, his name draws a blank response from most people today. One is reminded of the wisdom of the poet's words that the good which men do is "oft interred with their bones." For the colossal good that this man did lies deeply buried in the past by the prevailing liberal Establishment that he strenuously opposed.

Martin Dies was a seemingly ordinary young Democrat congressman from Texas elected in 1930 to the House while still only 29 years old. Born in Colorado City, Texas, in November 1900, Dies grew up in East Texas, graduated from the University of Texas, and received his LL.B. degree in law from the National University in Washington, D.C., in 1920. In the same year, he married and began the practice of law in Marshall, Texas.

A rugged individualist from the beginning, Dies has been described as a husky six-footer with the bulldog look of a squared, cowpuncher face. But this man was far from ordinary — in fact, he was astonishing. Smack in the middle of the blatant pro-Communist climate in the wake of Franklin D. Roosevelt's ascendancy to the White House in 1933, Martin Dies, a Democrat, took it upon himself to buck his own party's rabid opposition to investigating Communist subversion and infiltration of government, academia, labor unions, and the media. He became the first chairman of the House Committee on Un-American Activities in 1938 and led its efforts until 1945. For effectively exposing Communist subversion he was viciously attacked, just as Senator Joseph McCarthy was in the 1950s.

In this day of the supposed "end of Communism" it is difficult to understand the sacrifice and courage Dies' decision meant in the 1930s. The influx of Marxists, pinkos, socialists, fellow

travelers, and New Deal leftists who followed Roosevelt to Washington had taken over all forums and drowned out other voices.

Prior to Roosevelt, four Presidents had refused to recognize the Soviet Union, so revolted were they by the Soviet's brutality, perfidy, and revolutionary aim of overturning governments and social institutions worldwide. Yet in 1933, much to Dies' dismay, Roosevelt handed Soviet envoy Maxim Litvinoff a letter of recognition in exchange for a letter promising that the Soviets would not allow subversive groups to operate in the United States. The next day, the Communist International announced it would pursue exactly such activities while Litvinoff assured the comrades that the letter was a mere scrap of paper that would soon be forgotten in the realities of Soviet-American relations.

Following U.S. recognition of the Soviet Union, the picture of Washington —

Opposition from the top: Martin Dies, as chairman of the House Committee on Un-American Activities, ran into opposition from President Roosevelt when the committee started investigating Communists. As Dies recalled, Roosevelt once stated: "Well, you know, all this business about investigating Communists is a serious mistake."

as described by Dies in his 1943 book *The Trojan Horse in America* and in his 1963 autobiography *Martin Dies' Story* — defies belief. It was literally open-house at the White House for revolutionaries of every stripe, including Earl Browder, General Secretary of the American Communist Party, who came and went at his pleasure even though deserving Democrats could not gain an audience with the President. Communists, fellow travelers, socialists, and, of course, the indispensable dupes were all protected, encouraged, and even pardoned for unlawful acts by the Roosevelt administration. A sort of pro-Marxist frenzy swept over Washington. Businessmen were encouraged to give away trade secrets and technical know-how to the Soviets. High U.S. government officials were in frequent attendance at Soviet Embassy parties, where there was plenty of champagne and much talk of revolution, including such plans as requiring corporations to have a federal permit in order to operate. It was against this Red tide that an alarmed and distressed Martin Dies decided to swim.

Aware that the growing strength of the American Communist Party depended largely on subversives who were not even American citizens, Dies' first move was to introduce a bill to exclude and deport alien Reds. But his warning that the American Communist Party was "directed and controlled by Moscow," recently substantiated by the release of KGB files, was mocked. And his bill, which passed the House, was prevented from coming to a vote (and was therefore allowed to die) in the Senate by liberals led by Robert LaFollette of Wisconsin.

But Dies had just begun. In 1938 he accepted Roosevelt's urgent plea to chair an investigation into un-American activities. It is something of a puzzle as to why Roosevelt wanted such an investigation and wanted Dies to head it. Dies came to believe that Roosevelt felt confident he could force the committee to limit its investigation to Nazis and Fascists. But master of manipulation that Roosevelt was, it's more likely that his real objective was to cause Communism to be sen-

When Dies made it clear he intended to fully investigate Communism, liberal reaction was sure and swift. Every federal department, especially the Department of Justice, which Dies had expected would provide information, rejected his requests and refused to cooperate.

sationalized as the *only enemy*, thus diverting attention from his own seizure of power, while media ridicule of accusations of Communists in high places would cause Dies' claims to be discredited. Something of this sort did, indeed, happen.

When Dies made it clear he intended to fully investigate Communism as a kissing-cousin of the other two totalitarian "isms," the liberal reaction was sure and swift. Every federal department, especially the Justice Department, which Dies had expected would provide information, rejected his requests and refused to cooperate.

Although it was common knowledge that under President Herbert Hoover the records of the Communist Party, including its full membership list, had been seized by the government, these records had been destroyed or disappeared. Dies was forced to begin from scratch in an atmosphere that could not have been more hostile. Government employees became indignant and abusive, ridiculing the Committee's documented findings and parading in protest. Men and women in high positions were sponsoring, endorsing, or joining front organizations that supported Communist "ideals." Government officials defended employees found to be disloyal, refusing to fire them. Yet during the seven years that Dies chaired the House Committee on Un-American Activities, which became almost universally known as the Dies Committee, open hearings were held in every principal American city (where they were disrupted by riotous mobs), and a tremendous record of Communist subversive activities was amassed through the seizure of records of 160 Communist organizations.

Specifically, what kind of activities was the Committee charged with exposing as un-American? Obviously, rooting out disloyal government employees was of prime importance. Dies cited examples of the kind of routine hiring that was going on; for instance, a fellow named John Herling was offered a government post which he declined in writing, stating that he believed "in the abolition of the capitalist system." Herling also scorned the administration's radicals who tried to rationalize the need for the position. In other words, here was a man rejecting a New Deal job because it wasn't Red enough. Eventually, however, he was mollified and persuaded to accept the post of principal consultant to the Office of Coordinator of Inter-American Affairs. Another fellow named David Saposs, a pro-Communist activist who urged workers to "take control of industry and government and build a workers' Republic," was hired as chief economist of the Labor Relations Board and later became assistant to the chief of the Labor Division of the War Production Board. When another person named Sam Schmeller was fired from the FBI in 1935 because of his Communist activities, in a few weeks he was appointed to the Social Security Board and became a leader in the American Peace Mobilization, a Communist front that promoted and organized sabotage strikes.

Although the Dies Committee had no authority to fire anyone from his government post, it reported to the Executive the names of more than 5,000 employees with Communist records. But this was like running to the police only to find they are complicit with the criminals.

Dies pointed to the Office of War Information as being the perfect spot in government for radical propagandists; it had enormous power, prestige, and vast funds, all mobilized to pour out "information." Stunning lies and distortions in

reports from this office calling Chinese Communists "agrarian reformers" shocked John Birch as an Army intelligence officer in China — before he was brutally bayoneted to death by these "peaceful reformers," a crime that was covered up for years in order not to shatter the government's perfidious myth.

According to Dies, it was incredible how Communists found their way into the Office of War Information, the Federal Communications Commission, and the radio stations through the device known as the Trojan Horse, a reference

Opportunity missed: When Leon Trotsky, at the time living in Mexico, offered to appear before the Dies Committee to expose vast numbers of Communists throughout the Americas, the Roosevelt State Department refused to cooperate, making it impossible for Trotsky to come to the U.S.

to the famous Greek stratagem by which Troy was conquered. This tactic originated at the Seventh World Congress of the Communist International in Moscow in 1935, when thousands of comrades gathered from Communist Parties throughout the world.

One of the most successful areas of Trojan Horse infiltration was labor unions. In 1937, employees at the Fisher Body Works in Flint, Michigan, entered the plant, sat at their machines, refused to work, and refused

to leave. The sit-down strike was born. A court order to leave was defied and jeered. When the sheriff asked Governor Frank Murphy for help, Murphy refused; instead, he arranged for negotiations between union officials and the company. Condoning this illegal, revolutionary-style seizure of private property led to 250 sit-downs in the Detroit area alone. At the request of Vice President John Nance Garner (one of the few top officials not infected with the Marxist virus, he refused to run for a third term with Roosevelt), Dies gained House passage of a resolution to condemn and curb sit-down strikes. But Roosevelt refused to support it, and liberals in the Senate defeated it to the roaring approval of a violent mob in the gallery. (Dies observed that the importance of Committee moves could be gauged by the fierceness of the opposition. This one was a whopper.) So was set the precedent for the whittling away of property rights — a lesson well learned by conditioned students who staged the outrageous sit-downs and destruction of private university property in the 1960s, forcing spineless (or sympathetic) university presidents to cave in to their ultra-left, Marxist demands.

When the Dies Committee investigated the Detroit upheavals, sworn testimony revealed that well-known Communists had instigated and directed the sit-down strikes. These Communists also directed the mob of 15,000 men who barricaded the State Capitol and, armed with clubs, prepared to march on the University of Michigan. Michigan State Police sat by helplessly with no instructions from Governor Murphy; the governor was in daily communication with Roosevelt, who advised him not to use state troops in the face of open insurrection. When the Committee exposed these facts, Roosevelt assailed Dies with the usual accusations of absurdly false charges, although the main Committee witness was the Chief of the Michigan State Police.

Dies produced evidence that the leadership of 12 of the constituent unions of the CIO were either card-holding members of the Communist Party or subservient followers of that Party's line.

539 ON PAY ROLL OF GOVERNMENT LINKED TO REDS

Listed as Members of Radical League.

BY WILLARD EDWARDS.
[Chicago Tribune Press Service.]

Washington, D. C., Oct. 25.—An uproar on the floor of the house followed the publication today of a list of 539 government officials and employees who are members of the American League for Peace and Democracy, an organization which has the financial support of the communist party of America.

539 ON PAY ROLL OF GOVERNMENT LINKED TO REDS

Revealed as Members of Radical League.

[Continued from first page.]

the communist party, and receives $2,500 yearly from the communist party."

Some 200 government employees listed by the Dies committee are employed in key positions where they are in position to direct or influence subordinates in their departments.

A list of these employes by departments with their positions and sal-

CHICAGO DAILY

Named in Red Rep

Edwin S. Smith. Dr. Louis Bloch. Alice Barrows.

Agnes Chase. Willard W. Beatty. Hildegarde Kneeland

counsel, $8,000.
Plotka, Norman L., attorney, $2,600.
Potamkin, Lawrence, attorney, $4,000.

Jung, Theo, edi
Liss, Samuel, a
Marshall, Robe

Hundreds exposed: Long before America heard of Joe McCarthy, Martin Dies effectively exposed hundreds of Communist subversives working in the U.S. government. In 1939, for example, the Dies Committee made public a list of 539 government officials and employees who were members of a Communist front organization.

Former American Communist Party functionary Benjamin Gitlow wrote in his celebrated book *The Whole of Their Lives* that "it was Stalin himself who told us that he would rather get one union official into the Communist Party than 10,000 rank and file members." Dies produced Communist literature stating that union strikes are viewed as dress rehearsals for violent revolution; nevertheless, with protection from on high, Communist infiltration of unions ran rampant.

For instance, the notorious Communist Jack Stachel was given general supervision of trade unions while B.K. Gebert was assigned to organizing and directing strikes. William Weinstone, a member of the Central Committee of the Communist Party, was in charge of activities in the United Automobile Workers. In 1935 Stachel reported that "the old, conservative leadership of the [American Federation of Labor] is tottering.... Henceforth organized labor is definitely on the road toward bitter and gigantic class battles...." Communist records obtained by Dies indicated that leaders assumed great credit for organizing the steel, automobile, rubber, glass, and textiles industries. But the ordinary union worker, fed a diet of class

hatred and resentment against management, was ignorant of the fact he was being used to carry out Communist objectives.

Well-meaning citizens were deceived in many other ways. One was by the use of words. Although the Dies Committee exposed numerous Nazi and Fascist fronts that folded due to scathing publicity and administration opposition, it was a different story when it came to Communism. Of more than 600 Communist or Communist front organizations exposed, the majority simply sneered at the Committee, changed their names to high-sounding titles (such as Committee for the Protection of the Bill of Rights or China Welfare Appeal), and continued their activities unopposed by either the administration or the media.

This sort of problem was made more difficult when Roosevelt refused to cooperate with the Committee to obtain testimony from Leon Trotsky, then living in exile in Mexico. A bitter enemy of Stalin (who had been quicker to seize power), Trotsky offered to appear before the Committee to expose Stalinists in America and explain their conspiracy.

Dies knew that Trotsky possessed an invaluable list of every member of the Communist Party in the U.S., Mexico, and South America, which Trotsky was eager to turn over to the Committee. Yet, when Dies requested a visa for Trotsky, the State Department responded that it could not guarantee Trotsky's protection and that, if Trotsky came to the U.S., Dies would have to be personally responsible for his safety. Although Dies challenged this double standard, pointing out that protection had been provided for other controversial figures, in the end he was forced to abandon this extraordinary opportunity to obtain revelations that our security agencies could have used to smash the many spy rings engaged in the theft of military, scientific, and diplomatic secrets so desired by the Soviets.

Undeterred by ridicule, threats (the IRS audited his papers for six months), or bribes (even the promise of the Vice Presidency if he would simply keep his mouth shut), Dies continued his crusade, while the liberals, with their customary hypocrisy, assailed him for violating freedom of thought and speech. Dies went to great lengths to explain that our Republic has to have a way to prevent revolutionaries from using civil liberties to destroy civil liberties; that Communists were serving a foreign dictator committed to the destruction of our country; and that, of all the methods of defense, fearless exposure was the mildest and most effective means.

Dies remained always vigilant against reckless charges or character assassination, more concerned with facts than opinions and with specific proof than generalities. As an experienced attorney, Dies was well aware of what was admissible in court, what constituted proof of subversive activity, and what was an honest difference of opinion. The record shows that the Committee held to these standards throughout, balancing the demands of the Constitution with the imperatives of national security. No one has ever produced evidence that Dies was other than fair, straightforward, and honest, or that he ever maligned anyone.

But there were no such standards when it came to mercilessly maligning Dies. In *Martin Dies' Story*, Dies discusses the corruption that overtook our once-factual media in the 1930s. Prior to this time, he says, most newspapers took pride in being objective, confining their opinions and prejudices to their editorials. During the 1930s, this standard swiftly deteriorated as reporters and columnists joined in all-out support for the Liberal Front. Their favorite victim was the Dies Committee; their chief weapons were irony, ridicule, invective, and vituperation. Reporters from the United Press, many of them Communist sympathizers, were particularly vicious; even those from the staid Associated Press were openly hostile. Many reporters were members of the Newspaper Guild, an affiliate of the CIO so far to the Left that the Committee found that the New York City chapter actually was Communist controlled.

Americans will surely be surprised to learn that in 1939, long before Senator Joseph McCarthy's time, Martin Dies publicly disclosed a list of 539 government officials and employees, including numerous high-salaried New Dealers, whom he charged with being members of a Communist-funded and -controlled organization, the American League for Peace and Democracy (notice the high-sounding title). Needless to say, Dies was bitterly lashed for calling the League Communist. Many years later, in his pamphlet *Socialism in America*, former Secretary General of the U.S. Communist Party Earl Browder identified the League as an arm of the Communist Party, which "rose to become a national political influence ... on a scale never before reached by a socialist movement claiming the Marxist tradition.... Right-wing intellectuals complained that it exercised an effective veto in almost all publishing houses against their books, and it is at least certain that those right-wingers had extreme difficulty getting published."

These revelatory words of Browder's should stun us into a realization of the extent of the menace that Dies clearly perceived and was pitting himself against — that is, our country's disastrous turn to the Left and the writing into law of Marxist/Socialist tenets masquerading under the name of liberalism.

In the mid-1960s Dies wrote a series of articles for *American Opinion* magazine (a precursor to THE NEW AMERICAN); in one of those articles he discussed some of these hidden inroads, unfortunately taken for granted by most Americans. For instance, the very first plank of Marxist doctrine is government ownership of the land and abolition of private property. In 1954 Dies persuaded the House to require the first inventory of government land ownership; he was shocked to discover that federal, state, and local governments owned a third of the land in the United States. Since then the overall figure has exploded to more than 40 percent.

Dies stressed that the most important attribute of ownership is control, without which the paper title is meaningless. In the gradual program of communizing a nation as defined by Marx, the state might first seek control without appropriating the title. This is what has happened to American agriculture. As the number of farms drastically decreased, the number of employees in the federal Department of Agriculture drastically increased and expenditures for subsidies exploded. With the handouts came Roosevelt's Agricultural Adjustment Act and the socialization of this huge and crucial section of our economy. Hundreds of federal mandates determine what crops may be planted, what crops must be withheld, how much may be planted, where produce may be sold, to what use one's own produce may be put, and what price the farmer receives for crops sold as well as those never planted.

Dies lamented how the effect of this control of farming became far-reaching and profound, resulting in the obliteration of small farmers whose assigned quotas were too small to sustain a livelihood. Millions of Americans, especially black Americans, were forced to move to big

Dies remained always vigilant against reckless charges or character assassination, more concerned with facts than opinions and with specific proof than generalities. No one ever produced evidence that Dies was other than fair, straightforward and honest, or that he ever maligned anyone.

Agricultural agony: Roosevelt's Agricultural Adjustment Act helped socialize the agricultural sector of the American economy, ruining the livelihoods of small farmers and creating vast pools of new welfare recipients in the cities, a situation lamented by Dies.

Library of Congress

cities, where, qualified only for farm labor, many ended up on welfare. Thus from this one Act we got not only federal control of almost all farming land and the consolidation of farming in a few "agri-businesses," but a powerful impetus for the emerging Welfare State, political manipulation of blacks, and today's enormous inner-city problems.

How can Roosevelt's shocking coddling, protection, and promotion of Communists and their objectives be explained? In his 1963 autobiography Dies reasoned, more lucidly than most and largely from firsthand knowledge, that there were two closely related prongs to Roosevelt's pro-Communism. One was the crass buying of votes for which he was willing to harm his country; the other was that Roosevelt was actually a philosophical Communist — that is, a Communist sympathizer.

As evidence for his conclusions, Dies relates the following examples of Roosevelt's mindset: In 1938 Roosevelt tried to persuade Dies to abandon his aim to expose Communism in the CIO. As recounted by Dies, Roosevelt told him in a face-to-face meeting:

[I]f you expose the Communists in the CIO, the CIO will turn against the Democratic Party. If we lose the CIO in some of the eastern states, we cannot win an election....

Yes, there are Communists in the CIO. Some of them may be in positions of leadership as you say. I think, however, that you exaggerate the seriousness of Communism. The Communists have just as much right in the CIO as anyone else.

Dies reminded us that Winston Churchill, in *The Hinge of Fate*, quoted a note he had received from the President: "I know you will not mind my being brutally frank when I tell you that I think I can personally handle Stalin better than either your Foreign Office or my State Department. Stalin hates the guts of all your top people. He thinks he likes me better, and I hope he will continue to do so."

By 1940 the Dies Committee had established the fact that thousands of Communists and their stooges and sympathizers were on the government payroll "boring from within." Dies went to Roosevelt with the membership records and asked for something to be done. As recounted by Dies, Roosevelt became very angry and replied: "I have never seen a man with such exaggerated ideas about this thing. I do not believe in Communism any more than you do, but there is nothing wrong with the Communists in this country. Several of the best friends I have are Communists."

Telling the tale: In his 1963 autobiography *Martin Dies' Story*, as well as in his book *The Trojan Horse in America*, Dies tells the story of Communist subversion in America.

In 1943, Roosevelt told William Bullitt, our first Ambassador to the Soviet Union: "I have a hunch that Stalin doesn't want anything but security for his country, and I think that if I give him everything I possibly can and ask for nothing from him in return, he won't try to annex anything and will work for world democracy and peace."

Also in 1943, Roosevelt's devoted friend, Archbishop (later Cardinal) Francis Spellman, took notes on Roosevelt's remarks during a lengthy conversation. Unfortunately for mankind, those notes were not published until 1963. If Roosevelt had been exposed instead of idolized, the appalling tragedies resulting from our pro-Communist foreign policies might have been averted. Spellman's notes revealed that Roosevelt told him that the world would be divided into "spheres of

influence"; that he (Roosevelt) hoped the Soviets would get 40 percent of the capitalist economy of Europe; that the European countries would have to undergo tremendous changes in order to adapt to the Soviet Union; that China would get the Far East; and that there was no point to opposing Stalin because he had the power and it was better to give in gracefully.

From whence came this worldview? Dies believed it flowed partly from the influence of Roosevelt's closest confidants, such as the fanatically pro-Communist Harry Hopkins and the Soviet agent Alger Hiss, and partly from Roosevelt's insufferable egotism, which led him to believe he could carve up the world at will.

In 1945, broken in health and dispirited from political ostracism, Dies retired from politics. The final straw had come when the White House ordered the Justice Department to disregard his findings and Justice branded them unreliable, in spite of the fact that they contained the names of Alger Hiss, Nathan Witt, Edwin Smith, Lee Pressman, Donald Hiss, and others named years later as members of the Red underground. Yet in 1952, fully recovered and urged to run again, Dies was re-elected to the House as Congressman-At-Large to fight once again for the truth. In a remarkable triumph, he received 1,979,889 votes from the people of Texas, more than the combined votes cast for all the other Texas representatives. Yet his own Democratic Party knifed him. Sam Rayburn, Speaker of the House, kept him off the House Committee on Un-American Activities he had so superbly chaired. Instead, this invaluable asset to the anti-Communist cause was assigned to Merchant Marine and Fisheries. In 1959 Dies returned to the practice of law in Texas, where he died in 1972.

Martin Dies should be gratefully remembered as a valiant warrior; a man of great perspicacity, dedication to duty, perseverance, and honor; and a beacon of strength and integrity in the perpetual struggle for truth and liberty versus the consummate evil of our day. ■

Persecuted Paladin

Despised and defamed by the Establishment, Senator Joseph McCarthy has been vindicated as a true champion of freedom.

by Robert W. Lee

CORBIS/Bettmann

It has been said that a man's character may be judged as much by the enemies he earns as by the friends he makes. By that standard, the late Senator Joseph McCarthy was indeed of noble character. He had the right enemies.

Merriam-Webster's Collegiate Dictionary defines "McCarthyism" as "a mid-20th century political attitude characterized chiefly by opposition to elements held to be subversive and by the use of tactics involving personal attacks on individuals by means of widely publicized indiscriminate allegations esp. on the basis of unsubstantiated charges." That wrongheaded wordsmithing appears in the dictionary's tenth edition, published in 1996 at the very time when documents from files of the old Soviet Union, and declassified data from our own government, were substantiating the Wisconsin senator's warnings about Communist infiltration of our government. In March 1996, *Washington Post* columnist Edwin Yoder complained that the task of explaining "McCarthyism" to young Americans was being complicated by the "post-Cold War materials now spilling from U.S. and Soviet archives" which "show that the Soviet Union had a surprising number of spies in the U.S. atomic bomb program and elsewhere during and after World War II." Yoder lamented that "allegations of Soviet spying were among the staples of the McCarthy period," and that many Americans might "conclude that the latest disclosures vindicate Sen. Joe McCarthy and his imitators."

Which they do, placing the credibility of McCarthy's bitter longtime critics on the line. Anti-McCarthyite Godfrey Sperling of the *Christian Science Monitor* lamented in November of last year that he was "most unhappy over efforts in some quarters to rehabilitate the justly earned disrepute of this irresponsible politician who ruined the lives of so many people," even though "there is, indeed, growing evidence that McCarthy got it 'right,' back in the 1950s when he charged that there were communist spies among our leading cit-

CORBIS/Bettmann

"Tail Gunner Joe": McCarthy's good-natured remark about shooting down coconut trees from the rear-gunner position of a dive bomber has been used by his enemies to belittle his military accomplishments. The truth is that McCarthy not only waived a military exemption to join the Marines during WWII but also volunteered for the dangerous rear-gunner assignment on numerous combat missions. Admiral Nimitz praised him for his "meritorious and efficient performance of duty."

newspaper put it, administering "justice promptly and with a combination of legal knowledge and good sense."

During World War II, his judicial status exempted him from military service, but he waived the exemption and enlisted in the Marines. He was sworn in as a first lieutenant in August 1942, then served as an intelligence officer for a bomber squadron stationed in the Solomon Islands, where he volunteered to fly in the dangerous tail-gunner's seat on numerous combat missions. His main duties were analysis and evaluation of raw data obtained mainly by aerial photography.

During 30 months of active duty, McCarthy earned a Distinguished Flying Cross and an Air Medal, was unanimously praised by his commanding officers, and received a citation from Fleet Admiral Chester W. Nimitz, commander-in-chief of the U.S. Pacific Fleet during the war, for "meritorious and efficient performance of duty" and "courageous devotion to duty" as an observer and rear gunner aboard a dive bomber in his Marine squadron in the Solomon Islands.

McCarthy briefly returned to the bench after the war, but in 1946 opted to run for the U.S. Senate. In the Republican primary, he upset longtime incumbent Senator Robert La Follette, a leader of the state's Progressive Party that was by then affiliated with the GOP. McCarthy went on to easily defeat the Democratic candidate by more than 250,000 votes.

According to many of McCarthy's critics, it was not until the fall of 1949 that he first showed an interest in the issue of Communist subver-

sion, which he thereafter exploited for personal political advantage. But University of Wisconsin historian Thomas C. Reeves has documented that "McCarthy's interest in the Communist issue went back to the 1930s." It had been raised during the 1946 Senate campaign, when he (correctly) claimed that his opponent had been endorsed by the *Daily Worker*, official newspaper of the Communist Party, USA. And in April 1947, he had told the *Madison Capital Times* that his top priority was "to stop the spread of Communism."

During a 1952 speech in Milwaukee, Senator McCarthy stated that May 22, 1949 marked the beginning of the fervent public phase of his anti-Communist crusade. It was on that day that Secretary of Defense James Forrestal was found dead of what was said to be suicide on the grounds outside the U.S. Naval Hospital in Bethesda, Maryland. In *McCarthyism: The Fight for America* (1952), the senator recalled that prior to becoming acquainted with Forrestal, he had "thought we were losing to international Communism because of incompetence and stupidity on the part of our planners. I mentioned that to Forrestal. I shall forever remember his answer. He said, 'McCarthy, consistency has never been a mark of stupidity. If they were merely stupid they would occasionally make a mistake in our favor.'"

McCarthy told his Wisconsin audience that the "Communists hounded Forrestal to his death. They killed him just as definitely as if they had thrown him from that 16th-story window."

In the fall of 1949 three men brought to McCarthy's office a lengthy FBI report alleging extensive Communist penetration of the State Department. State had been notified of the report in 1947, but had ignored it. Three other senators had been asked to utilize the information to help awaken the American people to the Marxist threat, but they had declined. Only McCarthy had the gumption to tackle it.

On February 9, 1950, he leveled his first public charges about security risks in the State Department during an ad-

izens." Sperling stated that he "won't have McCarthy rehabilitated even if history may find that he was 'closer to the truth than those who ridiculed him,' as one columnist [Nicholas von Hoffmann] put it recently [on April 19, 1996] in *The Washington Post*."

Joseph Raymond McCarthy was born in Grand Chute Township, Wisconsin, on November 14, 1908. After completing four years of high school in a single year and making honor roll, he attended Marquette University, graduating in 1935 with a law degree.

McCarthy was a Democrat at the time, and the next year was elected president of the Young Democratic Clubs of Wisconsin's seventh district. He ran for District Attorney that year, finishing second to the Progressive Party victor, but ahead of the Republican candidate.

By 1939 he had shifted to the GOP, and was elected a circuit court judge, the youngest in state history. The Tenth Wisconsin Circuit had a backlog of some 250 cases, but by working long hours (often presiding past midnight) and eliminating red tape, Judge McCarthy quickly cleared the backlog while, as one local

dress to a Republican women's group in Wheeling, West Virginia. He began by quoting from Karl Marx, Vladimir Lenin, and Josef Stalin regarding their stated goal of world conquest, asserting that "today we are engaged in a final, all-out battle between Communistic atheism and Christianity."

He blamed the fall of China and other countries to the Communists during the previous six years on "the traitorous actions" of the State Department's "bright young men," specifically mentioning such leftist luminaries as John Stewart Service, Gustavo Duran, Mary Jane Keeney, Julian Wadleigh, Harlow Shapley, Alger Hiss, and Dean Acheson. But the segment of his speech that "lit the fuse," as it were, was his claim: "I have in my hand 57 cases of individuals who would appear to be either card-carrying members or certainly loyal to the Communist Party, but who nevertheless are still helping to shape our foreign policy."

McCarthy referred to a letter that Secretary of State James Byrnes had sent to Congressman Adolph Sabath (D-IL) in 1946, in which Byrnes asserted that State Department security investigators had declared 284 persons unfit to hold jobs in the Department because of Communist connections and other reasons, but that only 79 had been discharged, leaving 205 still on the payroll. McCarthy told his Wheeling audience that while he did not have the names of those 205, he did, as noted, have the names of 57 others. When he addressed the Senate on the subject 11 days later, an additional 24 had been added, bringing the total to 81.

There was, in other words, a rational basis for each of the figures (57, 81, and 205) which he had cited, yet his enemies sought (and still seek) to make it appear that he was erratic, confused, and pulling figures out of thin air. The ludicrous numbers game served to divert attention from the crucial question of whether there were still persons within the State Department — regardless of how many — whose loyalties ran to a hostile foreign power.

McCarthy's February 20th Senate speech took some six hours to deliver, due to constant interruptions and harangues by hostile colleagues such as Majority Leader Scott Lucas (D-IL), Brien McMahon (D-CT), Garrett Withers (D-KY), and Herbert Lehman (D-NY). McCarthy identified each case by a number, rather than a name, believing that "if I were to give all the names involved, it might leave a wrong impression. If we should label one man a Communist when he is not a Communist, I think it would be too bad." But on numerous occasions Senator Lucas demanded that McCarthy make the names public, which he persistently refused to do.

In the wake of McCarthy's charges, the Senate convened a special subcommittee of the Foreign Relations Committee to scrutinize his evidence. Chaired by Senator Millard Tydings (D-MD), its mandate was to conduct "a full and complete study and investigation as to whether persons who are disloyal to the United States are, or have been, employed by the Department of State." The hearings quickly degenerated, however, into an investigation of McCarthy himself, and after 31 days of testimony the subcommittee predictably branded McCarthy's accusations a "fraud" and a "hoax," and cleared (as being neither Communist nor pro-Communist) all 100-plus persons whose names he had submitted. The subcommittee also concluded that the State Department had an effective security program.

During the hearings, McCarthy had introduced public evidence regarding nine persons: Haldore Hanson, Gustavo Duran, Dorothy Kenyon, Frederick Schuman, Harlow Shapley, Esther Brunauer, John Stewart Service, Philip Jessup, and Owen Lattimore. Evidence relating to the first six showed that two (Hanson and Duran) had been identified under oath as Communist Party members; three (Kenyon, Schuman, and Shapley) had joined numerous Communist fronts and had backed other Red causes; and one (Brunauer) had sundry Communist ties that would eventually result in dismissal

"Today we are engaged in a final, all-out battle between Communistic atheism and Christianity."
— Senator Joseph McCarthy
February 9, 1950

from the State Department (in June 1952) as a security risk.

The high-profile cases were those of Service, Jessup, and Lattimore.

• **John Stewart Service:** In 1945, Service had been arrested for furnishing classified documents to the editors of the Communist magazine *Amerasia*. The Truman administration covered up the scandal and Service was not fired, prosecuted, or otherwise disciplined. During the Tydings Subcommittee hearings, Senator McCarthy produced substantial evidence that Service had been "part of the pro-Soviet group" that sought to communize China. Nevertheless, the subcommittee concluded that Service was "not disloyal, pro-communist, or a security risk."

Over the next 18 months, the State Department's Loyalty Security Board cleared Service four times, but in December 1951 the Civil Service Commission's Loyalty Review Board found that there was "reasonable doubt" about his loyalty and he was ousted from the State Department.

• **Philip Jessup:** McCarthy claimed that Jessup had an "unusual affinity for Communist causes," and the record showed that he had indeed belonged to at least five Red fronts, had close ties to many Communists, and was an influential member of the Institute for Pacific Relations, which would two years later be described by the Senate Internal Security Subcommittee (SISS) as "a vehicle used by Communists to orientate American Far Eastern policy toward Communist objectives." The Tydings Subcommittee snubbed it all.

• **Owen Lattimore:** Lattimore was one of the principal architects of the

Naming names: The list of highly placed subversives exposed by McCarthy includes (from the left) John Stewart Service, Philip Jessup, and Owen Lattimore, all of whom were protected by the Establishment.

State Department's pro-Communist Far Eastern policy. During a closed session of the Tydings Subcommittee, Senator McCarthy referred to Lattimore as State's "top Russian spy." That charge was leaked to the public, not by McCarthy, but by anti-McCarthy columnist Drew Pearson. McCarthy subsequently modified the accusation, acknowledging that he might "have perhaps placed too much stress on the question of whether or not he has been an espionage agent." He pointed out, however, that "13 different witnesses have testified under oath to Lattimore's Communist membership or party-line activities." The Tydings Subcommittee whitewashed Lattimore, but in 1952 the Senate Internal Security Subcommittee reported that "Owen Lattimore was, from some time beginning in the 1930s, a conscious articulate instrument of the Soviet conspiracy." The SISS asked the Department of Justice to have a grand jury determine if Lattimore had committed perjury during sworn testimony before the subcommittee. Lattimore was subsequently indicted on six counts of lying under oath, but when two of the counts were dismissed on technical grounds, the government opted to drop the case altogether, leaving his formal guilt or innocence in legal limbo.

Of the 110 names McCarthy gave to the Tydings Subcommittee, 62 were at the time employed by the State Department. Though the subcommittee cleared them all, within one year a State Department Loyalty Board instigated proceed-

ings against 49 of the 62, and by the end of 1954, 81 of those on McCarthy's list had either resigned from their government posts or been dismissed.

The GOP regained control of both the Senate and House following the 1952 elections, and McCarthy became chairman of the Government Operations Committee and its Permanent Subcommittee on Investigations. He no longer had to rely solely on speeches and other public pronouncements to warn the American people about Communist subversion, but was now able to conduct public hearings about disloyalty and incompetence in government. During his tenure, the subcommittee held 169 public and closed hearings and interrogated more than 500 witnesses. Extensive waste and mismanagement were uncovered in the Voice of America, while the exposé of Communist penetration of the Government Printing Office led to the removal, or further investigation by the FBI, of 77 employees and an overhaul of the GPO's security system. Scrutiny of defense plants included testimony from 101 witnesses, two of whom supplied information documenting efforts to establish Red cells within the plants. Thirty-two persons were eventually fired or suspended and security regulations were tightened.

Dentist Irving Peress was drafted into the Army as a captain in October 1952 and assigned to Camp Kilmer, New Jersey. One month later he refused to answer questions on a Defense Department form about mem-

bership in subversive organizations. In April 1953, the Surgeon General of the Army recommended that Peress be dismissed from the service. Instead, he requested, and received, a promotion to major.

Peress was subpoenaed to testify before the McCarthy Subcommittee on January 30, 1954. He invoked the Fifth Amendment 20 times when asked about his alleged membership in the Communist Party, his attendance at a Communist training school, and his efforts to recruit military personnel into the party. Two days later, McCarthy wrote to Army Secretary Robert Stevens, summarizing the testimony and requesting that Peress be court-martialed. He also wanted to know who had authorized Peress' promotion to major. That same day, Peress requested an honorable discharge, and was granted one the next day by his commanding officer, Brigadier General Ralph W. Zwicker.

McCarthy summoned General Zwicker to testify at a closed session of the subcommittee on February 18th. Zwicker was evasive, hostile, and uncooperative, and changed his story three times when asked if he had known at the time he signed the discharge that Peress had refused to answer questions posed by the subcommittee. McCarthy became increasingly exasperated, and, when Zwicker responded to a hypothetical question by saying that a general who ordered the honorable discharge of a major known to be a Communist should not be removed, expressed his opinion that Zwicker was not fit to wear the uniform of a general. McCarthy was subsequently attacked for supposedly "abusing" Zwicker and impugning his patriotism.

It was also during McCarthy's investigation of Communist influence in the Defense Department that his subcommittee heard testimony from FBI undercover informant Mary Stalcup Markward, who had belonged to (and held high positions in) the Communist Party of the District of Columbia from 1942 to 1949. Mrs. Markward testified that a Pentagon code clerk named Annie Lee

Moss had been a member of the Communist Party until her name was removed from the party's roster in 1945. Mrs. Moss had not been expelled, Mrs. Markward explained; it was party policy to remove from its rolls the names of those members who applied for or entered government service.

Mrs. Moss had been hired by the government in January 1945 as a clerk in the General Accounting Office. She later worked in the Pentagon cafeteria, and in 1950 secured a job in the Office of the Chief Signal Officer. After she was cleared by a loyalty panel in January 1951, her subsequent duties included the receipt and transmission by telegraph and radio of coded and plain text messages and communications originating overseas for the Army Signal Corps, the State Department, the Army Security Agency, the Central Intelligence Agency, and the General Staff.

The day after Mrs. Markward completed her testimony, Mrs. Moss (who did not testify at the time due to illness) was suspended from her job. However, she was reinstated later that month in a nonsensitive position.

Mrs. Moss testified before the McCarthy Subcommittee on March 11, 1954. That night, CBS news journalist Edward R. Murrow included a segment about the hearing in his network news program, closing with Senator Stuart Symington's assertion to Mrs. Moss: "If you are not taken back by the Army, come around and see me and I'll get you a job." Five days later Murrow devoted his entire *See It Now* program to the Moss incident, asserting that "the line between investigating and persecuting is a very fine one, and the junior senator from Wisconsin has stepped over it repeatedly. We must remember always that accusation is not proof, and that conviction depends upon evidence and due process of law."

Even today, the Moss case is portrayed by McCarthy's enemies as a classic example of how his supposedly "irresponsible methods" were employed to "destroy innocent persons."

Yet for more than four decades the truth about Annie Lee Moss has been a matter of public record. In 1958, the federal Subversive Activities Control Board, after scrutinizing pertinent FBI documents, reported: "The situation that has resulted on the Annie Lee Moss question is that copies of the Communist party's own records, the authenticity of which the party has at no time disputed, were produced to it (Exhibits 499 to 511 inclusive), and show that one Annie Lee Moss, 72 R Street, S. W., Washington, DC, was a party member in the mid-1940's." This was, indeed, the same Annie Lee Moss.

Evidence implicating another 155 defense workers was gathered by McCarthy's investigators, but they were never questioned under oath. At about the same time, efforts of the Eisenhower administration to bring an end to McCarthy's investigative efforts began gathering momentum.

The Army Signal Corps installation at Fort Monmouth, New Jersey had been developing defensive devices against atomic attack, and was deemed to be one of our nation's most vital security posts. Although the FBI had earlier warned the Army about security breaches at the facility, little heed was paid until McCarthy launched an investigation in 1953. During 1953 and early 1954, his subcommittee heard from 112 witnesses in open or executive hearings regarding the situation at Fort Monmouth. As a result, the Army suspended or discharged 35 persons as security risks, only to have the Army Loyalty and Screening Board (ALSB) reinstate all but two, with back pay.

McCarthy demanded the names of the 20 civilians then serving on the board. When he threatened to issue subpoenas, if necessary, key personnel within the Eisenhower administration met secretly to upgrade their anti-McCarthy strategy. Subsequent events would mark the shift of McCarthy's own primary focus — from Red infiltration to who was protecting the subversives.

A clandestine meeting was held on January 21, 1954, in the office of Attorney General Herbert Brownell. Those present included U.S. Ambassador to the UN Henry Cabot Lodge, Deputy Attorney General William Rogers, White House Chief of Staff Sherman Adams, White House aide Gerald Morgan, and Army Counsel John Adams. It was Adams who inadvertently let the skunk out of the sack by mentioning the meeting during testimony at the Army-McCarthy hearings a few months later.

On the right track: The record shows that McCarthy did not attack the innocent but exposed the guilty. He did not engage in a witch hunt, but uncovered a vast conspiracy that had penetrated the U.S. government and could not tolerate the light of exposure. Ironically, documents released from both the Soviet archives and the U.S. National Security Agency in the 1990s confirmed the Red penetration.

After learning of the meeting, Senator McCarthy wanted to know what had transpired, and why, but on May 17, 1954, President Eisenhower issued an executive order forbidding any employee of the Defense Department "to testify to any such conversations or communications or to produce any such documents or reproductions." It was a devastating attack on the constitutional system of checks and balances. From then on, members of the executive branch refused to cooperate with McCarthy's investigators and other congressional probes, citing the Eisenhower executive privilege directive as their excuse for withholding information from Congress and the public.

On March 11, 1954, in accord with a strategy that had been discussed during the January 21st meeting, the Army charged McCarthy with seeking preferential treatment for a former subcommittee staffer, G. David Schine, both before and after Schine had been drafted into the Army in November 1953. McCarthy countercharged that the allegations were made in bad faith, and were designed to prevent his subcommittee from continuing its probe of Communist subversion at Fort Monmouth and from issuing subpoenas for members of the ALSB. A special committee was appointed to take testimony about the conflicting charges. The Army-McCarthy hearings began on April 22, 1954.

The most memorable (because it was so widely publicized by the anti-McCarthy media) incident during the hearings occurred on June 9th, when Army counsel Joseph Welch baited the McCarthy Subcommittee's chief counsel, Roy Cohn, by challenging Cohn to get 130 Communists or subversives out of the defense plants "before the sun goes down." The sarcasm angered McCarthy, who interrupted to say that if Welch was so concerned about persons aiding the Communist Party, he should check on a man in his Boston law office named Fred Fisher, who had once belonged to the National Lawyers Guild (NLG), an outfit that Attorney General Brownell had described as "the legal mouthpiece of the

Archive Photos

Valiant voice: Not only McCarthy's friends but his political enemies admired his courage. As Senator John McClellan, who had voted to condemn McCarthy, put it: "He was a man of courage. No enemy can ever say otherwise."

Communist Party." Welch then delivered his famous lines accusing McCarthy of "reckless cruelty" and concluding: "Let us not assassinate this lad further, senator. You've done enough. Have you no sense of decency, sir, at long last?"

The implication that McCarthy had revealed something new was ludicrous. Fisher's connection with the subversive NLG had been reported a few weeks earlier by the *New York Times*. Welch had selected Fisher as an assistant in the case, but on April 16th the *Times* had printed a photo of Fisher and a story about his removal from the Welch team because of his past association with the NLG. Five days later, Fisher's link to the NLG was again publicized by the *Times* in connection with a story about the Schine controversy.

After hearing 32 witnesses and two million words of testimony, the committee concluded that McCarthy had not himself exercised improper influence in behalf of Schine, but that Roy Cohn had engaged in some "unduly persistent or aggressive efforts" on Schine's behalf. The committee also concluded that Army Secretary Stevens and Army Counsel Adams had "made efforts to terminate or influence the investigation and hearings

at Fort Monmouth," and that Adams had "made vigorous and diligent efforts" to block subpoenas for members of the Army Loyalty and Screening Board "by means of personal appeal to certain members of the [McCarthy] committee."

Having emerged from the Army-McCarthy hearings unscathed (except for matters attributable to misleading media spin), McCarthy then became the target of yet another investigation — the fifth in five years! — when Senator Ralph Flanders (R-VT) introduced a resolution on July 30, 1954, accusing him of conduct "unbecoming a member of the United States Senate." This was the same hypocritical McCarthyphobe who had two months earlier told the Senate that McCarthy's "anti-Communism so completely parallels that of Adolf Hitler as to strike fear into the hearts of any defenseless minority." Eventually, the original charge metastasized into 46 separate counts of supposedly improper conduct, and another special Senate committee, this time chaired by Senator Arthur V. Watkins (R-UT), was established to scrutinize them.

Following two months of hearings, the Watkins Committee recommended that McCarthy be "condemned" (not "censured," a significantly stronger penalty) on two of the 46 counts, neither of which had to do with his anti-Communist investigations, and both of which were as baseless as the 44 that were dropped.

The first count alleged that McCarthy had in 1952 "failed to cooperate" with a Senate subcommittee that had investigated a motion by Senator William Benton to expel him from the Senate. McCarthy had declined the committee's "invitation" (he was never subpoenaed), and never in Senate history had a member been disciplined for spurning a mere "invitation" to appear before a Senate panel. McCarthy had expressed his willingness to appear voluntarily, if he and his counsel were allowed to cross-examine witnesses called against him, but he was denied that right. The matter was forgotten for two years, until resurrected for the condemnation resolution.

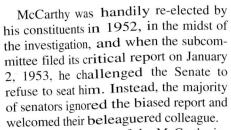
McCarthy was handily re-elected by his constituents in 1952, in the midst of the investigation, and when the subcommittee filed its critical report on January 2, 1953, he challenged the Senate to refuse to seat him. Instead, the majority of senators ignored the biased report and welcomed their beleaguered colleague.

The second count of the McCarthy indictment claimed that he had abused General Zwicker during their February 18th confrontation. Many senators felt, however, that McCarthy's conduct toward the general had been at least partially justified, due both to Zwicker's deportment that day and because he had shown contempt for the subcommittee by disregarding chairman McCarthy's letter of February 1st, then honorably discharging Irving Peress the next day.

The Zwicker count was dropped, but replaced at the last minute with a substitute that castigated McCarthy for, in essence, exercising his right of free speech outside the Senate chamber. He was scolded for making statements about fellow senators which, compared to the verbal abuse to which he himself had been subjected both on and off the Senate floor, were models of decorum. Senate rules provided that senators who referred to colleagues in a discourteous manner *on the floor* could be called to task, but outside criticism was subject only to the jurisdiction of courts under libel laws. The Senate could *expel* a Member for any reason (a penalty never seriously considered in McCarthy's case), but was not vested with power to otherwise punish members for speeches, statements, or even acts committed outside its chamber.

Nevertheless, the original first count, and the substitute second count, were approved by identical votes of 67 to 22, with all 44 Democrats (and one Independent), and 22 of 44 Republicans, voting to convict. The only Democrat to neither vote nor state his position was Senator John F. Kennedy, who was hospitalized that day.

McCarthy clearly did not merit the double-standard denunciation which has been so egregiously twisted and distorted over the years to defame his memory.

Senator McCarthy and wife Jean, who were married in 1954, adopted a baby daughter, Tierney Elizabeth, in January 1957. A few months later, on April 28th, the senator became ill and was admitted to the Bethesda Naval Hospital. He was diagnosed with acute hepatitis, an inflammation of the liver. His critics have claimed that he was an alcoholic, but

William Rusher, counsel to the Senate Internal Security Subcommittee in 1956 and 1957, who met McCarthy repeatedly on social occasions, has said that "he had at one time been a heavy drinker, but in his last years was cautiously moderate," a conclusion bolstered by the senator's demeanor during the Army-McCarthy hearings, and the nature in which he handled his daily workload, speaking engagements and other public appearances, and family duties during those last years.

Joseph McCarthy died in the hospital on May 2, 1957, at age 48. He became the first senator in 17 years whose funeral services were held in the Senate chamber. More than 30,000 Wisconsinites filed through St. Mary's Church in Appleton to pay their last respects. During special memorial services in the Senate on Au-gust 14, 1957, then-Majority Leader Lyndon B. Johnson, who had voted to condemn him, stated: "There was a quality about the man which compelled respect, and even liking, from his strongest adversaries. [He] had strength ... great courage ... daring ... [and] had a rare quality which enabled him to touch the minds and hearts of millions of his fellow men." And Senator John McClellan, who had also voted to condemn, declared: "It has been said here that he was not the first to call the country's attention to the dangers of the Communist conspiracy ... but no one warned and alerted the people of this country more effectively than did Joe McCarthy during the time he had the opportunity to guide the Committee on Government Operations and the subcommittee thereof, the Permanent Investigating Subcommittee. I admired Joe McCarthy because of his courage. He was a man of courage. No enemy can ever say otherwise."

McCarthy was attacked for the "methods" he employed, but those methods posed his greatest danger to the forces he was fighting. His Marxist enemies did not like his objective, which was to get rid of Communism, but they were even more alarmed that instead of simply fighting Communism on some ideological level, he had decided that the way to slow and eventually rout the Red juggernaut was to expose individual Communists and pro-Communists. He was right; and he was vilified not because he "smeared innocent people," but because he identified and exposed culpable ones. Any inaccuracies in his charges (admittedly there were some) were always pointing in the right direction. His methods were no different than those employed by other senators who were applauded for their vigorous cross-examination of, say, organized crime figures. The difference was the target.

Joseph McCarthy boldly told the truth about Communism in America, and those who had the most to lose refused to believe him, which explains much about where American politics and culture stand today. ■

control center of an invisible government which intends to make the United States a dependent province in a one-world socialist system." And then this straightforward evaluation of public education from the October 1979 issue of *American Opinion*, a forerunner of THE NEW AMERICAN: "[W]hat we still call free public schools are costly government schools. The thrust of government schools is not educating children, but mashing them down to a low level of mediocrity; squeezing them into a common mold prescribed by agitators, sociologists, Marxist militants, and venal politicians; cultivating a crowd culture which makes human beings blind conformists in all things involving intellect and spirit, but renders them violent anarchists when seeking gratification of their appetites or acting in a mob."

To understand the mind that makes such blunt sense, one must know more about the man. In a promotional piece for his weekly *Dan Smoot Report*, the Missouri native told his readers that "my father was a dirt-poor farmer ... a tenant on his father-in-law's place when I was born. He had little formal schooling, but taught me to love books. Before I entered a one-room county schoolhouse for my first year of formal learning, I had already read such books as *David Copperfield*, *Moby Dick*, *Treasure Island* and *Uncle Tom's Cabin*."

Born in 1913, he was orphaned at age ten. By age 14, he was on his own and traveling the hobo circuit by rail. During that time, he said, he "did just about every kind of manual work that boy, or man, ever did for a living: from chopping cotton in Arkansas to shining shoes in Denver; from mining coal in southern Illinois to riding fence on a great, sprawling ranch in western Nebraska. At the age of 14, I even got one job stirring mash at a moonshiner's still in western Kentucky.... I had a wonderful time. The depression left no scars on me."

By 1931, Smoot's wanderlust had taken him to Dallas, Texas, where, over the next ten years, while working full time jobs ranging from warehouse work to front office clerk, he got married (she 16; he 20), earned a high school diploma, and received B.A. and M.A. degrees from Southern Methodist University.

In 1941, he accepted a teaching fellowship at Harvard University while

Hoover's FBI: As a "G-Man," Smoot — a hobo turned Harvard scholar — investigated Communist subversion and became a ghost writer for J. Edgar Hoover.

studying for a doctorate in American Civilization. In his 1993 autobiography, *People Along the Way*, Smoot recounted that the "Harvard faculty I had occasion to visit with were puzzles to me — their attitude toward America was quite different from anything I had ever before encountered. I am talking about my peers in graduate school, some of them starting their second years as teaching fellows, though all of them were younger than I was.... They were from affluent, prominent families. Yet, they seemed to be ashamed of America, or to hate her. At any rate they were contemptuous of my patriotism, which struck them as mawkish, anachronistic, flag-waving."

On December 7, 1941 this patriotic teacher and his wife heard the frightful news about Pearl Harbor on the radio. Smoot recalls: "We did not say anything [until] she turned toward me saying 'I suppose you will be joining the Army?'"

"Marines, I hope," was the reply.

But minor physical flaws, including flat feet, made him unacceptable to any branch of the military. It was ironic since Smoot was in excellent shape — and proud of it — and had been at one time on his way to becoming a competing gymnast. When his wife, Betty, suggested the FBI as a way of serving his beloved America in time of need, he applied immediately. Smoot found a kindred spirit in the Bureau's doctor who said that flat feet shouldn't be a hindrance since the FBI didn't require G-Men to march. "I welcomed the job," he recalls in his autobiography, because it was "concerned with the security of the Country. I felt a patriotic obligation to find a civilian job wherein I could show my willingness to die heroically for my country."

Soon Smoot found himself settling into routine FBI field activities, from finding men dodging the draft to tracking down murderers on the loose. He remembers working on "criminal cases exuding the flavor of good detective stories ... some of it exciting, part of it a great deal of fun; but it did not satisfy my romantic notions of what a hale and hearty young American male should do when America the Beautiful was in danger."

In 1944, he was assigned to an FBI Internal Security Squad investigating Communist Party operations in Ohio. Now Smoot was in his element: "Agents warned me that working on communist cases was the dullest most useless work an Agent could do. I welcomed the job, however, because ... it might get me closer than I had been to defending my Country in time of war."

Smoot threw himself into this work, and with his characteristic love of the written word, he read Communist newspapers, magazines, pamphlets, and propaganda fliers, as well as such books as Karl Marx's *Communist Manifesto* and *Das*

Kapital, and Lenin's *Imperialism and the Highest Stage of Capitalism* — tomes he referred to as "gruesomely dull." It was the beginning of a life of investigating and analyzing Communism, and, more importantly, exposing the sinister machinations of those who manufacture the Red threat.

For more than three years, Smoot observed Communist Party members in action — as they infiltrated labor unions, agitated for a Moscow-friendly U.S. foreign policy, and exerted influence even within the American government. What he learned of Communist subversion during this work was to have a great effect on his later career.

When, after the war, lucrative offers were lined up for Smoot to return to Harvard — including a $5,000 Rockefeller Foundation supplement to his annual salary — he was convinced that he could not in good conscience return to teaching. "My investigations of communism had disclosed such a heavy infiltration of Marxist ideas (and individuals) into the American Academic community," he recalled, "that I did not want to be a part of

it anymore."

Moving up the ranks in the FBI, Smoot qualified as a firearms instructor and was assigned to the roster of the agency's speakers bureau. In short order he found himself in Washington, D.C., where he ghost wrote magazine articles, newspaper guest columns, book prefaces, and speeches for FBI Director J. Edgar Hoover himself.

Ever restless, in 1951, after ten years with the FBI, Smoot "yearned to do something [else] for America. I knew a great deal about the international socialist conspiracy, but what could I do?" His malaise about the conflict between his patriotic concerns, and his commitment to a career he now found routine, grew to be too much.

On the day he resigned from the FBI, a friend of a friend introduced Smoot to H.L. Hunt, the Texas oil tycoon who had just created *Facts Forum*, a Dallas-based educational campaign to fight Communism. Hunt wanted both sides of important issues ex-

"When we build the central government into an all-powerful colossus ... we place our freedom and our lives in the hands of political quacks and witch doctors in Washington whose power to destroy us is unchecked and unlimited."

— Dan Smoot

plained to the American people so they could better discern between the fallacies of socialism and benefits offered by the free enterprise system. Smoot's job was to pick the subjects and presenters, and then moderate what followed. While the Establishment media were offering Hobson's choices — false alternatives in public policy debates — Smoot's straight-shooting style was evident right from the start: The first program was entitled "Should the U.S. get out of the UN and get the UN out of the U.S.?" and the second broadcast was on the topic "Stop Foreign Aid: Yes or No?"

Facts Forum was initially a locally televised 15-minute debate between two high school students with Smoot as the researcher and host, but the program was soon being filmed in Washington, D.C. and nationally syndicated (no network would give the Hunt/Smoot venture a platform). The pupils were replaced by congressmen and other public policy leaders but, Smoot remembers, the youngsters had done a better job than the public officials ever did because they "hit the questions head-on, from opposite viewpoints; I could never get politicians to do that." Smoot eventually developed the format into a one-man show: He researched, wrote, and delivered both the left and the right side of the issues. Within three years his broadcasts were heard on 350 radio stations and 80 television outlets, reaching some 20 million people weekly.

Although he was presenting a strong conservative message, Smoot was in a relatively safeguarded position. Backed by the financial security of H.L. Hunt, he had

AP/Wide World

Mr. and Mrs. H.L. Hunt: The richest man in the world by the time this photo was taken (1972), Hunt had hired Smoot in 1951 to host the TV program *Facts Forum*. Under Smoot's guidance, the program, in TV and radio formats, eventually reached 20 million people weekly.

become a well-known and influential conservative, yet for editorial "balance," he had to yield half of his weekly presentation to the liberal side of any issue. Listeners and viewers of the program sent in well over 100,000 letters of inquiry and encouragement during his stint with *Facts Forum*. Many of them said, however, that "the two sided program confused people who were not already well acquainted with the great fundamental struggle of our time: collectivism versus individualism," Smoot remembers. "I resigned from *Facts Forum* in June, 1955 … to give only one side — the side that uses old-fashioned American, constitutional principles as a yardstick for measuring all important issues."

Smoot had in mind an independent free-enterprise publication. He realized his goal with the first issue of *The Dan Smoot Report*. The first issue, "This Is My Side," was mailed on June 29, 1955 to the thousands of people who had sent him fan mail. The inaugural

On his own: Resigning from *Facts Forum* in 1955, Smoot struck out on his own with *The Dan Smoot Report*. After a shaky start, it became a great success.

newsletter observed that "when we build the central government into an all-powerful colossus — as we did under Roosevelt and Truman, and continue to do under Eisenhower — we place our freedom and our lives in the hands of political quacks and witch doctors in Washington whose power to destroy us is unchecked and unlimited." Dan Smoot was off and running.

The new operation, however, faced significant challenges. It was initially, for instance, run on a shoestring: "The dining room table was my desk.... My typewriter was the old Underwood upright I had bought and learned to use in 1931," he writes in *People Along the Way*. Even worse, "paying for the printing and mailing of the first issue took all the money we had."

Although Smoot and his wife figured their publishing venture had to be built on a minimum of 2,000 replies, the net return of that first prospecting package was only 900 subscriptions. Accompanying those checks however, came more than 500 letters saying in essence, "Thank God for what you're doing.... America needs this kind of analysis.... You have given us new hope.... Please don't stop!"

Thank goodness he read his comment mail instead of just counting the money. Smoot recollects: "Our hours were very long and our income very short that first year; but there was never a year in our married life we enjoyed more." A feeling many small entrepreneurs know well.

The Left had long sneered at Dan Smoot as the spokesman for the "Texas Oilionaires" through his association with H. L. Hunt. Now on his own, that reputation still haunted him. "The legend that I was H.L. Hunt's hired voice … never did die. Many conservatives rejoiced in it. It meant that I had all the money I needed for my work." That legend, though, was far from the truth. Undercapitalized, and with no advertising income, *The Dan Smoot Report* struggled on the road to success. But, after just one year in business, he took another step of faith by adding a broadcast version of his *Report*. His entire broadcasting network

in 1956 consisted of only four radio stations — far from the heady days of *Facts Forum*. But Dan Smoot had graduated early, with high honors, from the School of Hard Knocks. He knew what he believed in was right; that the whole venture was the right thing to do; and that with hard work — and God's blessing — *The Dan Smoot Report* would succeed by some measure of His will.

In 1957, after just one year of broadcasting, *The Dan Smoot Report* could be heard on 150 radio stations reaching an estimated audience of 16 million people. By the early 1960s, a televised version of the *Report* was aired on more than 150 television stations as well. Time slots on each broadcast outlet were negotiated one station at a time, however, as no network would sell time to a conservative broadcaster.

The Dan Smoot Report, in its printed form of eight pages, covered a variety of topics, and in typical Smoot style, carried such titles as:

• Congress or Dictator's Assembly? (7/9/62);
• Planned Dictatorship (6/3/63);
• Revolution and the National Council of Churches (5/16/66);
• UN: A Nest of Communist Spies (12/14/70);
• Moochers and the Miserable Congress (1/25/71).

Beyond some seemingly startling headlines always lay a painstakingly researched argument. *The Dan Smoot Report* for January 18, 1965, headlined "What Are We Doing in Vietnam?," contained 34 footnotes. The newsletter for March 16, 1970, headlined "Equal Tyranny is Still Tyranny," an issue devoted to the forced busing of schoolchildren, ostensibly to integrate classrooms, cited 25 references over four pages. Tens of thousands of Americans relied on the meticulously documented newsletter each week for letters to the editor, for debates over the backyard fence, and for contacting Congress. Indeed, this writer's personal collection of annual bound volumes of *The Dan Smoot Report* include copies bought at used bookstores — heavily un-

derlined by, and with marginal notes from, the original owners.

Subheads, which broke up the newsletter copy, almost always included one called "What You Can Do." For September 30, 1963, Smoot suggested that his readers

> ... study the voting records of Representatives and Senators to determine which ones show understanding and respect for the Constitution. All who do not should be voted out of office.... A Congress composed of men with enough brains and integrity to uphold the Constitution, would scrap our no-win, no-defense policies and initiate a program, infinitely less expensive than the present one, which would defend the United States against foreign enemies.

As was typical of the Smoot style, there was nothing ambiguous in his suggestions.

Smoot's efforts drew praise from one of America's greatest patriots, Robert Welch. In 1958, at the founding meeting of the John Birch Society, Welch observed: "I think that *The Dan Smoot Report*, because it is fairly short and is quite suitable to pick up for reading during fifteen minutes of waiting time, should be in just as many doctors' and dentists' offices as possible." Circulation figures indicate the newsletter was finding even wider distribution than waiting rooms. From a low of 3,000 subscribers in 1956, *The Dan Smoot Report* was mailed to 33,000 in 1965, and upwards of 50,000 in later years. But those numbers are only paid subscribers; in 1961 alone, more than 1,300,000 copies of *The Dan Smoot Report* were distributed around the nation.

From the Left, Smoot's influence was regularly pointed to with alarm; he was portrayed as an "ultra-conservative broadcaster" in a spate of scaremonger books such as Richard Dudman's *Men of the Far Right* and William Turner's *Power on The Right*. In their 1967 book *The Radical Right*, Benjamin Epstein and Arnold

Forster said: "Smoot takes a back seat to no one on the Radical Right in warning against the current trends in Washington. In September, 1966, for instance, he summed up the record of the 89th Congress by declaring: 'In one year (1965), the 89th Congress, under President Johnson's drive for "consensus," enacted unconstitutional, socialistic legislation more damaging to the cause of freedom than *all* legislation enacted during the administrations of Franklin D. Roosevelt, Harry S. Truman, Dwight D. Eisenhower, and John F. Kennedy.' " In the liberal mind, of course, such an observation is anathema.

Four times annually *The Dan Smoot Report* published tabulations of key U.S. House and Senate votes. Always to the point, Smoot assigned each member a "C" for Conservative and "L" for Liberal on each vote cast. This was his idea of truth in labeling.

In his writing and speeches, Dan Smoot consistently used the term constitutional conservative or simply constitutionalist when describing the kind of po-

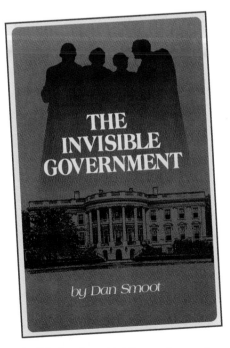

Pathfinder: Smoot led the way in exposing the activities of the Council of Foreign Relations in his underground best-seller, *The Invisible Government.*

> *"It does little good in the battle against socialism to send to the federal Congress men who are just conservatives.... The only answer is for the people to elect to Congress constitutional conservatives...."*
>
> — Dan Smoot

litical leadership America needed (and still needs). In political action he was always sure to carefully differentiate between those public servants who understood the real yardstick of American liberty — the Constitution — and those politicians who wanted just a little less government intrusion in our lives. His report for December 29, 1969, entitled "Can Conservatives Save the Republic?," explains it this way: "It does little good in the battle against socialism to send to the federal Congress men who are *just conservatives....* The only answer is for the people to elect to Congress *constitutional* conservatives who stand immovable on the principle that, no matter how popular or well-meaning a program, the federal government cannot legally participate unless clearly authorized by some specific grant of power in the Constitution."

Smoot also consistently espoused the philosophies of freedom that formed the basis of the Founding Fathers' conception of liberty during the formation of the United States. On the issue of gun control, he said a "free man must have [an] unrestricted right to own and use personal weapons, in defense of his family, his home, and his own person against ... an invading army, an agent of an internal political conspiracy, or a common criminal." On the nature of equality, a concept often twisted into new and novel meanings by leftist partisans, Smoot observed that the "Christian concept of equality of men ... has nothing to do with my income or my health or my environment. It simply gives me — a little, imperfect man, born in sin — an individual personal relationship with God: A relationship equal to that of any other man on earth." Significantly, Smoot realized that these values were under attack by a conspiracy that, in the end, would see the United States destroyed in favor of an all encompassing world-state. "Somewhere at the top," he said, "are a few sinister people who know exactly what they are doing: They want America to become part of a worldwide socialist dictatorship...."

Dan Smoot's observations had impact far beyond his regular readership and listeners. Over the years his authoritative analysis has been cited in books ranging from John Stormer's best-selling political action manual *None Dare Call It Treason* to Rousas J. Rushdoony's historical study *The Nature of the American System*.

Generations of constitutional conservatives have benefited from Smoot's groundbreaking news-letter/broadcast. But today, long after his retirement, conservatives still owe him a specific debt of gratitude for his 1962 book, *The Invisible Government*. An exposé of the elitist Council on Foreign Relations (CFR), *The Invisible Government* forever changed the way anti-Communist activists looked upon their enemy. For those who were confused by the no-win, dead-end approach to the menace of creeping socialism, Smoot explained that shadowy hands were at work behind the scenes. "I am convinced," he wrote in *The Invisible Government*, "that the objective of this invisible government is to convert America into a socialist state and then make it a unit in a one-world socialist system." His research into the inner workings of the CFR took "four years of detective work more exciting (and infinitely more important) than any FBI case I ever heard of," he writes in his autobi-ography. "In 1957, I began making a chart of organizations mentioned in the news as supporting causes I knew to be communist causes," Smoot recalls. "It was not a communist apparatus. It was the Council on Foreign Relations," Smoot writes in his *People Along the Way*, "whose small membership roster included people like Harry Dexter White, Alger Hiss, and other communists, along with Presidents of the United States, Secretaries of State, heads of Wall Street brokerage firms, famous international bankers and their famous lawyers."

The Invisible Government was an underground best-seller; it is is said to have sold upwards of two million copies — and was in print for decades. It continues to be an important reference guide, although as Smoot modestly points out, subsequent conspiracy studies, such as James Perloff's *The Shadows of Power*, are better "than mine is, mine having gone into less depth into the CFR...." The truth is that, though many fine books on the conspiracy have been written since the appearance of *The Invisible Government* in 1962, Smoot's groundbreaking work undergirds most of them.

Health concerns forced Dan Smoot into semi-retirement in the early 1970s, and he combined his newsletter circulation with *The Review of The News* (a forerunner of THE NEW AMERICAN), where his "Dan Smoot Report" continued to appear on an irregular basis.

Now retired after a full and exciting lifetime of sacrifice to his beloved country, Dan Smoot offers this frank observation in his autobiography: "Wouldn't the job of putting constitutionalists in control of our federal government be like numbering sands or dipping oceans dry? No, it would be as easy as electing one constitutionalist to the U.S. House of Representatives from the Congressional District where you live. When people in two hundred and eighteen Congressional Districts do that ... they could starve the international socialist programs of the federal government.... For awhile it would be a valiant holding effort in Washington; but if your elected constitutionalists hold firm, victory will be inevitable." ■

Wise patriot: Smoot knew that saving the Republic "would be as easy as electing one constitutionalist to the U.S. House of Representatives" from each Congressional District.

Americanism's Standard-bearer

Robert Welch launched an unprecedented movement to expose and rout the worldwide collectivist conspiracy.

by William F. Jasper

How often has public calamity been arrested on the very brink of ruin by the seasonable energy of a single man?... One vigorous mind without office, without situation, without public functions of any kind ... I say one such man confiding in the aid of God, and full of just reliance in his own fortitude, vigor, enterprise, and perseverance, would first draw to him some few like himself, and then that multitudes hardly thought to be in existence, would appear and troop about him.

— Edmund Burke

To those familiar with the life, words, and works of Robert Welch, it must seem that Mr. Burke's lines above, though penned in 18th-century England, were written precisely and prophetically with this great 20th-century American patriot in mind. In this most calamitous of centuries, a great many heroic men have arisen in every land to fight the good fight — and to rally others in the fight — against organized evil, against totalitarian tyranny. Many of these valiant heroes perished in the brutal fray, their noble deeds known only to God, and their selfless sacrifices unremembered and unsung by their countrymen. Robert Welch recognized, as an "heir to the ages," and as a debtor to these courageous souls, a sacred obligation to carry on their fight. It was with a profound sense of duty to God, family, and country, and with a firm determination to stop, reverse, and rout the global advance of Communism, specifically, and collectivism, generally, that, in 1958, he founded the John Birch Society and dedicated the remainder of his life to this purpose.

If an important measure of a man is to be found in both the friends and enemies that he makes, then Robert Welch can be said, on this count alone, truly, to rank as a giant among men. During his lifetime, he was cursed by the worst,

It was with a profound sense of duty to God, family, and country, and with a firm determination to stop, reverse, and rout the global advance of Communism, specifically, and collectivism, generally, that, in 1958, Welch founded the John Birch Society and dedicated the remainder of his life to this purpose.

and blessed by the best, of humanity. He was repeatedly singled out for vicious smear treatment in the official Communist press — *Pravda, Izvestia, People's World*, etc. — which should have served as the highest commendation possible of his patriotism and the effectiveness of his crusade. Instead of coming to his aid and exposing these vile attacks for the lies they were, the "Liberal" press in America joined the attacks with even more malicious inventions and calumnies.

But if he was infamously reviled, he was also famously revered. Professor E. Merrill Root, the great poet and essayist, knew Robert Welch well and toiled alongside him for many years in his epic undertaking. He wrote affectionately of his friend and compatriot: "As you meet him in his quiet office … or as you see him in public at a meeting or a John Birch Society dinner, you feel a power. It is not what we call today 'charisma.' Robert Welch does not have that as (on different levels) a John F. Kennedy did, or a Theodore Roosevelt, or a Patrick Henry. There does not at first seem to be a flair, a personal magnetism, a something that reaches out and grasps you. It is a quiet power. It affirms and insists, through convictions, through an amazing knowledge, through a goodness and integrity that seem almost to be tangible. It is not oratory. He is not a spell-binder. He writes clearly, often brilliantly or eloquently; he writes better than he speaks. Yet somehow, something fundamental in the mind and the man, a grasp of things as they are,

a sincerity and integrity flow out of him and into his audience. His power lies in his goodness and his truth. I have felt this, I have seen this, and I bear sober witness to it."

"And no one can know him," continued the Bard of Earlham College, "under the weight of the world and the stress of his enemies, without reverence for his courage. Strong, I would say — stubborn, his enemies might say — in his conviction, his knowledge, his passionate desire to serve and save his country, he dares the cost and faces the danger fearlessly." Robert Welch's great character was complemented by an equally admirable intellect. In the introduction to G. Edward Griffin's excellent biography, *The Life and Words of Robert Welch*, Professor Root wrote: "Robert Welch lives inwardly on a high plateau of ideas, of ideals (based on reality), of values and meanings. As you will see, 'the realms of gold' where he most loves to travel, and in which he often stood 'silent upon a peak in Darien,' are mathematics and poetry! He has done advanced work in mathematics, which is worthy of interest because it shows his enchantment with the life of the pure mind, and with the abstract beauty of numbers. He found such joy in it that he could gladly have devoted his whole life to such studies."

However, one would certainly gather from the offerings of the hostile Establishment press that, in addition to being a wicked bigot, Robert Welch was also an illiterate bumpkin. The *Los Angeles Times*, for instance, in its January 8, 1985 obituary, stated that Welch was "not particularly well-educated in rural schools." That, of course, is patently absurd, as anyone familiar with the facts will immediately recognize. Robert Welch was a true genius, a child prodigy who began reading at two, tackled algebra at age six, read all nine volumes of John Clark Ridpath's formidable *History of the World* at age seven, and entered the University of North Carolina at age 12. He was a genuine "Renaissance Man," a world traveler, conversant in several languages, and an avid, lifelong student of history, language, philosophy, economics, mathematics, science, geography, chess, poetry, classical literature, politics, and other subjects.

The life of this remarkable man began at the turn of the century, on December 1, 1899, on a farm in Chowan County, North Carolina. He was schooled at home by his mother, Lina Welch, who not only nurtured young Robert's precocious intellect and love of knowledge, but also instilled in him good habits and strong moral convictions. Honesty, a strong work ethic, good manners, respect for one's elders, responsibility, generosity — these and other virtues were fused into the character of Robert Welch at an early age. When he entered high school at ten, he was already far advanced, academically, beyond the level of his older classmates.

Robert Welch entered the University of North Carolina at the age of 12, and graduated at age 16 in the top third of his class — in spite of a couple years when his grades fared poorly due to his frequent skipping of classes to pursue his interests in poetry, French literature, and chess. Meanwhile, the United States had entered World War I and so, at 17, he enrolled at the U. S. Naval Academy, probably the only plebe ever to start at Annapolis with a college degree already in hand. In 1919, with the war over and other interests beckoning, Robert Welch resigned from the Academy. After two years, he ranked fourth in a class of nearly one thousand cadets.

It was off to Cambridge, Massachussetts then and Harvard Law School for the young scholar. There Welch would clash repeatedly with a Marxist law professor by the name of Felix Frankfurter, whom Franklin D. Roosevelt would later appoint to the Supreme Court. After two and a half years at Harvard Law School, Welch determined to launch out into the business world. With a recipe for fudge and less than a hundred dollars capitalization, he launched his candy manufacturing enterprise. Later, he joined his younger brother James' candy firm, the James O. Welch Company, as its vice president. Over the years, he became a recognized leader in the business community, serving as vice

Child prodigy: Welch (in front) entered the University of North Carolina at age 12.

president of the National Confectioners Association and chairman of the Education Committee of the National Association of Manufacturers. In the latter capacity, Welch chaired bimonthly meetings across the United States for two years on the state of American education.

In 1946, Welch journeyed to England to study the destructive impact on that country of its socialist Labor Government. He was alarmed and distressed by the pursuit of similarly destructive policies by our own federal government. He was even more alarmed by the foreign policies of the Truman State Department, which were betraying our allies and assisting the establishment of Communist regimes in Europe and Asia.

In 1951, following President Truman's ignominious firing of General Douglas MacArthur, Welch penned his first major political work, entitled *May God Forgive Us*. It had begun as a lengthy letter to a friend outlining the calamitous results of America's post-World War II policies and the global Communist advance. Welch sent copies to several friends, and was soon besieged with requests for additional copies. He had several hundred copies printed up, which resulted in requests for *tens of thousands* more. We were at war with the Communists in Korea, and Welch's incisive analysis of America's defeats and retreats so soon after our victories over Germany and Japan struck a responsive chord with the American public. In 1952, conservative book

publisher Henry Regnery began printing *May God Forgive Us* in book form, and before year's end had sold 200,000 copies. Virtually overnight, Robert Welch had become one of America's top-selling anti-Communist writers.

In *May God Forgive Us*, Welch made clear his belief that the only reasonable explanation for the otherwise inexplicable series of Communist victories throughout the world was treachery and treason in our own government. He wrote:

> In China it was our ally Chiang Kai-shek whom we badgered, hamstrung, and abandoned; and tools of Stalin named Mao and Chou En-lai and Chu Teh whom we helped to take over Chiang's country. In Poland it had been our ally Mikolajczyk whom we deceived, abandoned, and disowned; and tools of Stalin with such names as Osubka-Morawski and Boleslaw Bierut whom we had helped to take over Mikolajczyk's country. In Yugoslavia it had been our ally Mihailovich whom we shamefully disowned, libeled, and allowed to be "legally" murdered for the Communists' propaganda purposes; and a tool of Stalin named Tito whom we helped to take over Mihailovich's country — for which Mihailovich had fought so hard and faithfully against our German enemies....
>
> For in all of the sociological equations that Stalin has solved in order to make these various conquests, there has been one dependable factor. This has been the moral support and the financial support of our government, however cleverly disguised and however skillfully the facts have been kept from the American people.

He was not making wild charges; he set out clear documentary evidence and differentiated between those who were Communist or pro-Communist, and those who were merely dupes, useful idiots, or unprincipled and ambitious climbers. "Let me make it crystal clear that I do not think Harry Truman is a Communist or a

sympathizer with Russian imperial ambitions," Welch wrote. "He is, I do think, a callous politician, with few scruples about the means used to achieve a political end." He was not so gentle with Secretary of State Dean Acheson, the architect of so many of our pro-Communist policies, and the friend and protector of Soviet agent Alger Hiss.

Nor did Robert Welch spare the American people their due share of guilt for allowing such monumental treachery to be carried out in their name. Speaking eloquently from the heart, he appealed to the American people to take off their blinders and shake off their complacency:

> What's the matter with us, anyway? Neither facts nor pictures seem to sink into our centers of feeling any more. They remain just words and lines and forms, objective phenomena outside the glazed surface of our noumenal existence. The physical suffering, the mental anguish, the never-ceasing terror of our fellow human beings, represented by these words and pictures, no longer reach through the glaze to activate our imaginations or to excite our sympathies....
>
> As we sit in our warm homes, after a happy meal with our families, and turn on our television sets or radios, it is hard for us to think of a man just like ourselves always half-starved, always half-frozen, haggard and hopeless, remembering the days when he too was free, as he is brutally driven to finish up the literal exhaustion of his body in labor for the benefit of the very tyrant who has enslaved him. It is harder still to remember that there are *millions* of such men; or that in the past six years, *six hundred millions* of our fellow human beings have been placed under the merciless heel of this monster and the bestial control of his henchmen and police.
>
> For the pusillanimous part that we have played in all this spreading horror; for our indifference to the grief of others; for our apathy to the

crimes we saw and our blindness to those we should have seen; for our gullibility in the acceptance of veneered treason and our easy forgetfulness even when the veneer had been rubbed off; for all our witting and unwitting help to the vicious savages of the Kremlin and to their subordinate savages everywhere, may God — and our fellow men — some day forgive us!

In 1954, Robert Welch's second explosive book, *The Life of John Birch*, appeared. He had stumbled across the amazing story of this American military hero and Christian martyr while conducting research in the congressional committee files in Washington, D.C.

John Birch, he learned, was a courageous, young Baptist missionary who had gone to China in 1940 to spread Christ's Gospel and work among the Chinese. When America entered into the war, Birch volunteered to join the Flying Tigers, General Claire Chennault's 14th Air Force. Because of his mastery of the Chinese dialects and his uncanny ability to blend in with the Chinese, he was assigned to develop an intelligence network throughout China. In 1942, Birch rescued a group of pilots who had parachuted into Japanese-occupied China after bombing Tokyo. Among the downed pilots he safely conveyed through enemy lines was famed aviator Colonel Jimmy Doolittle.

Throughout the war Birch served with distinction and bravery. He developed a full-fledged intelligence network, which became known as the "eyes and ears of the 14th Air Force" in China. As the conflict wore on, he was promoted to captain and was awarded numerous commendations, including the Legion of Merit. On August 25, 1945, ten days after the war ended, Captain John Birch was murdered by the Chinese Communists. An autopsy of Birch's body confirmed an eyewitness account that it was a deliberate, cold-blooded execution. This war hero was first shot in the leg, then, with his hands tied behind him, in the back of the head execution-style. Finally, his face was savagely mutilated with bayonets, presum-

ably to conceal his identity.

What most shocked Robert Welch, though, was the discovery of the fact that the circumstances of Captain Birch's death were deliberately covered up by the U.S. government. In 1950, Senator William Knowland of California charged on the floor of the Senate that news of the murder had been smothered by Communist sympathizers to conceal the true nature of Mao Tse-tung's "agrarian reformers" who were trying to oust Chiang Kai-shek's government. If the truth about this Communist atrocity had been known, it would have been far more difficult for Stalin's agents in the State Department to sell its pro-Mao policy to the American public.

Among the explosive revelations Welch included in *The Life of John Birch* was a confidential memorandum dated June 10, 1947 from the Senate Appropriations Subcommittee to Secretary of State George Marshall. It stated:

It is evident that there is a deliberate, calculated program being carried out not only to protect Communist personnel in high places, but to reduce security and intelligence protection to a nullity....

On file in the [State] Department is a copy of a preliminary report of the FBI on Soviet espionage activities in the United States, which involves a large number of State Department employees, some in high official positions. This report has been challenged and ignored by those charged with the responsibility of administering the Department....

The memorandum then named nine of the employees who it said "are only a few of the hundreds now employed in varying capacities who are protected and allowed to remain despite the fact that their presence is an obvious hazard to national security." Why was the Truman administration protecting all of these subversives and security risks?

Welch intensified his study of global political developments, including trips to many foreign lands to see firsthand what

was happening. He became friends with some of the leading anti-Communist leaders of the world and developed contacts that would prove vitally important in years to come. In 1955, he visited President Syngman Rhee of South Korea, who later wrote to him: "I must confess I did not know we had such a staunch ally and champion as you in America." He also met with Generalissimo Chiang Kai-shek in 1955, and again ten years later.

By 1956, Welch knew he must do more in the fight to save America, and so he left the candy business to publish a "now-and-then magazine" called *One Man's Opinion*. After his death in 1985, his widow, Marian Probert Welch, wrote concerning his decision to launch his crusade nearly 30 years earlier:

When he was age fifty-six, friends asked my husband why he was giving up a small but hard-earned measure of success and future promise in a business career, and foregoing a chance for comfort and ease at last, to embark on a new venture which they knew would lead to heavier responsibilities than ever before. He referred them to his poem "At Twenty."

Robert was aware of the long travail of men laboring over centuries to achieve what he called "this continuity of generations" of intellectual wealth, which we enjoy today but which so many of the contemporary generation insist on ignoring. My husband grieved over today's revolt against traditions and mores, for he knew and loved our culture so long in the making. As an "heir of all the ages," he realized he could not afford the luxury of standing by to watch the loss of what had been won for us by successive generations of brave men over those countless years. And so, with the magazine *One Man's Opinion*, Robert Welch embarked on a crusade that became The John Birch Society. Keeping his pledge "At Twenty," he *tried* — and he never regretted it.

Here is that inspiring verse which the idealistic young scholar wrote during his first year at Harvard in 1919:

> If, fifty years from now, when I survey
> The scanty roll of things that I have done,
> I find a score of visions unfulfilled
> And victories I dreamed of still unwon,
> I'll doubtless see mistakes that I have made
> And places where I lost because I picked the losing side;
> But not a failure shall I find
> In the trail I've left behind,
> Where I might have won but didn't, just because I never tried.

As the circulation to his journal skyrocketed and demands for coverage of more issues increased, Welch changed the title of his publication in 1958 from *One Man's Opinion* to *American Opinion* in order to accommodate the contributions of other authors. *American Opinion* (the immediate predecessor to THE NEW AMERICAN*)* quickly became the premier forum of analysis and commentary for America's top anti-Communist, free market thinkers and writers. They included: Westbrook Pegler, Dan Smoot, George S. Schuyler, Taylor Caldwell, Henry Hazlitt, E. Merrill Root, Medford Evans, Dean Clarence Manion, Representative Martin Dies, Senator William Knowland, Harold Lord Varney, Ludwig von Mises, Hans Sennholz, Charles Callan Tansill, and others.

But Welch knew that much, much more must be done to stop and reverse the deadly course on which America was heading. Following Edmund Burke's counsel, this "one vigorous mind without office, without situation, without public functions of any kind," determined to "first draw to him some few like himself."

Late in 1958, Robert Welch extended invitations to 17 men to meet him for a two-day presentation on an urgent matter. Eleven of the 17 accepted and joined him in Indianapolis on December 8th and 9th. This group was heavily represented by former officers of the National Association of Manufacturers who, through their association with Welch, had gained a great deal of respect for his knowledge of contemporary affairs. His in-depth, two-day survey of the state of the world was a brilliant but grim examination of the current Communist/collectivist threat to America and the Free

Founder and namesake: Welch (foreground) saw in missionary-soldier John Birch (background) those heroic qualities that exemplified the goodness of America and mirrored the noble character traits that would be necessary for victory.

World. He did not pull any punches about the total inadequacy of the myriad of anti-Communist organizations opposing the Communist juggernaut. "At present," said Welch, "we are in the position of trying to defeat a disciplined, well-armed, expertly commanded army with a collection of debating societies. And it can't be done."

The constantly changing, elected leadership, parliamentary structure, and democratic methods of most voluntary organizations could not possibly provide the kind of efficiency, effectiveness, and steadfastness of purpose that would be essential to success in this fight. Only completely determined, solid, monolith-ic, principle-based leadership could provide an organization protection internally against infiltration, splintering, and inside fighting. At the conclusion of this presentation, Welch announced his plan to begin building a national, grassroots, education/action organization that *would* be capable of defeating the enemy arrayed against us. He intended to name it, he said, after John Birch, whose heroic qualities exemplified everything that was good about America and mirrored exactly the noble character traits that would be necessary for victory in this epic struggle. And so began the John Birch Society, an organization Welch led for the next quarter of a century.

World events soon vindicated many of the predictions and warnings presented by Welch at that founding meeting (the transcript of which became *The Blue Book of The John Birch Society*). He had told the Indianapolis attendees, for instance: "If you have any slightest doubt that Castro is a Communist, don't. If he is successful, time will clearly reveal that he is an agent of the Kremlin."

But Welch did not wait for "time" to reveal what was already obvious. In the February 1959 issue of *American Opinion*, he published a concise but withering exposé of Castro's Red bona fides. That was followed in April with the entire issue of *American Opinion* devoted to fully documenting "the fact that Castro was, and all of his adult life had been, a vicious, lying, brutal, murdering Communist." If such a statement seems self-evident today, please be informed that at the time Comrade Fidel was being celebrated as an *anti-Communist*. According to the Eisenhower administration, the *New York Times*, the U.S. State Department, Harvard University, *Reader's Digest*, and virtually the entire Establishment media chorus, Castro was the "George Washington" of Cuba.

The same chorus heaped scorn and ridicule on the Birch Society founder for daring to besmirch their darling Fidel, and for two years kept bleating their unalloyed praises of the new Cuban "liberator." Some of these self-anointed "experts" continued their adulation even af-

"If there had been even one chapter of the John Birch Society in Havana prior to 1959, working to expose Castro as Robert Welch was at the time, Cuba would not have fallen to Communism."

— *Major Pedro Diaz Lanz*
Former chief of Castro's Air Force

ter Castro, having consolidated his power, himself came forward to boast that he was indeed a Communist and had been one all along. All of which went a long way toward establishing the credibility of Robert Welch and the Birch Society with all who had eyes to see.

One individual who fit that category was Major Pedro Diaz Lanz, who joined the Society's speakers bureau and traveled the nation exposing not only Castro's revolutionary agenda as the Kremlin's new Viceroy for Latin America, but the campaign of deception in this country supporting that agenda. "If there had been even one chapter of the John Birch Society in Havana prior to 1959, working to expose Castro as Robert Welch was at the time, Cuba would not have fallen to Communism," said Major Diaz Lanz, who was Castro's Air Force chief and one of the regime's top officials when he defected and escaped to the U.S. in 1959. Like thousands of other Cubans who had fallen for Castro's propaganda, Diaz Lanz lived to regret his dangerous ignorance and naiveté.

The American people were becoming more and more outraged and were demanding to know how it could be that our government had made yet another terrible mistake, this time installing a Red dictator on our very doorstep. Intending no compliment to Welch or his fledgling Society, but hoping simply to deflect attention from the duplicity and treachery of his own administration, President Eisenhower claimed: "Only a genius and a prophet could have known for sure that

Cuban Premier Fidel Castro was a Communist in the 1950s."

In its first months of existence, the Society scored a major victory by organizing a nationwide protest against the 1959 Eisenhower-Khrushchev Summit and the exchange visits in Moscow and Washington planned for the two leaders as a send-up before the summit. The JBS hastily organized the Committee Against Summit Entanglements, with Robert Welch serving as chairman. Joining him as vice chairmen were former Ambassador Spruille Braden, businessmen William Grede and Alfred Kohlberg, Dean Clarence Manion of Notre Dame Law School, and General Albert C. Wedemeyer. Another 60 prominent Americans came aboard as members. The Committee ran full-page ads, with the whole roster of the Committee appearing as its signature, in the *New York Times*, *Chicago Tribune*, *Detroit Free Press*, *Dallas News*, *Cincinnati Enquirer*, *Arizona Republic*, and scores of other newspapers throughout the country.

Public reaction was so favorable to the Birch ad campaign, and so unfavorable to President Eisenhower's overtures toward the "Butcher of Budapest," that Khrushchev's anticipated propaganda coup was a crashing failure and the Eisenhower return visit to Moscow was called off. Once back in Moscow, a furious Khrushchev delivered a scathing speech reporting on his visit. "There are forces in the United States working against us," he said. "They must be publicly whipped, subjected to the torments of Hell!"

A few months later, in 1960, Communist Party leaders from over 80 nations were summoned to a meeting in Moscow and directed to wage a "resolute struggle against anti-Communism." The U.S. Senate Internal Security Subcommittee conducted hearings about this important directive and on July 11, 1961 published a report entitled *The New Drive Against the Anti-Communist Program*. It included the following passage: "For the first time, the world Communist network, in a basic policy and operational document, specifically referred to the anti-Commu-

nist movement in the United States, recognizing that it had reached proportions large enough to constitute a main — if not the main — danger to Communist progress in our country...."

In 1963 a report of the California State Senate noted of the same Moscow directive: "So far as the American Communists were concerned, this was an order — plain and incontrovertible. It was not lightly printed. It was an implementation of orders from the highest source of the world Communist movement, and it was therefore imperative that the Party here do everything in its power to render the Birch Society, the anti-Communist schools, and all of the other rising anti-Communist organizations ineffective...."

The torments of hell were not long in coming. The Communist attack was launched on February 25, 1961, with a lead smear in *People's World*, an official newspaper of the Communist Party, under the headline "Enter (from stage right) the John Birch Society." The Society found itself falsely accused of racism, anti-Semitism, fascism, Nazism, Ku Kluxism, and the entire litany of defamatory labels. Birchers were called paranoids, extremists, radicals, super-patriots, hatemongers, bigots, subversives, lunatics, and fanatics.

Like the defamatory attacks against the JBS carried in *Pravda* and other Soviet publications, the *People's World* article would have had little effect on its own, since few Americans read it, and fewer still placed any credibility in an openly Communist publication. However, when *Time* magazine, and then much of the rest of the "mainstream" media, quickly followed with a sustained torrent of screeching tirades echoing the same charges as the *People's World*, it was evident to all knowledgeable anti-Communists that the Society was in for a smear the likes of which had not been seen since Senator Joseph McCarthy had been singled out for similar treatment a decade earlier.

Joining in the vicious attacks on the Society were many of the Establishment politicians, industrialists, and financiers who had been longtime apostles of appeasement of and cooperation

Renaissance man: Welch, with wife Marian and a portion of his personal library, was an avid, lifelong student of history, language, philosophy, economics, mathematics, science, geography, chess, poetry, classical literature, politics, and other subjects.

with Communism. Many of these individuals, though wealthy capitalists, had often used their tremendous power and influence to undermine and destroy our anti-Communist allies in other countries, provide massive economic, technological, and military aid to Communist regimes, and stop the investigation and exposure of Communists in the federal government and other centers of power here in the United States.

Robert Welch, like many other anti-Communists, grappled with a dilemma. Many of these wealthy and influential individuals had proven by their repeated actions that they were working consciously in concert with the Communists and that they favored convergence of the United States with the Communist countries into a world government under the United Nations. But they were not, as far as anyone knew, members of the Communist Party. What exactly was their relationship to the Communists and how could they be properly designated? Through his own intensive historical research, and that of many others, Welch came to understand that the Communist Conspiracy was but the overt, militant arm of a much larger and older conspiracy.

The origins of the Communist Conspiracy, which by 1960 claimed roughly 40 million members in its 81 Communist Parties throughout the world, could be reliably traced back beyond 1848, when

Karl Marx penned the infamous *Communist Manifesto* for the Communist League. In fact, the bloodline of the Communist Conspiracy ran directly back to the French Revolution of 1789 and to the secret group that orchestrated the bloody events of that period, the Order of the Illuminati. Founded in Bavaria in 1776, this occult, criminal cabal was dedicated to the destruction of Christendom and the establishment of a "new world order" under the global dominion of its secret brotherhood. In very short order it had established a network throughout Europe and recruited to its membership powerful and wealthy individuals. During the 19th century, this same evil camarilla provided the brains and the motive force behind the series of revolutions and wars that rocked Europe and destroyed the established order, preparing the way for the Communist takeovers of the 20th century.

In his famous 1964 speech, "More Stately Mansions," Robert Welch outlined the history of this incredibly ruthless "Master Conspiracy," of which the Communists are only the most visible and openly militant arm. This was developed further in his brilliant 1966 essay, "The Truth In Time," and in subsequent essays in *The John Birch Society Bulletin* and *American Opinion*. In his 1966 essay he introduced the term "Insiders" to identify the inner, ruling clique of this Satanic conspiracy.

Dr. Medford Evans, author of *The Secret War for the A-Bomb*, as an administrative officer on the atomic bomb project, got a close-up look at the interaction of Insiders and Communists. He became a loyal friend of Robert Welch and a longtime contributor to *American Opinion*. "Welch insisted, over and over," wrote Dr. Evans in a 1985 encomium to his departed friend, "that the danger was

not a body of ideas (important as they are) so much as a body of men, particularly a group of individually capable men in league with each other — a powerful conspiracy seeking ever greater power."

The Insiders and Communists were (and are) not much perturbed by the many anti-Communist and patriotic groups that restrict their opposition to the "field of ideas." What they can't tolerate is individuals and groups who expose the Communists and the Insiders behind and above the Communists. That the Birchers were hitting the mark was evident from this Communist Party fusillade that appeared in *People's World* of March 18, 1967: "The John Birch Society is the largest and most sophisticated 'anti-Communist' organization in the United States. The Right is a seething mass of over 4,000 organizations, bewildering in their titles, aims and diversity. Of all these groups, only some 30 distinct organizations appear to be of national importance, and the prime one is The John Birch Society."

In his "If You Want It Straight" essay in the July 1977 JBS *Bulletin*, Welch expounded on just why the conspirators were so upset:

The John Birch Society set out early to build up a properly staffed educational army which was to create the only form of opposition that the Insiders of a Master Conspiracy did not know how to overwhelm or to destroy. This growing opposition consisted of exposing the background, methods, purposes, and progress of that Conspiracy so as to generate more public understanding of what was taking place, and a resulting grass-roots resistance to many of its projects....

[O]ur operation was based on the membership formula. Nor do we mean a temporary and tenuous membership in some political action group; or in some academic propaganda organization where the members' contact with headquarters was only by mail. The basic features of our organizational pattern have been continuous, palpable, and real. We required regular periodic meetings and specific activities that were carefully planned and coordinated. And the cost of supplying able officers, whom we call our field staff, for inspiring, guiding, and supervising these several thousand platoons or chapters, has been so great that not a single other American organization in this fight against the Conspiracy has even attempted to maintain a paid and professional field staff. Yet this very sound and solid core of all our effort is what caused the Insiders to be so disturbed and frightened by The John Birch Society that they set out almost at once to destroy it.

Indeed. The Insiders realized almost immediately that this was not just another "debating society." They were facing a monolithic organization of highly educated, highly motivated constitutionalist activists carrying out a concerted, coordinated action agenda under the direction of a very capable and determined leader who could not be bribed, corrupted, intimidated, or diverted. They understood that Robert Welch was not bluffing when he said, "We do not intend to devolve into any loose organization, but to become a more tightly knit and more effective brotherhood with every passing month. We know what we want and where we are going, and we mean business every step of the way."

Moreover, this organization did not get diverted and bogged down in politics. "Education is our total strategy and truth is our only weapon," Robert Welch repeatedly reminded members of the Society. He had the wisdom to recognize that the prerequisite for any positive, long-lasting political progress was the creation of an informed electorate. And that could only be created through a core base of activists who are committed to constitutional principles above political personalities and party agendas. While encouraging members to be politically active as responsible citizens, the Birch Society has never endorsed, supported, or promoted candidates

for elective office, or aligned itself with any political party. Through its educational strategy, the Society set out to bring about "less government, more responsibility, and — with God's help — a better world." It soon established a nationwide network of local chapters guided by a full-time, paid field staff, a book publishing arm, bookstores, audio and film production, a speakers bureau, specialized ad hoc committees, and a host of other weapons of truth for its educational army.

Unforgettable farewell: Welch was in extremely poor health when the John Birch Society held its 25th anniversary celebration in 1983. Mustering the strength to make what would be his last public appearance, he moved many of the 1,200 present to tears and received a standing ovation that lasted for many minutes.

In 1983, just days before the Soviets shot down the airliner that was taking him to Korea, Congressman Larry McDonald — who had become chairman of the John Birch Society earlier that year, the same year Welch (then 83) transferred the reins of leadership — stated of his mentor: "As a true pioneer, Mr. Welch has cleared the land, removed the stumps, and helped to push out of the way the boulders that were before us. It is now time for us to develop the field, enrich the soil, and prosper for the benefit of future generations of Americans and other heirs of our once great civilization." Welch suffered a stroke by year's end — just days after the Society's 25th anniversary celebration at which, in poor health, he mustered the strength to bid his farewell. He passed away in January 1985.

The current president of the Society,

John F. McManus, worked closely with Robert Welch after joining the staff of the organization in 1966. "What an incredibly marvelous man he was and how very fortunate for America that we have had the benefit of his profound knowledge, wisdom, courage, tenacity, and foresight," he told THE NEW AMERICAN recently. "I truly believe that the freedom fight would already have been lost long ago, and America would already be submerged in a one-world socialist dictatorship if not for the 'seasonable energy' of this single man."

"Every day we see confirmation of the wisdom and warnings of Robert Welch," says G. Vance Smith, CEO of the John Birch Society. "I am especially impressed with his extraordinary foresight in creating a principle-centered organization that could withstand incredible smears as well as the test of time. Mr. Welch recognized, even if others did not, that the mere publication of truth was not sufficient to rout the Conspiracy. The dissemination of truth will have its desired effect only when it is put to use as part of an organized concerted action program, with thousands of dedicated members pulling together."

Dr. N.E. Adamson, Jr., a retired Boston surgeon now living in Charlottesville, Virginia, was the youngest member of the original Council of the John Birch Society, which provides advisory leadership to the organization. Last year, while giving this writer a tour of Thomas Jefferson's University of Virginia, he reflected on his long, close association with Robert Welch and his four decades in this epic undertaking. "I am sure we will never fully realize how truly blessed we have been to have had the benefit of Robert Welch's incomparable vision and leadership," he said. "All Americans owe him a tremendous debt of gratitude. What is especially important to me is that this vital organization, which he founded and led so capably, and which is needed now more than ever, is still here today, fighting the good fight, firmly committed to the same principles and purpose. We should all thank God for Robert Welch." ∎

About the Authors

All of the profiles in this book originally appeared in THE NEW AMERICAN *magazine. The list of contributors follows.*

Mark Samuel Anderson is a newspaper reporter and columnist in Michigan.

Gary Benoit is the editor of THE NEW AMERICAN.

Steve Bonta, a regular contributor to THE NEW AMERICAN, is a linguist currently working on a Ph.D.

Thomas R. Eddlem, a regular contributor to THE NEW AMERICAN, was director of research for the John Birch Society at the time he wrote his contribution (the C.S. Lewis profile) to this book.

Peter B. Gemma, a free-lance writer, is a fundraising and public relations consultant.

William Norman Grigg is a senior editor of THE NEW AMERICAN and the author of *Freedom on the Altar: The UN's Crusade Against God & Family.*

Jane H. Ingraham, a regular contributor to THE NEW AMERICAN, is a lifetime student of the freedom philosophy, and a longtime political activist and writer.

William F. Jasper is a senior editor of THE NEW AMERICAN and the author of *Global Tyranny ... Step by Step: The United Nations and the Emerging New World Order.*

Robert W. Lee, a regular contributor to THE NEW AMERICAN, is the author of *United Nations Conspiracy.*

John F. McManus is the publisher of THE NEW AMERICAN, the president of the John Birch Society, and the author of *The Insiders, Financial Terrorism: Hijacking America Under the Threat of Bankruptcy,* and *Changing Commands: The Betrayal of America's Military.*

Fr. James Thornton, a regular contributor to THE NEW AMERICAN, is a priest in the Eastern Orthodox Church.